The Jesus Dialogues

The Jesus Dialogues

Jesus Speaks with Religious Founders and Leaders

BRENNAN R. HILL

RESOURCE *Publications* · Eugene, Oregon

To my beloved wife, Marie, and to my treasured family, Ami and Ed, Marie, Natalie, Lauren, BJ and Allie, and Grant.

Contents

Introduction

You are about to engage in a privileged opportunity—to listen in as Jesus sits down in sacred places with the founders and leaders, both female and male, of many religions. Uniquely, all come on an equal basis, not as true or false, authentic or pagan, orthodox or heretic. Rather, each religious founder and leader represents a tradition that has somehow been revealed by the divine.

The similarities among religions are striking, the differences profound, the divisions both among and within the religions are deep and abiding. All of this enlightens us on the mysterious complexity, the elusive nature of divine truth. It demonstrates that the problems of intelligibility lie not in the Source of revelation, but in the receivers. Humans "see in a glass darkly" and are limited by their innate inability to grasp the ungraspable, understand that which is beyond understanding, or experience what is beyond experience.

The differences among these religions perhaps also arise from the diversity of historical cultures, languages, and historical periods. The limitations of the founders themselves as well as the shortcomings of those who follow religions are perhaps other factors that add to obvious differences among religions. At the same time, these variations can manifest the elusive character of religious truth.

The similarities among the religions are profoundly encouraging. They point to a common Source, a universal human understanding, a valid experience of Truth, as well as an awareness of Truth's ultimate Oneness. And yet the Mystery remains. The Divine is beyond our understanding, our stories, beliefs, metaphors, symbols, and ceremonies. The perennial search goes on, but hopefully amidst more human religious unity and commitment to common action.

We begin with the Abrahamic religions from the Middle East, Judaism, Christianity, and Islam. They are linked by efforts toward reform, with Jesus as a Jewish reformer and Muhammad viewing his revelation as a reform of both Judaism and Christianity. First, Jesus dialogues with the central figure of his own Judaic religion, Moses, and his sister, the prophetess Miriam. They discuss some of the biblical stories on the origins, development, and history of Judaism and Christianity. Attention is also given to the sacred scriptures of these two great religions, their beliefs about God, and the rituals that they celebrate. The focus then turns to the later history of Judaism and Christianity, the divisions, persecutions, and how modern Jews and Christians are addressing contemporary issues.

Then Jesus converses with the great founder of Islam, Muhammad, and with his influential wife, Khadijah. The Prophet's unique life is discussed as well as the amazing revelations he received from Allah over a number of years. The dialogues compare and contrast the teachings of the New Testament and the Quran and takes up such contemporary issues as *jihad*, nonviolence, the succession of leadership, the identity of Jesus, as well as how Muslims and Christians deal with ecology and women's issues.

The next chapters contain dialogues among Jesus and key figures in the ancient Indic religions: Hinduism, Buddhism, and Jainism. All three arise from the religious traditions of India. Buddhism represents a reform of Hinduism, and Jainism is related to both in terms of principles such as ahimsa and strict asceticism. The origins, history, beliefs, cults, and modern concerns with world issues of these religions are discussed and compared to those of Christianity. Then there is a dialogue between Jesus and the founder of Sikhism, Nanak. Nanak's revelations are thought to transcend other tradtional religions such as Hinduism and Islam.

Next Jesus converses with the key figures of two of the religions of the Orient: Taoism and Confucianism, comparing the main elements of these religions with those of Christianity. The next dialogue is among Jesus and key figures in indigenous religions from Africa and the Americas. Noted here are many traditions that still impact believers in the United States, and indeed in many areas all over the world. The last chapter deals with the importance of interfaith dialogue and how such exchanges might be carried out productively.

Throughout, the discourse is carried out respectfully, with all participants truly learning from each other, politely disagreeing, and relating to each other with genuine friendship. Scriptural parallels begin each dialogue, women religious leaders are heard with deep regard for their equality, and common concerns for addressing issues are presented.

And now you are invited to listen in on these stimulating, informative, and inspiring conversations.

Acknowledgments

Many thanks to all the fellow travelers and guides who accompanied me throughout the world and to all those who assisted me in my efforts to understand and experience the religions of the world. Much gratitude toward my wife, Marie, for being my traveling companion and for her expert proofreading of the text, and to Sue Goldberg for her superb copy-editing.

Chapter 1

Judaism

~~~ Jesus with Moses and Miriam

Can a woman forget her nursing child,
or show no *compassion* for the child of her womb?
Even these may forget,
yet I will not forget you.

—ISA 49:15 *(EMPHASIS ADDED.)*

As he went ashore he saw a great crowd: and he had *compassion* for them,
because they were like sheep without a shepherd; and he began to teach them
many things.

—MARK 6:34 *(EMPHASIS ADDED.)*

Jesus: Moses, I am so delighted to meet you and your sister, Miriam—both
great prophets of my religion. You know, I am sure, that I was born a Jew
and died a Jew. I have always honored you as a leader of my religion. It saddens me that our two traditions separated from each other. My desire was to
reform my own religion rather than begin a new one.

Moses: Jesus, we too are honored to meet you and to sit here on this hillside overlooking Jerusalem, an important city for many religions. Miriam and I have always been close. As you know, when I was a baby, she put me in a basket to be saved from Pharaoh's wrath. Miriam arranged that our mother, Jochebed, be hired as a nurse in the court. Later, Miriam played a prominent role in our exodus from Egypt and led the celebration when we crossed the Red Sea to gain freedom.

Jesus: I am pleased to be with you, Miriam. My beloved mother has the same name! I am always glad to see women counted among the prophets. You too bear the Spirit of God and bring forth God's revelation. My apostle Paul also spoke of women as prophets in the early Christian communities.

Moses: You mentioned that you did not want to start a new religion, but wanted to reform Judaism. It grieves me also that my people now have a separate religion from yours and that there exists such deep division and misunderstanding among many of our followers. Over the centuries, Jews have suffered such horrible persecutions from Christians! We must discuss this regrettable history in more detail later.

Jesus: Please share some of your story with me, Moses.

Moses: As you know, Judaism began long before me, though I lived more than a thousand years before you were born. Our father Abraham, our great originating patriarch, lived possibly thousands of years before me.

We might review our stories for those who are listening to our dialogue. As Torah reveals, Abram (his original name) was called by God to leave his land of Ur (probably in Iraq) and go to a foreign land, where he would begin a great nation and bless all the communities on earth.

Abram must have been a man of great faith because he picked up his family and traveled until he came to the land of Canaan. There God changed Abram's name to Abraham and made a solemn covenant with him that is still the centerpiece of our religion: "And I will give to you, and to your offspring after you, the land where you are now an alien, all the land of Canaan, for a perpetual holding; and I will be their God" (Gen 17:8). Henceforth, we would view ourselves as a chosen people, and our male children would be circumcised as a sign of this sacred covenant.

Jesus: I want my followers to see themselves as a chosen people also, but not in any exclusive sense. "Christians," as they now name themselves, are called to proclaim to all people that they are chosen to be in a covenant with the Creator as God's beloved people.

Moses: Yes, but often your followers have thought that the so-called "New Testament" replaced our "Old Testament" and viewed Jews as in need of conversion. Vatican Council II changed that thinking and now your covenant is described as being in continuity with ours. And, of course, Islam is included in what is termed the Abrahamic religions, the People of the Book. All of us need to alert people everywhere that they are God's people.

Miriam: Well, let's go on with our story. You men tend to be too theoretical. Religion is about people. According to our faith stories, Abraham and his wife Sarah had a son Isaac, who in turn with his wife Rebekah had two sons, Esau and Jacob. The latter's name was changed to Israel, and his sons generated the twelve tribes of Israel. This marks the beginning of a new people founded by these fathers and mothers, beginning with Abraham and Sarah. One of Jacob's sons, Joseph, was sold into Egypt. He prospered there. During a famine, he welcomed Jacob and his family into Egypt where they all thrived.[1]

Moses: And that is when I came into the picture. Torah tells of a new pharaoh coming into power who enslaved the Israelites. At one point, he decided to kill all our babies. So to save me, Miriam put me in a basket and set me afloat in the bushes along the Nile. As she watched, I was retrieved by Pharaoh's daughter and taken to the palace, where I was raised in courtly comfort. As a young man, I was strong and impetuous. At one point, I got into serious trouble for killing an Egyptian who was abusing a Jew. I fled to the desert, where I lived as a shepherd for a number of decades.

Jesus: There is a similar story surrounding *my* birth when Herod slaughtered innocent babies after hearing that a new king was born. My stepfather Joseph was alerted in a dream to take me into Egypt so that my life could be saved.

Moses: As the story goes, one day God suddenly spoke to me from a burning bush and directed me to return to Egypt and free my people. It was a scary mission, but I followed God's command and returned to Egypt. For quite some time, I was unable to persuade pharaoh to let my people go. It

1. Ska, *The Exegesis of the Pentateuch*, 33ff.

was only after a series of disasters and the death of Egypt's firstborns that the pharaoh decided to capitulate.

Soon after we left, the pharaoh sent troops after us, but their chariots got mired in the quicksand of the sea where we had crossed safely. This was our "Passover," and our people still celebrate this event every year.

Jesus: It is heartening to hear your firsthand account of those ancient times. I have so many treasured memories of celebrating Passover with my family and then later with my disciples. My last supper with my disciples was in fact a Passover dinner, which I transformed into a commemoration of my death on the cross the next day. Since that time, my disciples have celebrated that sacred meal in my memory, as I had asked them.

Moses: After my people escaped Egypt, we wandered in the desert for forty years. Those were trying times with much hardship over which my people complained a great deal. But God was always with us. At one point, on a mountain called Sinai, God gave me the Law, the Commandments, to show my people how to live good lives.

Jesus: My followers still cherish the commandments, Moses. And you are recognized as a great leader. Some even refer to me as the "new Moses."

Moses: Thank you, Jesus. It really upset me that after all my work for my people, God did not deem me worthy to enter the Promised Land. It broke my heart that I had to die without ever being able to see my dream fulfilled in the land of Canaan. Nonetheless, there is some consolation in the recognition accorded me by my people who still hold me up as their greatest prophet, liberator, and lawgiver.

Jesus: I cherish this sacred history, Moses. When I was young I remember those wonderful family gatherings on our rooftop, where it was cool, and we would talk about times past. I remember being taught that Saul united the tribes and became the first king. He wasn't keen on David, that young upstart shepherd who gained recognition by killing the Philistine, Goliath. Saul drove David out of the country. Then, when Saul died, David returned and became our greatest king. His son Solomon was the next king, who consolidated and organized the nation. He also built the first Temple and has been recognized for his wisdom.

Miriam: Indeed. We honor David as our greatest king, and his sayings and prayers have always been a source of inspiration. I know that you, Jesus, are called "Son of David."

Jesus: I have always prayed David's psalms, and in fact had one of his prayers on my lips as I died on the cross: "My God, my God, why have you forsaken me?"

Miriam: That was indeed a painful time for you and your family, Jesus. I am so sorry that some of our Jewish leaders played a part in your unjust condemnation and crucifixion. It seems that they could not tolerate your challenges to their hypocrisy and authority.

Moses: I too regret what happened to you, Jesus. So often my people have been blamed for your death, and we have even in modern times been called "Christ killers." I am sure that you know that there were only certain individuals that hated you and plotted against you, and not the Jewish people. Your first disciples were all Jews, and many honored you as a Jewish reformer.

Jesus: That is very true, Moses, and there is certainly no basis for the anti-Semitism that has existed throughout history. You are my people and always will be. Now let's get on with exploring our history.

Moses: Well, after Solomon's death, the kingdom began to fall apart. We became two kingdoms: Judah in the south and Israel in the north. Those were troubled times. Israel became unstable and later was conquered by the Assyrians. Its leaders were exiled.

Later, the Babylonians came into power, invaded Judah, and deported Judah's wealthy, its professionals, and its craftsmen to Babylon. Eventually, they raided the Hebrew treasury and then leveled the city of Jerusalem, along with its Temple.

Fortunately, the Persians came along next and allowed many Jews to return to Jerusalem so that they could rebuild their lives as well as their Temple.

Jesus: I remember hearing from my parents that all this happened about five hundred years before I was born. That was about the time that the Jews put together our sacred Torah as well as the Talmud and the commentaries on Torah. We can discuss these texts later. Please review for me what came to be called the Second Temple period.

Moses: That was a time of great development in Judaism, but also a period when there was serious division among Jews, as well as more devastating conquests.

When the Jews came back from Babylon to Judah and rebuilt the city and Temple, the Samaritans to the north of Judah did not recognize these new developments. They were unwelcoming and hostile. They rejected the new Temple and the priesthood in Jerusalem. The Samaritans believed that they had the authentic practice of Judaism and had the real Temple. They were not about to recognize these strangers from Babylon.

Jesus: How unfortunate! I recall the hostility of the Samaritans in my day, and how dangerous it was to travel through their area going from my home in Galilee to Jerusalem for the feasts. There were wild animals and thieves in the mountains, and the Samaritans were extremely hostile and dangerous.

But they weren't all unkind. I told a story about a man who got robbed and was rescued by a good Samaritan. There is also another story about a much-married Samaritan woman with whom I struck up a conversation near Jacob's well. She actually went into the city and brought out folks to hear my preaching.

Miriam: Well, that wasn't the end of the conquests. About three hundred years before you were born, Alexander the Great incorporated our area into the Greek Empire. The Greeks left a lasting impact on our people. The Hebrew Bible was actually translated into Greek. I know for a fact that your own Scriptures, Jesus, were also written in Greek.

There was a serious protest in Judah about 150 years before you were born. At that time, our people rebelled against the Seleucids who were trying to stop us from practicing our religion and who wanted us to be Hellenized. Jewish families, like the Hasmoneans and the Maccabees, revolted and took over Judah. It was during your grandparents' time that the Romans came in and took over Palestine.

Jesus: Yes, I was told that the Romans took all the good land and drove the Jews into the hinterlands up north, where peasants like us had to work as tenant farmers. Much of the best crops where taken by the Romans, and we had to pay very high taxes to lease the lands.

The Romans put us under the direct authority of that tyrant Herod, who was only part Jew! He had been a lowly and ruthless sheriff, but the Romans raised him up to be a puppet king. He and his family were corrupt and lived luxurious lives at our expense.

I clearly remember that after I was arrested, it was the Roman procurator, Pilate, who sent me to Herod to humiliate me in front of my own Jewish rulers. I gave the old fox little satisfaction; so, after ridiculing me, Herod sent me back to the Romans who were in charge of Jerusalem. Only the Romans had the power to sentence me to death by crucifixion, and so my enemies shouted and intimidated him to crucify me.

Pilate even tried to get out of it by offering the choice to free me or some ruthless murderer, Barabbas. Can you believe that the mob chose to free him! I was devastated and knew that my fate was sealed. It was so hard for me to hear my own people, whom I had taught and healed, shouting: "Crucify him!" I felt so betrayed! First my own apostle, Judas, turned me over for thirty pieces of silver, and then some of my own people wanted my body to be torn apart by scourging and then to be hung naked on a cross until I could no longer breathe. I had done nothing to deserve such horrible punishment, and it was all I could do to forgive my enemies and die with love and compassion for all people.

Miriam: What a horrendous ordeal for you, Jesus! I am so sorry that you had to go through all of that, and at the hands of some of our own people.

Moses: You were subjected to the cruelest punishment of those times. Some of our Jewish leaders certainly turned on you! And Pilate, the Roman leader, was such a coward to give into the mob and use his authority to impose such a death.

Tell me, Jesus, who were some of the other Jewish leaders that you had to contend with at that time?

Jesus: Well, I remember that the Pharisees were a formidable group. They have a bad reputation and are considered to be hypocrites. I know that I was rough on some of them and called them "whited sepulchers," "blind fools," and "snakes." I could get carried away sometimes when I witnessed evil behavior.

Actually, many of the Pharisees were good men. They were a sect among our people who gained prominence during the exile when there were no priests and no Temple. Pharisees kept ritually clean by staying separate from the people. Some of them were good examples of how to be a Jew; some labored as social workers among the poor and taught Torah. During my time there were two outstanding teachers: Hillel and Shammai. Both had their own schools and often differed in their interpretation of Torah.

I remember hearing that Shammai declared that a man needed a serious reason to divorce his wife, but Hillel said that just about any reason would do—even if he didn't like her cooking![2]

Miriam: It is regrettable that only the negative aspects of Phariseeism are remembered in our own day since we still use the word in a pejorative sense.

Jesus: How true, Miriam. Some of the Pharisees in my day approved of my teaching and would come around secretly at night to hear more. Most were traditionalists who believed in the resurrection of the dead in the final time. Many of them were deeply spiritual and good servant-leaders.

But some hated me because of my popularity as a teacher. They resented the fact that I had little formal training and no official authority. Some were shocked when I healed on the Sabbath and hated me so much they wanted to see me killed. Some were fakes and hypocrites, and, when I told them so, their hostility increased.

Moses: What did you think of the Scribes during your time?

Jesus: The Scribes were a diverse group. Some were mere copyists of the Torah. Others were learned scholars and accomplished theologians who actually contributed to the development of the oral tradition. The Pharisees and others recognized their authority and were open to new interpretations.

Miriam: Your Gospels also speak of the Sadducees. Who were they?

Jesus: The Sadducees of my day were the rich, noble Jews who lived in luxurious homes in Jerusalem. Among them were the priests and elders who controlled the Sanhedrin, the "Supreme Court" for Jews of that time. They decided tax and land disputes as well as criminal punishments. I was taken before them on a number of trumped up charges of blasphemy, of all things. Everyone knew that never in my life would I "curse God."

The Sadducees, recognized only the written tradition and were quite conservative.[3] It was much as it is today in the Church: some recognize the authority of great scholars, but others only give authority to what is officially written down by the magisterium.

The Sadducees gained much of their wealth through heavy taxes, land rental by poor farmers like my family, and the huge sums taken in from

2. Bowker, *Jesus and the Pharisees*, 89–93.

3. Saldarini, *Pharisees, Scribes and Sadducees in Palestinian Society*, 1–45.

countless pilgrims who were required to celebrate the Jewish feasts in Jerusalem. They also made a fortune on the money-changing needed to pay the fees in Jewish shekels to enter the Temple or buy animals to be sacrificed by the priests. Roman coins or monies from other areas were not acceptable. Sadducees also accumulated huge sums of money on the required purchase of sheep and birds offered for slaughter.

This explains why they were so incensed when I turned over their tables and drove the greedy vendors out of God's house. Even though I was against violence, I really lost it that day when I observed all the corruption in the Temple.

Moses: What did you think of the Zealots? I have heard there were ex-Zealots among your disciples.

Jesus: During my time the Zealots had not yet formed into an official party. That would come later. But we did have organized terrorists who, like most of us, resented the Roman domination of our lands and people and wanted to be free of their control. These terrorists resorted to whatever violence they could perpetrate in order to put fear into the hearts of the Romans and keep them off balance. They would stab Roman soldiers in the marketplace, burn down Roman homes, and break into their armories and steal weapons. They would disrupt Roman religious services to the gods and goddesses. Their motto was the old Hebrew slogan: ". . .I have been very zealous for the Lord, the God of hosts. . ." (1 Kgs 19:10).

I chose several reformed Zealots to be my disciples. As I mentioned earlier, Pilate offered to free a Zealot—Barabbas—or myself, when we were both up for execution. The people chose to free the terrorist! Eventually, they founded an official party and instigated a full-blown revolution around 70 CE.

Miriam: Who were the Essenes? I know that some of their writings were discovered in modern times. They sound like a strange group to me.

Jesus: Well, they were a bit strange—they kept to themselves and always seemed to be looking down at their sandals. A very exclusive group indeed! I had little contact with them.

The Essenes of my day seemed to be a large, reclusive Jewish sect that lived strict ascetic lives in towns and in the desert. They did not accept the validity of our Temple in Jerusalem or our priests. Their largest community was in Qumran near the Dead Sea, a god-forsaken location, if there ever was one. They believed that the Messiah would come to them at the end-time.

As it turned out, the Romans wiped them out during the Jewish revolt at the end of the first century.

Miriam: Sounds like an unusual group. We Jews can be clannish at times, but we usually don't cut ourselves completely off from everyone!

Jesus: Getting back to our history, let's talk about the changes that occurred in Judaism after my death. I know that most of my early followers were Jews and continued to practice their Jewish faith and worship in the Temple. Eventually, their beliefs in me as the Messiah were not acceptable. The Jews and Christians tragically separated, especially after the Romans destroyed the Temple.

Miriam: The revolutions against the Romans and the destruction of the Temple were a terribly painful period in our history. For a time, Jews were excited and proud that we were going to be able to throw off the yoke of the Romans and be a free nation once again. But it was not to be. The beautiful Temple was burned down, and its very stones were dismantled. Our people were slaughtered and dispersed.

Jesus: How did this revolution ever get started? I cannot imagine a group of poorly trained Jews taking on Imperial Rome.

Moses: The revolution began about forty years after your death. Rome had controlled the city with a weak procurator and hired brutal, but often ineffective, soldiers from other countries to guard Jerusalem. The Zealots you spoke of had become a strong party, and they led the revolution. We were able to take over Jerusalem from the Romans in 70 CE. But Rome sent reinforcements, and after a bloody struggle Titus led his better trained and armed Roman legions to conquer Jerusalem. Our sacred Temple was destroyed, and many of our people were either slaughtered or fled into exile.

The so-called Western or Wailing Wall, where Jews pray today, is the foundation wall from that Temple that the Romans destroyed. Today you can see pilgrims from all faiths worldwide stuffing their prayer intentions into wall crevices and praying with bowed heads. It is most inspiring! The last few popes have prayed at this wall and inserted their petitions in its cracks.

Miriam: To go on with our story—fortunately, a sizable community of Jews was able to flee north to Yavne, led by the great Yochanan ben Zakkai. Once there, he and a number of scholars began to determine the official canon of the Hebrew Scriptures. They organized prayers, rituals, and the Passover Seder meal.

It was like Judaism was starting all over! Since there was no longer a temple, priests, or Sadducees, there would no longer be animal sacrifices. The Pharisees reconstituted a Sanhedrin, and rites were formulated to ordain rabbis, who would function as the Jewish teachers. This was indeed a new form of Judaism.[4] This is usually called the Rabbinic Period of Judaism because we moved from Temple worship and animal sacrifices led by priests to different rituals and practices led by rabbis.

Jesus: I am amazed at how different the rabbinic Judaism was from the Jewish religion that I knew! I am aware that my movement also experienced some dramatic changes during this period as well. The Jesus movement, which some called "The Way" and the Romans dubbed "Christianity," continued to attract Jews. In time, however, the message spread to Gentiles. This was due largely to the work of my apostle Paul. The movement spread through Syria, Greece, Turkey, and even to Rome.

There was much turmoil in the movement. Some of the faithful wanted converts to be circumcised and honor the dietary laws of the Jewish tradition, but Paul insisted that this was not necessary. Peter and Paul engaged in a vigorous debate about this issue that is recorded in Christian Scripture.[5] Ultimately, Paul prevailed and Christians began to move away from Jewish customs.

Miriam: I am amazed at how little Christians today know about Judaism. Many of them are not even aware that you, Jesus, are a Jew.

Jesus: That is odd indeed. Many Christians think that I was one of the first Christians. It is clear to me that if one doesn't understand Judaism, it is difficult to understand Christianity!

But nevertheless, the break between our religions was final and irrevocable. While the early Christians went to Temple, new followers met in house-churches, usually in secret, because the Romans and some Jews persecuted them. The Eucharistic meal that I left them as a legacy was the centerpiece of their meetings, and they shared stories from my days with them. Thankfully, they followed my lead and included women in their various emerging ministries.

4. Neusner, *Judaism*, 111.

5. See Gal 2:11–13.

Much to the dismay of the Jews, Christians did not participate in the revolution against the Romans. Instead, they fled Jerusalem to the surrounding areas and avoided the conflicts.

Miriam: We felt betrayed by the Christians, but we soldiered on, and our rebellions continued, even after Jerusalem and the Temple were destroyed. Decades later there was another major uprising. Our people were soundly defeated again and were forbidden to enter Jerusalem.

Fortunately, some Jewish leaders were able to reconcile with the Romans, and Jews were able to get established in Galilee, your home province. There they set up academies and began to work on compiling the oral teachings in the Mishnah. By then, more than half the population of Jews lived outside of Judah. They began adapting to these cultures and developing new forms of Judaism. Now both the oral and written traditions were used to shape the beliefs.

Torah and loving kindness became the two pillars of Judaism. Atonement for sin by animal sacrifice was replaced by sincere repentance (*teshuvah*). This was especially emphasized on the High Holy Days of Rosh Hashanah and Yom Kippur. The Torah became the center of our worship, and the Mishnah (c. 220) became the source of great learning.[6]

Jesus: During those early centuries, the Christians also developed new forms. A priesthood, somewhat modeled after the Jewish priesthood, was developed, as well as leadership models (deacons and bishops). Since Jewish priests had abstained from sexual intercourse before they led Temple rituals, a similar kind of abstinence was to be practiced by Christian priests. This gradually developed into priestly celibacy, but the practice was not universally enforced for many centuries, and then only in the Western church.

Early on, the official priestly ministries were restricted to males, but women were ordained to many other ministries. Much of ministry centered on service, especially to the poor—and there were plenty of poor to serve!

It was only many centuries later that the hierarchical and priestly offices centered on having special powers (consecrating host/wine and forgiving sins). By then, women were excluded. They could serve, but special powers were not extended to them, nor were they allowed to participate in decision-making or voting.

Miriam: Sad to say, our experience is similar. During the Rabbinic Period we were largely patriarchal and gave little attention to the role of women.

6. Holtz, *Back to the Sources*, 84.

Much of the discussion centered around the Jewish Scriptures. It had taken centuries to settle on a canon or authoritative list of Jewish Scriptures.

Our central notion with regard to scripture was Torah and that can mean many things. There is a useful story about the two great teachers you mentioned earlier, Shammai and Hillel. A heathen went to Shammai and said, "Convert me on condition that you teach me the entire Torah while I am standing on one foot." Shammai turned angry at such insolence and drove the heathen away with a stick. The heathen made the same offer to Hillel. Hillel said, "That which is hateful to you, do not do to your neighbor. This is the entire Torah. The rest is commentary—go and learn it." The heathen was converted!

Jesus: Interesting! Hillel was simply quoting what I call the second of the greatest commandments as it is in Lev 19:18. (Love your neighbor as yourself: there is a version of this in most religions.) In my teachings, I added the first great commandment: "You shall love the Lord your God with all your heart, and with all your soul, and with all your might (Deut 6:5)."

What are some other meanings of Torah?

Moses: Well, Jesus, I guess I would say that the broadest meaning of Torah is "all Jewish study of Torah," which includes Mishnah and Talmud. Mishnah is the collection of the oral tradition. Talmud expands the Mishnah with debates, commentaries, and interpretations.

But strictly speaking, Torah is composed of the first five books of the Hebrew Bible: Genesis, Exodus, Leviticus, Numbers, and Deuteronomy. The Hebrew Bible also consists of the Prophets and Sacred Writings, which include the Psalms, Proverbs, Job, Ecclesiastes, Song of Songs, the book of Ruth, Lamentations, the book of Esther, the book of Daniel, the books of Ezra-Nehemia, and Chronicles.

Jesus: Moses, your Hebrew Scriptures have certainly gone far beyond what we studied in my time. I must say that I like the way modern rabbis are trained in open debate and critical thought about your scriptures. Our seminary training is generally done in very traditional fashion, and our new candidates are often protected from open debate and critical thinking.

Miriam: We Jews are somewhat baffled by your scriptures and how quickly they appeared. Ours developed over many centuries. They make up a whole library, and we aren't even sure of authorship. Your scriptures seem to have been written within several decades after you died!

Jesus: That's true, Miriam. The first Gospel, Mark, was written about thirty years after my death, and the others appeared soon after. Gospel authorship is unclear, but they were named after disciples. Paul's earlier letter, the first one to the Corinthians, was written just twenty years after my death. The last Gospel, John, was written about seventy years after my passing.

That being said, it still took centuries to come to a final conclusion as to what should be included in the Christian Scriptures. A Christian bishop, Marcion (d. 160), rejected the Jewish Creator God as well as the goodness of creation and insisted that the Hebrew Scriptures not be included in the Bible. His views were rejected, and the Hebrew Scriptures were retained.

Miriam: I have heard comment about Gnostic Gospels, but they are not included in your New Testament. Why is that?

Jesus: So-called Gnostic communities, who rejected the physical world and any notion that I was truly human, developed their own gospels. Mainline Christianity rejected these texts. They disappeared until 1945 when copies were discovered buried in Egypt. Some Christian scholars see much value in these gospels, while others reject them. The Gospel of Thomas and others have been the subjects of extensive research in modern times.

So you can see, even though our scriptures were written soon after my death, it took a long time to reach a final decision about what the Christian Bible would be. As early as the second century, the Fathers seem to be working with a set collection. The great early preachers such as Ambrose (d. 397) and Augustine (d. 430) drew their sermons from a "Bible."

It seems that the texts of the Christian Bible were officially decided in 382 CE. The texts include the Hebrew Scriptures, the four Gospels, the Letters of Paul, The Acts, other inspired letters, and the book of Revelation. Jerome (d. 420) was commissioned by the pope to do his classic translation of the Bible into Latin. It would be a millennium before the Bible could be translated into other languages.

Miriam: I find all that history confusing. In our day, we didn't even have scriptures or a Bible. We just had oral traditions that we passed down from one generation to another. The beliefs that are within the tradition—those are what are important to me. I would like to talk more about our beliefs.

Moses: Well, I will go first. In my view, the two central beliefs of Judaism are: the One God and the Covenant. The stories in the Hebrew Scripture reveal how the Hebrews struggled with the belief in one God and at times fell back into polytheism. The final outcome of this struggle was a solid belief that there is but One God.

That belief is the main reason why Jews do not accept that you are the Son of God or divine, Jesus. I don't want to offend you, but if you are divine, that would seem to indicate that there is in fact more than one God. By the same token Judaism has not been able to accept the Christian teaching on the Trinity: Father, Son, and Holy Spirit. To us, that sounds like three gods.

Jesus: I am not offended. I have known your position with regard to me for many centuries. I understand and respect your beliefs. All I can say is that Christians firmly believe in just one God. They believe that I am that one God made incarnate, coming as a human being. I am the One God in the flesh. The Trinity is a theological model that was proposed by Augustine. This teaching insists that there is but one God, but that this one God is manifested as the Father, Son, and Holy Spirit. God is one but is revealed as Creator, Savior, and Inspirer. I think we can agree that all images and models of God are only human images and in no way explain the unfathomable Mystery that God is.

Miriam: I knew that was coming. We certainly have images of God in our Hebrew Scriptures that cause great pain and confusion.

Jesus: Yes, Miriam, many Christians are shocked at some of the images of God in the Old Testament. They read of God portrayed as a violent warrior, a condemning judge, and a cruel punisher for sins. They find it difficult to accept a God who orders plagues, kills firstborn children, or orders the killing and enslavement of women and children as the prizes of war. So often this God comes across as vengeful, judgmental, and violent. I know you have many more loving and compassionate images of God in your scriptures, and I hope those would become more familiar to people.

My experience of God was deeply intimate and personal. The loving Creator God was compassionate and forgiving. As the Son of God, I personified that image.

Now, I hope that I have not offended *you!*

Miriam: Not at all, Jesus. You know, my brother Moses used to bear responsibility for writing the Torah, but scholars now know that these stories were written by different hands long after his death. They are symbolic teaching stories and should not be taken literally or even as historical writing.

Once, when he was speaking of God, Isaiah the prophet declared: "For my thoughts are not your thoughts, neither are your ways my ways."

The Mystery of God is beyond our comprehension and words. These early stories present primitive attempts to understand God. Often, human anger, desire, revenge, and cruel actions were projected onto God.

I know you offer other more positive and tender images of God, Jesus. One of your favorites was "Father," and you further refined that intimacy by calling God "Abba," or Dad.

But you know, you also used some scary images of God, like your description of the last judgment where the sheep and the goats get separated or where you describe God as throwing people into the outer darkness, or casting them into Gehenna.

Jesus: You got me there, Miriam. I guess I carried some of my negative Jewish images of God into my teachings. Sometimes I lost my cool, especially when I confronted hypocrisy. But for the most part, in my life and the way I dealt with people, I portrayed God as healing, forgiving, and loving.

Miriam: I know that some of your people get very edgy about feminine images of God, and some even think that is "pagan." Actually, we Jews have used many feminine images of God in the scriptures: a woman giving birth, a mother, a nursing mother, a protective mother. Lady Wisdom is described as present at creation.

I am glad to see that you were true to that tradition when you referred to yourself with the feminine image of a "mother hen." And at one point you portrayed God as an old woman searching for a coin. But for the most part, you stuck with the image of Father.

Jesus: Yes, Miriam, and I am aware that most Jews have long moved beyond the warrior God—the angry, condemning, punishing God—and worship a Divinity of benevolence and love.

By the way, I've seen lots of the warrior God imagery among all of our followers, especially during WWII (God is my co-pilot; God hates our enemies) and after 9/11 (Why is God punishing us?). I know that Jews still have some old-guard worshipers of the warrior-God in Israel too, but I recognize that the vast majority of Jews are peace-loving people.

Miriam: I wonder if you could connect this conversation to your teachings on nonviolence.

Jesus: I have had an extremely difficult time convincing my followers that they are to be nonviolent people. I made some radical statements about "turning the other cheek," loving your enemies, and forgiving "seventy times seven," but my teaching has been watered down with the so-called "just war theory." In modern times, people such as Martin Luther King Jr., Dorothy Day, the Berrigan brothers, Thomas Merton, and John Dear have taken my teachings against violence and war seriously, but they were often criticized for doing so and even silenced.

Moses: Our people value peace, but there has also been at times a vengeful spirit (an eye for an eye and a tooth for a tooth). Throughout history we have often had to be on the defensive against the attacks on others. This has been the case in modern Israel, but I have to admit we have at times been harsh on the Palestinians. That whole situation seems to be beyond resolution.

Miriam: I'd like to address the notion of covenant, which is so central in our tradition. That has certainly been a point of controversy between Jews and Christians. Many Christians see the Jewish covenant as the one that has prefigured the Christian religion, rendering our covenant obsolete. Even in the New Testament one gets the impression that your coming as Messiah was predicted by our prophets. Jews don't accept that notion of prophecy nor do they accept that you are the Messiah.

Sorry, Jesus, but we just cannot accept that you are the Son of God or the Messiah!

Jesus: I understand, Miriam. That difference between us goes back thousands of years, and we must simply agree to disagree. It certainly doesn't help when Christians "pray for your conversion."

As for the covenant, Christians honor the sacred covenant made between God and people. They believe that they are the children of God and my brothers and sisters. Unfortunately, my followers have often seen their "new" covenant as supplanting your covenant. They have read "children of God" in an exclusive fashion.

I taught inclusivity and wanted my message of love and compassion, which is vintage Judaism, to be preached to all nations. It is not a question of "we are saved and you are not," which was often the Christian attitude toward members of other religions and even toward other Christian churches. Whether they are in a religion or outside of religion, people of all nations, colors, and sexual persuasions are all called to share in God's life here and hereafter.

Most of my original followers were Jews and saw my coming as the fulfillment of their longing for a Messiah. The Gospel writers selected passages from the Hebrew Scriptures that seemed to express their Jewish longing for my coming. It's doubtful that those Jewish prophecies specifically had me in mind when they were spoken. My followers are strongly committed to the belief that I am their Messiah. That is certainly one area where we have a deep disagreement.

Moses: Well, maybe we better cool this discussion down a bit and discuss our celebrations and feasts. As you know, we Jews see the holiness of time, and we celebrate the past as though it was still going on.

Passover is a major celebration for Jews. It is called Passover because it recalls that the angel of death passed over the doorposts marked with lambs' blood and spared the Jewish families. On that night we celebrate the Seder meal at home with many foods symbolic of the first Passover.[7]

Jesus: I celebrated this feast many times with family and friends. As I mentioned earlier, I celebrated this meal with my disciples—our "last supper" together—the night before I died.

Moses: We have other important feasts that we celebrate: Pentecost, or Shavu'ot, which celebrates the harvest and commemorates the giving of Torah at Mt. Sinai; Hanukkah, often around your Christmas, when we celebrate the miracle of the oil—lamps that burned for eight days with little oil after our victory over the Seleucid Greeks and rededication of our Temple in 164 BCE; and Purim, when we commemorate how Esther saved our people.

Jesus: My followers also celebrate many feasts. The main ones are Christmas, which commemorates my birth. This is preceded by a period of preparation called Advent. A time of penance precedes the commemoration of my suffering and death during Holy Week. That week ends with our most important feast, Easter, which celebrates my resurrection from the dead. Other feasts, such as Pentecost (the birth of the Church) and those honoring my mother and saints, are also celebrated in some of my churches.

Miriam: Jesus, I am struck at how the feasts we celebrate reveal our different views of history. We see Passover and the liberation from Egypt as central, and I suspect that your followers cannot relate to that at all. By the same token, your death and resurrection have little or no meaning for Jews. Sadly, even though you are a Jew, our religions have become so divided.

Jesus: It seems like division is characteristic of religion, both among the religions and even within each religion. I know I prayed for oneness for my

7. Neusner, *The Way of Torah*, 140ff.

people and your covenant with God was to be one, but it hasn't worked out that way, has it?

I am sure you are aware of the early divisions among Christians: the heresies, the split between East and West, the separations of Protestant and Catholic, and all the divisions that still go on in both of the movements. I know you also have endured your share of divisions.

Moses: You already mentioned some of the various divisions among Jews during your time: the Essenes, Samaritans, Sadducees vs. Pharisees, Zealots, and others.

After the destruction of Jerusalem, Jews no longer had a center and began to adapt to many other cultures, even more than they had during the Diaspora (the scattering of Jews to other countries). Rabbinic Judaism helped stabilize our religion, but our encounters with Christianity and Islam especially affected us. We were often oppressed and even forced to convert.

After Christianity became the dominant religion in the Roman Empire in the fourth century, we were often marginalized and isolated. We used these periods to better develop our commentaries (Mishnah and Talmuds).

In the areas where we fell under Islamic rule, we enjoyed even more freedom to develop our traditions. During the medieval period we reveled in our Golden Age of literature, poetry, philosophy, and religious writing in Islamic Spain. All that ended when the Christians drove Islamic power out of Spain, along with the Jewish people in the fifteenth century. We were dispersed to North Africa, the Balkans, and the Middle East and became known as the Sephardic Jews. Even earlier, in the twelfth century, we dispersed from the Mediterranean and settled in Germany, other parts of Western Europe, and the Slavic countries as the Ashkenazi Jews.[8]

Miriam: Our great medieval scholars also shaped Judaism—people such as Judah Halevi and Moses Maimonides. In the eighteenth century the great scholar Moses Mendelssohn encouraged Jews to be well educated, free, and critical in their religious views. Thus we Jews have always valued the finest education for our children. This has been one reason why we have been able to be so successful as a people.

Our medieval mystical tradition, the Kabbalah, was also influential and was revived by the Hasidic Jews in the eighteenth century. Kabbalah became strong in the Slavic countries.[9]

8. Corrigan, *Jews, Christians, Muslims*, 344. Also see http://www.nbcnews.com/science/science-news/most-ashkenazi-jews-are-genetically-europeans-surprising-study-finds-f8C11358210.

9. Feldman, *Fundamentalism of Jewish Mysticism and Kabbalah*, 32ff.

Moses: There is still a strong bond among Jews, which is amazing when you think of our many divisions. Some of our divisions are fairly recent, dating back to the nineteenth century when Jews were free to live in Europe and adapt to the various national cultures.

Orthodox Jews resisted adaptation to culture because they maintain that Torah was divinely given to Moses and is not subject to change. As a result, they choose a very strict approach to Judaism's language, laws, lifestyle, dietary practices, and rituals. Among the Orthodox Jews, there is still debate over how much Jews may adapt to the cultures where they live.[10]

Miriam: I find Reform Judaism very interesting because they are free to adapt to cultures, which has always been a Jewish gift. This movement began in nineteenth century Germany. Reformers began to worship in German rather than Hebrew. They accepted the human authorship of Torah and employed a critical, rather than a literal, approach to their Scriptures.

Conservative Judaism tries to take the middle path. They endeavor to adapt to culture and modern biblical scholarship, but at the same time they strive to avoid excesses. Reconstructionist Judaism is another movement that often holds secular views about religion.

Jesus: Both of our religions have been persecuted, but I must say, I have never seen religious people suffer the way you have and, shamefully, often at the hands of Christians.

Our persecutions have been many. In the beginning, Christians were hunted down by the Romans because we did not accept their gods and goddesses nor the divinity of the emperor. Some Jews saw us as idolaters because Christians worshiped me as the Son of God. In addition, faithful Christians throughout the centuries were exiled or executed because they were considered to be heretics. Many Christian women who were mystical and filled with the Spirit were burned at the stake as witches.

Local hostile people led by Oriental leaders in China and Japan, as well as by African and Native American chieftains, often killed our missionaries. In the twentieth century, many thousands of Christian leaders and ministers have been imprisoned or killed during the Nazi regime in Europe, as well as Russia, Central and South America, Africa, and China.

Moses: As you know, Jews were conquered and oppressed by the Assyrians, Babylonians, Persians, Greeks, and Romans. Christians often saw us

---

10. de Lange, *The Penguin Dictionary of Judaism*, 464ff.

as "Christ-killers." After Christianity came into power in the fourth century, Jews lost much of their property, were forced into ghettoes, and were often compelled to convert.

Under Islamic rule we fared somewhat better. Even though we were often obliged to wear distinctive clothing, pay high taxes, and had restricted religious freedom, we were typically given autonomy and not pressured to convert.

At times we were protected by some of the popes, but during the Inquisition we were tortured and killed as heretics or for refusing to convert. In Europe we were even blamed for the Black Plague! Many Jews in the Middle East were slaughtered during the Crusades. During the Protestant Reformation, Martin Luther turned many against us and urged his followers to burn down our synagogues for the honor of God and Christianity. We were often persecuted in the Ukraine and in Russia. So often we moved from being tolerated to being hated and persecuted. It became difficult to trust. A change of leadership meant that we could lose everything.

Miriam: No doubt, the Holocaust (*Shoah*) during last century was the most horrific experience the Jews have ever had. There was a determined effort to kill all the Jews in Europe, and in the end more than six million Jews were slaughtered. One and a half million Jewish children were killed, most of them in the concentration camps. Along with them, six million others, including political dissidents, Slavs, homosexuals, the disabled, elderly, and others considered to be "inferior" were gassed and cremated in industrial fashion.

Such horrors bring to mind a passage from Jeremiah: "Thus says the Lord, A voice is heard in Ramah; lamentation and bitter weeping. Rachel is weeping for her children; she refuses to be comforted for her children, because they are no more" (Jer 31:15).

Jesus: What is so difficult to understand about the Holocaust is that most of the main perpetrators of these horrors were Christians. Hitler and most of his closest associates were Christians; some were Catholics. What could they be thinking to even call themselves my disciples and yet be filled with such hatred and carry out such slaughters? I am embarrassed to have most of them in any way associated with my church. Neither before their cowardly suicides nor at their trials or executions did I hear them honestly admit their atrocities or show repentance.

How did the Jews ever manage to carry on in their religion after these unspeakable crimes against them?

Moses: This was a deep trauma for the Jews. Some began to doubt that there was a God. Others felt that God had let them down by not coming to their aid. Christian countries had shut their doors to them.

Strangely, not much was said for some time; apparently, the horrors were repressed. Then, in 1960, Adolf Eichmann, one of the masterminds of the whole plan of "extermination" and the man who supervised the transportation of millions of Jews to the camps, was captured in his hiding place in Argentina. Eichmann was put on trial, convicted, and executed in 1962. That trial seemed to trigger memories of the Holocaust. Many wrote and spoke about their experiences, and soon Holocaust museums were set up in Jerusalem and Washington, D.C.[11]

Jesus: It seems like the establishment of the State of Israel gave many Jews hope. They were now back in the land that had been their home.

Miriam: Yes, Jesus. It was good to be back in our homeland. But it has been a constant struggle to maintain our security there. Modern Israel has an interesting history. Interest began with the Zionist movement in the nineteenth century, led by Theodor Herzl (d.1904). Zionists wanted the Jews to have their own homeland in Palestine, which was part of the British Empire. After WWII, many Jews aspired to immigrate to Palestine, but the British objected. The Jews revolted, and there was violence. At the same time, in 1947, worldwide sympathy escalated for the Jews due to the horrors of the Holocaust, and the United Nations partitioned two separate states: one for the Jews and one for the Arabs. The Arabs objected, and there were several wars, which Israel won. The victories resulted in more land for Israel. Since then, there has been ongoing hostility between the Jews and Arabs. Now efforts are being made to establish two different states—Israel and Palestine.

Jesus: If I may, Miriam and Moses, I'd like to turn our conversation to an important topic: how our traditions have dealt with women. Both of our religions have had serious issues regarding the rights of women. As you know, I took a very liberating view of women in my day. I objected to the one-sided divorce laws that enabled only a man to divorce his wife—sometimes for trivial reasons. I opposed stoning women for adultery and even risked harm to myself to stop such a practice on one occasion. I healed both women and men as equals. I taught women at a time when they were not allowed to study Torah. And most uniquely, I chose men and women as my

---

11. Neville, *The Holocaust*, 275ff.

disciples and sent them all forth to preach the word. No other rabbi had ever done that.

Mary Magdalene was one of my closest disciples. I appeared to her first when I was raised from the dead. My beloved mother, Mary, played an important role in continuing my mission of love and service.

In my day, the priesthood and all the Jewish offices were held by men. It was a patriarchal religion, and I was a strong advocate for change. My movement was based on equality, collaboration, and loving service. Power was to be "for" not "over."

Miriam: This is a favorite topic of mine, and I like to get up on my soapbox about it. We all know that for millennia Judaism was largely a patriarchal religion. Women were purchased in arranged marriages as teens and spent their lives keeping house and caring for the needs of men. They had few marital, divorce, or inheritance rights. Men held all the positions of authority. Only men were taught the trades.

Thankfully, things improved in the Rabbinic Period. Women were no longer purchased for marriage, and their consent was required. They were given some rights for inheritance, divorce, medical care, and for participation in business. Since they always had religious leadership rights in the home, their influence became more significant once the rituals shifted from Temple to the home. Still, the woman's role was largely to be mother and homemaker.

I am quite proud of the roles that women have played in Judaism. We have had so many outstanding women throughout the ages. One thinks of Sarah, the wife of Abraham; Rachel, the wife of Jacob; Rebekah, the wife of Isaac and the mother of Jacob and Esau; Hannah, a prophetess and mother of Samuel; Deborah, the Prophetess; and Queen Esther.

Today modern Jewish women are making new advances. They now have come to realize that Torah and its commentaries are written by men, with little attention given to women. They see that men have largely portrayed God in their own image and likeness, as warrior, judge, and avenger.

Women want a place at the table to study and interpret Scripture from the feminine perspective.[12] Women also want equal roles as teachers and leaders of services, inclusive language in their prayers and song, and an active role in the decision-making offices.

12. Dorff and Newman, *Contemporary Jewish Theology*, 132ff.

Moses: Many of these changes seem to be coming too quickly for some of our people. The Orthodox Jews experience the most difficulty because they believe that Torah is directly from God and, therefore, cannot be changed.

Reform Jews have been the most open to change. They have women cantors and rabbis, and women are equal at services. Women can now hold important positions of authority and can study Torah. There is a bat mitzvah for girls as a counterpart to the bar mitzvah for boys.

Conservative Jews have moved in the same progressive direction, but at a much slower and considered pace. Orthodox Jews are slower in making these changes. Some have initiated parallel rabbinic studies and the office of Rabbinic Assistants. More women can study Torah and often form their own prayer groups.

Miriam: Some shocking scenes have been occurring at the Wailing Wall in Jerusalem over the rights of Jewish women. Some women, including Orthodox women, have demonstrated at the Wall. They have faced opposition from ultra-Orthodox groups. These women have been fired on with tear gas and physically assaulted and even threatened with years of imprisonment if they read Torah publically, blow the ram's horn, or wear prayer shawls. Can you imagine, Jesus? How is this "created in the image and likeness of God"?

Jesus: There are so many sacred Jewish beliefs that conflict with this kind of negative attitude and behavior against women. We believe that God is beyond gender. Moses, God told you, "I am who am." That is existence beyond gender. All our images are drawn from human life and imagination. God is beyond all those images and existed long before them. Human fathers have only been around for about one-hundred thousand years. God is eternal and beyond any image.

Miriam: Jewish women today want the fullness of Torah, not just a Torah conceived and written by men. Women want to reexamine the Torah from a feminine perspective and feature accounts of the women in the Bible. Women want to examine the laws of Torah to determine if they are just and honor the dignity and equality of women. They expect equal opportunity for Torah education, teaching, and leading rituals.

Jesus: Well, it looks like we are all facing the same challenges here. Christianity is also quite patriarchal. Many of our Protestant churches have made headway with regard to the leadership and the ordination of women, but the Eastern and Western Catholic churches show little progress.

In Catholicism, there is a strong resistance to ordaining deaconesses, despite centuries of such ordinations. Even stronger is the resistance to the ordination of women. Pope Francis, who insists that women are equal and wants them to have more significant roles in the church, says that the ordination of women is not open for discussion. Since the church authority is centered in ordination, it will be difficult for Pope Francis to promote the equality of women.

Miriam: Sometimes I lose patience with the lack of leadership opportunities for women, but in another arena, that of the environment, we are finding more common ground.

Moses: It seems that many contemporary Jews are getting involved in the environmental movement. That should not be surprising since we have such a beautiful creation theology. We believe that the "earth is the Lord's," that creation is good, and we are its caretakers.[13] Modern Jews have incorporated their appreciation for the beauty of the earth into their Sabbath observance.

Miriam: We have always believed that we are "the people of God," called by God to a covenant that requires us to obey the laws of God. By the way, Jesus, it's important to note that we don't believe that the Fall occurred after the forbidden fruit was eaten. Christians seem to have made too much of that disobedient act, holding that it caused death itself and the degradation of humankind from birth.

Our tradition tells us that humans are born with goodness, but with the potential to break God's law. And we are now beginning to see that God's law is that we be good stewards of God's creation. Jews are to be a light to all people. Creation is from the hand of the Creator and needs to be cared for and sustained.

Jesus: Yes, I know our religions differ here. Even among Christians there are diverse views about original sin. Augustine, who developed the theology of original sin, maintained that humans were born as "masses of damnation," without God's grace and requiring baptism to be saved. Therefore, he concluded that unbaptized babies went to hell. That teaching was later softened to "limbo," where such babies could enjoy natural happiness but were deprived of the vision of God. The notion of limbo has now been dropped from the Catholic tradition. The whole matter is placed in the hands of a loving and merciful God. The prevailing Christian view now is that humans

13. Benstein, *The Way into Judaism and the Environment*, 6ff.

are all born as children of God, but into a sinful world and that all have an inclination to sin.

Christians today seem to have a much more positive view of human nature. Many see all people as sharing God's grace. The world is viewed as God's creation. Humans must overcome their inclination to be greedy and wasteful with regard to the Earth and its resources.

As both of you said, we are all people of God and share in the Creator's desire to preserve and conserve the Earth.

Let's close our conversation by examining more fully our traditions on the issue of violence.

Moses: We already mentioned that some of our earlier traditions portray God as an avenging warrior. The Hebrew authors at times seem to project their dark side of anger, hatred, and cruelty onto God. There are some brutal statements in Torah, where the Lord gives his blessing to the slaying of thousands of enemy men, women, and children; the enslavement of prisoners of war and virgins of the enemy; and the stoning of people for their sins.

People should know that none of that is acceptable to Jews today. It simply comes from different eras and cultures. Those stories, symbolic or not, do not portray behavior that is approved today.

We are aware that some of these passages were used by Christians to justify slavery, and for that we are sorry. These biblical statements were taken very literally and out of the appropriate context of the ancient world.

Jesus: I was clear on my interpretation of the Jewish tradition. I did not subscribe to "an eye for an eye and a tooth for a tooth" mentality (Exod 21:24). I taught my followers to love their enemies and to pray for those who offend them. I taught them the Jewish belief in the sacredness of life and the solemn commandment: "Thou shalt not kill." Hatred and anger poison the soul. Only forgiveness and reconciliation are healthy for one's spirit.

I oppose war as a destructive evil that takes countless innocent lives and reaps only destruction. "Peace be with you" was my legacy to my followers after my Resurrection.

As for slavery, it was very much a part of the culture of my time. Neither my disciples nor I had slaves, but it was common among the wealthier citizens. It was so much a part of the culture that I opted to not confront it head on: I believed that my teachings on love and compassion would ultimately prevail. Tragically, it took many centuries before that happened. And even now, there are still new forms of slavery, including the abominable "sex trading" of young women.

Moses: As we all know, our greeting, *shalom*, means "peace be to you." Our prophets and the best of our tradition are dedicated to honoring the dignity of human life and striving to be peaceful. We condemn revenge and unprovoked aggression.[14] As one of our greatest teachers Hillel declared: "Be one of Aaron's disciples, loving peace and pursuing peace, loving humankind and bringing them near Torah."[15]

Miriam: Well, brothers Moses and Jesus, this was a wonderful and enlightening conversation. As a prophet, I pray that both of our religions will carry on their dedication to justice in this world. My sincere hope is that the peoples of our two ancient religions will continue to find common ground and grow closer.

Jesus: This conversation has given me new insights and appreciation for our shared history and values. I have been honored to spend this time with my Jewish sister and brother, sharing our common traditions as well those where we differ.

Moses and Miriam: Shalom! Peace and blessings on you and all the people of God.

SUGGESTED READINGS ON JUDAISM

Cohen, Shaye. *From Maccabees to the Mishnah*. Louisville: Westminster John Knox, 2006.

Drucker, Malka, ed. *Women and Judaism*. Westport, CT: Praeger, 2009.

Kaplan, Dana Evan. *American Reform Judaism: An Introduction*. New Brunswick, NJ: Rutgers University Press, 2003.

Satlow, Michael. *Creating Judaism*. New York: Columbia University Press, 2006.

Tirosh-Samuelson, Hava, ed. *Judaism and Ecology*. Cambridge, MA: Harvard University Press, 2002.

14. Schiffman and Wolowelsky, *War and Peace in the Jewish Tradition*, 517ff.

15. *The Mishnah*, Pirke Avot 1:12.

Chapter 2

Islam

∼ Jesus with Muhammad and Khadijah

. . .it is righteousness—to believe in Allah and the Last Day, and the Angels, and the Book, and the Messengers; to spend of your substance, out of *love* for Him, for your kin, for orphans, for the needy, for the wayfarer, for those who ask, and for the ransom of slaves; to be steadfast in prayer, and to practice regular charity. . .

—Qur'an 2:177[1]

And one of the scribes came near and heard them disputing with one another, and seeing that he answered them well, asked him, "Which commandment is the first of all?" Jesus answered, "The first is, 'Hear, O Israel: The Lord our God, the Lord is one; and you shall love the Lord your God with all your heart, and with all your soul, and with all your mind, and with all your strength.' The second is this, 'You shall love your neighbor as yourself.' There is no other commandment greater than these."

—Mark 12:28–31

1. Ali, *The Qur'an*, 7.9.

28

Muhammad: *As-salamu alaykum*, great prophet Jesus. It is pleasant sitting here with you on this hillside overlooking Jerusalem, the city that has so much meaning for our religions. As you know, I was born more than five hundred years after you and met many of your followers along the caravan routes. I have great respect for you. Respect for you is important in our religion too. I am so eager to learn more about you and your movement.

Jesus: Blessings on you, Muhammad, and on your wife Khadijah. Your religion, Islam, has certainly been a force in the world, and many of your followers are devout and peaceful people. I look forward to hearing more about you and your religion. First, tell me more about yourselves.

Muhammad: Well, I was born around 570 CE in Mecca, an arid city in the Arabian Desert. Mecca was a thriving oasis, where merchants and camel drivers gathered to refresh themselves and compare goods. It also was a place to sing and dance around the Kaaba, a cube-shaped building that contained images of the many tribal gods and goddesses. I was born into the Quraysh tribe, but, since I was a member of a poor clan and orphaned early, I did not benefit from the wealth and influence of that tribe. You see, my father died before I was born, and my mother died when I was six years old. I was raised first by my grandfather, and then by my uncle, Abu Talib, a merchant. My uncle gave me a job on the caravans, and I worked hard and traveled to many exotic places.

Actually, it was on one of my trips through Syria that I met a Christian monk named Bahira. He taught me a great deal about Christianity, which was popular in that area but widely diverse in its beliefs. Bahira and I became friends; I was stunned when he predicted that I was destined for greatness and would become a prophet of God.

Jesus: I can relate to your surprise at Bahira's predictions. I was equally surprised when my mentor, John the Baptist, said that he was not worthy to baptize me and indicated that he was only preparing the way for me. He even said that he was not worthy to buckle my sandal! And this from someone who has taught me how to pray in the desert, the meaning of deep repentance, and the notion of the kingdom of God. But go on. You were talking about your work with the caravans.

Muhammad: I grew into a powerful man and became a highly skilled caravan driver. When I was twenty-five, I apparently caught the eye of Khadijah, a forty-year-old woman who was successful in the caravan business. She not only hired me, she also asked me to marry her, which was rather unusual in those days.

Khadijah: Indeed it was! Most marriages at that time were arranged when people were young. Being older, of course, that was not feasible. I was very much attracted to Muhammad the moment I saw him, so I just went ahead and proposed marriage to him.

Muhammad: After we married, we had seven children: three sons who died in infancy and four daughters. We also adopted Zayd and Ali, who was the son of Abu Talib. Abu had come on hard times, so I thought the least I could do for him would be to raise his son.

I understand that you never married. Wasn't that unusual for your times, Jesus?

Jesus: Yes, it was. Most young Jewish people had their marriages arranged when they were teens. In my case, my father died when I was young. It was more important for me to take over his trade and keep the farm running than to have my marriage arranged. By the time I left home at age thirty for my all-consuming mission to heal and to teach the kingdom of God, I hardly had time for a family. I didn't have a home or money to support them either. In addition, my life was cut short at thirty-three, when I was crucified.

But please tell me more about your life. My followers often have so many misconceptions about you.

Muhammad: Well, I became a family man and a partner with my wife in the caravan business. I continued to travel a great deal throughout the Middle East. What chaos in the world at that time! The two empires that dominated that area, the Byzantine to the east and the Persian to the west, were constantly locked in bloody struggles. I witnessed a great deal of struggle and brutality on my trips. Then, when I returned to Mecca, the corruption shocked me. The wealthy were greedy and out for pleasure. Poor widows and orphans were shunned and driven outside into the deserts and mountains to live like refugees. There were blood feuds and revenge killings among the clans. Women were just property, with no rights, and spent their lives serving their husbands. Daughters were seen as liabilities.

Religion had become much too superstitious. I couldn't keep track of all the gods and goddesses. Allah was a distant god who seemed to have been forgotten.

The Jews I met in my travels seemed to be in disagreement about many of their teachings. And the Christians were quite a mix. Some were living in the desert with their own interpretation of the Jesus tradition. Other groups had been ostracized because of their "heretical" views about your humanity or divinity. I could never understand why there was so much division within the Jewish and Christian traditions or even between their traditions.

Jesus: In the early centuries of the development of Christianity, there were many disputes about my teachings. We can discuss that in more detail later.

I can understand your reactions to the corruption and religious confusion of your time. I too witnessed much corruption and brutality in my day. The Herod family had been put in charge of several provinces of our area. They built enormous palaces and lived luxurious lives, funded by the tax burdens on the backs of the poor.

There was much religious confusion in my day. My people in Galilee were hated by the Samaritans in the central province. The Samaritans did not accept our Temple in Jerusalem or our priesthood. It was always dangerous to travel through that area. In the south by the Dead Sea, the Jewish Essenes lived in seclusion and also rejected our tradition of Judaism.

In Judea in the south, the Romans ruled with brutality. The procurator lived royally in Jerusalem and in his summer palace in Caesarea. The Romans worshiped many gods and goddesses and even held the corrupt emperor to be divine. The Sadducees were the wealthy Jewish landowners and couldn't care less about poor farmers and tradesmen like myself. Many of our Pharisees and scribes were leading double lives. Our widows and orphans lived in squalor also, and the lepers were shunned and cast out into the desert to live. Indeed, the political and religious corruption of my day and the oppression are some of the reasons I took on a mission for reform.

I was wondering, what religious group did you identify with early on?

Muhammad: I was attracted to the Hanifs. They refused to participate in all the superstition at the Kaaba and believed that there was but one God. I was influenced by them. At that same time, my distress about the corruption around me led me to go off into the mountains for retreats. There I spent many hours in meditations and had deep dreams.

On one occasion, when I was about forty years old, I was praying in a cave. Suddenly, I felt overpowered by a strong spiritual force. I was told: "Read in the name of your Lord who created man from an embryo; Read for your Sustainer is the most bountiful."[2] Then I began to hear about a

2. Ali, *The Qur'an*, Surah 96:1–3.

benevolent God who created humans and wanted to instruct them and to be intimate with them. I heard about the rebellion of God's people; I heard that Allah sees all, wants to be near us, requires adoration, and warns that those who resist him will be condemned.

The whole experience threw me into a panic. Was I being tricked by one of those *jinnis* that my people are so wary of? I fled to the top of the mountain and there met a spirit who told me that I had encountered the archangel Gabriel. I went home not wanting to have anything to do with this experience. If I spoke about it, people would surely think me to be insane or a charlatan.

Have you ever had an experience like this, Jesus?

Jesus: Yes. One occasion comes to mind. I was in the desert on retreat. I was exhausted, almost overcome with hunger and thirst, and quite afraid that the wild animals in the area would sneak up on me. Suddenly, a spirit spoke to me and asked me to turn the rocks into bread, which I admit would have tasted so good at the time. I was tempted to work a miracle, but, like you, suspected this was an evil spirit. I told the spirit that true bread was the Word of God. Then the spirit invited me to go up to the top of the Temple and throw myself off, telling me that the angels would save me. My faith told me that I should never tempt my God like that, and I refused. Finally, I was taken to the top of a mountain and offered the whole world as my empire if I would worship the spirit. I knew my God was a God of service and not domination, and I now recognize that I was in fact dealing with Satan. He left, and God's Spirit came and comforted me.

So what happened when you went home from your mountain retreat?

Muhammad: As soon as I got home, I sought refuge in my wife's arms, telling her that I might be losing my mind.

Khadijah: I wrapped my husband in a cloak, comforted him, and assured him that he was not going mad. I told him that he was too good a man for God to allow him to be so tricked.

I then consulted my cousin Waraqa, who had just converted to the Christian religion, Jesus. He came to see my husband and assured him that he was a truly good person and a genuine prophet. After this assurance, God remained silent for some time, and both my husband and I became skeptical of the whole matter.

Muhammad: Suddenly, one day, I was overcome by a great force and told that I was not demented, but was born with a sublime nature, was due unending rewards, and that I will be shown by Allah those who have gone astray from the path as well as those who are guided on the way. I now knew that I was being given a special mission to help my people.

My initial message was not about abuses in religion, but about the true nature of Allah and the need for social reform. I began to speak as a Messenger from God, from Allah, who was a good and loving Creator. I preached about Allah as "the most generous," "the most merciful." This was not the remote and dispassionate Allah of my Arabic people. Allah was the protector of the poor and underprivileged and called the greedy to turn from their selfish ways and to help the needy, the orphaned, and the beggars.

When did you get your calling to be a prophet, Jesus?

Jesus: First of all, it was fortunate that you had your wife Khadijah to turn to as you struggled with this calling. Women are often more sensitive and can know us better than we know ourselves.

I remember turning to my mother for advice. She told me that when I was conceived she heard a message that she would have a son. He would be a great person and would be called "the Son of the Most High." She told me that she often wondered what this meant. At one point, when I was only twelve, I had the notion that I was being called to be "about my Father's business," but she quickly took me back home and said I was too young. I do remember one occasion when we were at a wedding where the hosts were in danger of embarrassment because the wine they were to serve their guests had run out. She asked me to solve the problem. I said I was not yet ready for my mission, but she just gave me the nudge I needed to start. After I left home at age thirty, she would occasionally show up and see if I was all right. There were many rumors about me, and there were dangerous threats made against me. She knew, even before I did, that I was in harm's way.

As far as my calling to be a prophet, I think I first felt that when I was a reader in the synagogue and identified with the message of Isaiah.

Tell me more about your own mission.

Muhammad: Well, I started with my family and close friends. They joined me as companions and were called "Muslims," or those who submit to God. For a few years the people of Mecca did not notice the message. As my revelations developed, the people in the city began to realize that I was teaching: "There is no God but Allah, and Muhammad is God's messenger." The Quraysh leaders began to take notice because this challenged their beliefs in many gods, as well as the financial gains they made on all the pilgrimages and devotions at the Kaaba. I began to speak for God as his prophet, and I condemned their greed, tribal vengeance, violence, and idol worship at the Kaaba. In God's name I stood up for the poor and the outcasts and began to empower them. The local leaders began to turn on me.

Jesus: I can see similarities in my own mission. At first my message about God's love, the presence of the kingdom, and my miracles were well-received. But once I went after the pride, greed, and hypocrisy among some of my religious leaders, as well as the lip service of their prayers and rituals, I knew that their fear and hatred were being turned toward me.

So how did your leaders treat you?

Muhammad: First they tried to bribe me to be quiet. They often ridiculed me as I spoke to pilgrims visiting the Kaaba. Then they boycotted my clan, refusing to allow us to buy or sell, preventing us from even using the town's well. We were devastated by the ban. When they finally lifted the ban and things started to improve, both my beloved wife Khadijah and my protector Abu died. I was left vulnerable, and yet I continued to have my revelations. At one point I felt that I was transported to Jerusalem, where I encountered Adam, Abraham, Moses, and you, Jesus—all the great prophets of the past. I began to be physically abused and received death threats. It seemed obvious that I had to leave Mecca.

Jesus: So where did you go?

Muhammad: I had been invited to mediate some disputes in Yathrib about 250 miles north of Mecca. It is now called Medina. I went there, barely escaping plots to assassinate me or to kidnap me and hold me for ransom. Some of my followers gradually came to join me.

Did you experience such threats?

Jesus: Yes, early on when I worked miracles on the Sabbath, some began to plot my death. I confined most of my work to Galilee because it was dangerous for me to go to Jerusalem. In fact, it was there that I was arrested and crucified.

So what happened in Medina?

Muhammad: For the next twenty-three years my revelations continued, and I applied them to the people of Medina. I became their chieftain, and my revelations directed me to establish equality among the tribes and clans, to stop the blood feuds and revenge, and call for forgiveness and reconciliation among the people. I abolished the crippling taxes on the people and called for alms for the poor, the homeless, and the orphans. I freed slaves and gave equality to women, giving them their rights in inheritance, dowries, and ownership of property. After the death of Khadijah, I married several wives and took up residence with them near the mosque I had built for the community, so the people could meet and have regular prayer to the one God, Allah.

All the while, the tribes of Mecca continued to be my enemies. I attacked their caravans and took their goods for my people. Eventually, they marched on Medina, but we were able to defeat them and drive them back to Mecca. They attacked again; though I was wounded, we prevailed.

Jesus: This is one area where we differ, Muhammad. You became a warrior and went to battle with your enemies. I taught my followers to turn the other cheek when struck and to love their enemies and pray for those who persecute them. Now I know that many of my followers later turned to war, even religious wars, but I always taught the way of nonviolence.

Muhammad: I too was a person of peace, but I believed that one has a right to self-defense. Didn't your followers develop the "just war theory?"

Jesus: Indeed, they did—four hundred years after my death, when Christianity was the official religion of the Roman Empire. They borrowed the theory from the Romans, and you know the brutality of those people. I have never seen a so-called "just war," or a war that couldn't have been avoided by early negotiations or stern sanctions on those who threaten war. Wars that kill millions of innocent people can never be called "just."

So how did you resolve the conflict with Mecca?

Muhammad: The people of Medina began to lose patience with me. I had come as a peacemaker, and I was now leading them into wars as an aging military leader. Fortunately, I was able to gain support from many of the local Bedouins, so I led a pilgrimage of great numbers into Mecca. The leaders there were overwhelmed and had to stand aside, unable to resist. I went over to the Kaaba and destroyed all the images of the gods and goddesses, except, you might note, the image of you, Jesus, and of your mother, Mary. We don't worship either of you, but we do have great reverence for you. From that day forward the Kaaba was to be the house of the one God, Allah.

If I am not mistaken, Jesus, didn't you have some altercation at your Jewish Temple? Wasn't that an act of violence?

Jesus: You must be thinking of the time I visited the Temple in Jerusalem and was greatly angered by the crooked money-changing and marketing that was going on there. I was very upset and made a whip of rope, over-turned their tables, and drove those greedy people out of my Father's house of prayer. I did not consider this to be an act of violence because I was care-ful not to injure anyone. It only shows that we all have our faults—and that I truly lost it that day!

So what happened after you cleansed the Kaaba?

Muhammad: After that I was able to unite all the Arabs in the areas into Muslim tribes within a united religious and political order called the *um-mah*. I returned to Medina several years later and continued to lead my people. One day at prayer I felt very ill and returned to my residence, where I passed away. This showed my followers that, though I was the prophet of the one God, Allah, I was still a mere human. I had not named a successor, so my followers were faced with the challenge of continuing my mission.

What happened after your death, Jesus?

Jesus: I know that your followers believe that it was someone else, other than me, who died on the cross and that, instead, I directly ascended into heaven and remain there until the Last Days.

Here we have a great difference, Muhammad. It was I who died on the cross, executed by Roman and Jewish enemies. This event is central in all my Gospels and is depicted as my final act of love for all the people throughout the ages. Here I offered my life for the salvation of the world. And then, it was on the third day, God raised me from the dead, and I appeared to my disciples and many others as being in a new state of existence. It was only after some time that I returned to the Father, but my disciples believe that I am present to them always as their savior. As I promised, they experience my presence in the world, in themselves and others, in the sacraments, and in the Scriptures, for all time. In the Last Days, my followers expect my Second Coming, when I will proclaim that I am the savior of the world.

Muhammad, we know there are serious differences between Islam and Christianity, but that doesn't mean that our people can't love each other and see all as children of God or Allah. We just have to agree to disagree.

But let's move on. How did your people cope after you were gone?

Muhammad: After my death, my Muslim people recognized that I was the final prophet and that they needed to preserve my revelation.

I was not a reader or writer, so as I received my revelations over many years, I memorized them and recited them to my closest followers. They, in turn, either memorized them or wrote them down. These were considered to be the beautiful and inspiring words of God. After my death, the first caliph (deputy), Abu Bakr, following my orders, decreed that all written and oral memorizations be gathered into one text. Eventually, a definitive version, the Qur'an, was compiled. All other versions were destroyed. The Qur'an consists of 114 surahs or chapters and is arranged from the longest surahs to the shortest. This is considered to be the actual speech of God, as revealed to me, his prophet. To be authentic, it must be in our beautiful Arabic and is to be recited or read. Those who can memorize the entire text are greatly honored. The Qur'an is not a book, but rather the living word of God. To recite or listen to its haunting inner rhythms, tones, and guttural sounds in Arabic brings all Muslims inner strength, comfort, and solace. We also have the Hadith, which are not my direct revelations. They are some of my other words and deeds, as well as those of some of my early companions. There are many Hadith, and these range from being sound, to being good, to being weak, depending on how their authenticity has been rated by early evaluators.

I know your followers also have a deep reverence for the Word of God, Jesus. How does their understanding of the New Testament differ from the Muslim understanding of the Qur'an?

Jesus: I have to say, Muhammad, that your followers seem to be quite literal toward your revelations. They seem to be open to different interpretations, but they view your revelations as directly coming from God, word for word.

My followers take different approaches to my revelations. They believe that I am the Son of God and that my revelations were from God. Many of my teachings were also memorized, and oral traditions existed in my communities for some time after my death. Various authors, who are referred to as Gospel writers, gathered these oral stories and wrote unique compilations. Earlier views were that these were symbolic and metaphoric writings that contained my teachings. Later, some believed that God actually dictated my teaching to the Gospel writers. There were differences among the accounts, but the versions were put into a kind of harmonious union of one account. More recently, many of my believers hold that the Gospels are not so much the "words of God," but that they are the Word of God—stories and accounts based on what I said and did. They are "inspired" in that the writers were inspired by God to be true to my teachings. As you can see, among my believers, there are varying approaches to my revelations. They range from those who take the Scriptures literally to those who approach them critically as sacred literature. Somehow, the truth of my Gospel teaching seems to have survived all of this controversy!

Then, of course, there is the challenge of incorporation of the Hebrew Bible into the Christian Bible and seeing that also as revelation. Where do the Muslims stand on that?

Khadijah: Muslims recognize Jews and Christians as "people of the book" and their traditions as monotheistic religions. In fact, the Qur'an includes stories from both the Hebrew and Christian Bibles. At the same time, we hold that both the Jewish and Christian traditions had to be purified, corrected, and advanced by the final revelation that my husband received as God's prophet.

Jesus: You say that you are God's prophet, Muhammad. How do you see yourself in relation to other prophets and to me?

Muhammad: My revelation told me that Abraham was a Muslim and our founder. Both he and his son Ishmael built the Kaaba. Moses is the liberator and lawgiver. Moses was told of my coming and asked his people to honor me.

We have a deep respect for you, Jesus, and believe that you are a Spirit from God, who was born of a virgin and was a great teacher, prophet, and miracle worker. We do not believe that you are the Messiah, nor can we accept that you are divine because we believe in just one God. Neither is the teaching of Trinity acceptable to us because it seems to be three Gods. We do believe that you will come on the Day of Judgment.

Jesus: Well, that explains why there has been such a deep division between Muslims and Christians. Still, there must be respect and love among us. These differences should not be the basis for alienation.

Now, let's take a look at the laws of our traditions. Christians have many laws. We recognize the Ten Commandments. The church began to formulate its own books of laws in the Middle Ages, and now Eastern, Western, Protestant, and Catholic churches have their own laws or ordinances. The Roman Church has a collection of Canon Laws. My law, of course, is the law of love, and all other laws have to be measured by that virtue.

Where are your laws to be found?

Khadijah: Muslim law is also complex and diverse according to our own divisions. The Muslim word for law is *shariah*. Much of the law comes from the Qur'an or from our legal scholars, but there are many variations and interpretations. In our mosques, the Imams, or leaders, teach and lead their communities in legal matters. In the Sunni tradition there are four main schools of legal thought, and the Shia have their own distinct schools.[3]

Jesus: Do Muslims have some fundamental laws?

Muhammad: Yes, we call them the Five Pillars of Islam. They are mentioned in the Qur'an and developed in the Hadith. They are as follows:

1. The profession of faith (Shahada)
   This is to be recited everyday: "I testify that there is no God but God. I testify that Muhammad is the Messenger of God."

2. Ritual prayer (Salat)
   Muslims are required to pray five times a day, if possible in the local mosque.

3. Give alms to the poor. (Zakat)
   Muslims are required to purify themselves of greed and share what they have out of compassion for the needy. Muslims are obliged to give 2½ percent of their possessions to others.

4. The month-long fast (Sawm)
   This is during the month of Ramadan in late summer or early fall. The Muslim is obliged to fast from sunrise to sundown from food, drink, and sexual intercourse. It is time to reflect on Allah's blessings and give to the needy.

5. A pilgrimage to Mecca (Hajj)
   This pilgrimage, with all of its elaborate rituals, is to be made at least once in one's lifetime.[4]

Jesus: As I mentioned earlier, my fundamental law is the law of love—love of God and love of neighbor as oneself. Acts of love, rather than mere obedience to rules, should characterize my followers. They are called to be of service to others. The person who wants to be first is to be last and the servant of all. In addition, we value the theological virtues of faith, hope, and charity and the cardinal virtues of prudence, justice, fortitude, and moderation in all things. Christians are encouraged to pray regularly, to receive Eucharist, and to give to the poor. They usually fast during the church season of Lent to prepare for the week that commemorates my death and Resurrection. They often make pilgrimages to Palestine, my homeland; Rome, the center

3. See Kamali, *Shari'ah Law*.
4. See Hussain, *The Five Pillars of Islam*.

of Roman Catholic Christianity; and other important Christian sites. None of these are strict requirements.

How did Islam spread?

Muhammad: After my death, the caliphs spread my message among the Arab tribes. Within several decades, largely through conquest, Islam spread through the Middle East and then through large sections of Europe, as far away as parts of France and into Spain. They also moved into North Africa and Spain, and then east into Pakistan, China, and Southeast Asia. In the medieval period, they conquered Turkey and established the Ottoman Empire. The Muslim Empire became larger than either Greece or Rome. While Europe languished through the Dark Ages, approximately the fifth to the eleventh centuries, the Islamic Empire flourished with outstanding advances in science, commerce, scholarship, education, and literature.[5]

All of this conquest occurred after my death; it was done by the original caliphs, at first, as an effort to unify the Arab tribes. Later, it became an effort to gain dominance, land, and riches. That was not in my vision or teachings.

Jesus: I understand, Muhammad, because the same dynamic took place within my movement. I preached nonviolence, and for the first two centuries or more my followers were persecuted and even killed as martyrs. My Jewish reform grew into a religion of its own. Once Christianity was accepted within the Roman Empire and became the official religion of the empire, Christianity became part of the power structure. In turn, Christians persecuted the so-called pagans and destroyed their temples and statues.

Once the empire began to collapse, Christianity shifted its emphasis to the conversion of the so-called barbarians who were overrunning the empire: the Huns, Gauls, Celts, Anglo-Saxons, and others. My religion eventually became part of the political and military structures of Christendom and engaged in numerous conflicts and wars. Later, Christians engaged in the violent Crusades, the conquest of the New World, the religious wars of the Reformation, and the building of the enormous colonial empires.

What did your own revelation tell you about the use of violence? The 9/11 event in the United States and terrorism today have led many to associate Islam with *jihad*, or holy war, with its images of suicide bombers and roadside bombs.

---

5. Leaman, *An Introduction to Classical Islamic Philosophy*, 225–37.

Muhammad: First, let me point out that Islam is derived from the Arabic word *salaam*, which means peace. There are 1.6 billion Muslims in the world[6] and the vast majority of them are peace-loving people who work hard for a living and want to raise their children in a peaceful society.

My revelation taught me that all human beings are created by Allah and are called to return to their creator. The Qur'an teaches that God created humans in diverse genders, tribes, and nations "that they may recognize one another" and be friends, brothers, and sisters. For Islam, life is sacred and must be protected and preserved from violence. In the Qur'an, God says, "That is why we decreed for the children of Israel that whosoever kills a human being, except as punishment for murder or for spreading corruption in the land, shall be like killing all humanity; and whoever saves a human life, saves the entire human race."

I supported what would later be called the "just war," but forbade the killing of women, children, and aged. I strongly opposed and forbade the Arab blood feuds, tribal revenge violence, and repression by dictators. The Qur'an tells us that God calls humans to be just, do good, and be generous. It forbids indecency, impropriety, and oppression. Like many of your followers, Muslims support a "just war theory" that views war as a defensive, last-resort decision that protects noncombatants.

Let me address *jihad*. First of all, the word means struggle. It occurs thirty-five times in the Qur'an and, for the most part, refers to the human struggle against sin and evil—the struggle against greed, violence, and hatred. Here, *jihad* refers to the struggle for a peaceful and just world. There are more than seventy passages in the Qur'an in which war is prohibited.

Only four verses in the Qur'an are warlike. These are wrongly interpreted by extremists to allow for terrorism and revenge killings. The vast majority of my followers do not struggle over getting even with their enemies, but rather with making ends meet and raising and educating their children. They struggle to be good, prayerful, and just people, concerned about hunger, poverty, war, and unemployment.[7]

Jesus: Let's discuss the divisions in our religions, Muhammad. I know that your goal was to unite the Arab tribes and clans during your lifetime. How did that work out after your death?

6. PewResearch Religion & Public Life Project, "The Future of the Global Muslim Population."

7. See Noorani, *Islam and Jihad*.

Muhammad: Yes, my followers divided, Jesus. The first source of division was centered on the choice of my successor. Many in the community gathered and chose Abu Bakr, one of my close companions, to be in charge. They gave him the title of caliph. This upset those who wanted the succession to be by direct descendants, and not by selection. These people wanted Ali, my cousin and son-in-law who was married to my daughter Fatimah, to be in charge. In other words, my descendants would have the right to rule. Cries of tyranny and apostasy were shouted back and forth. The third caliph was murdered, and eventually Ali gained the leadership. Then, Ali was assassinated. Lines of conflict were drawn that remain today and include the Sunni and Shiite branches.

The Sunnis are a large majority of Muslims. The Sunnis (*sunna* means tradition) hold that the leader of the community (*ummah*) can be anyone who follows and teaches the tradition as interpreted by learned scholars. The Sunnis follow the Qur'an, the Sunna (accounts of what I said and did), as well as scholarly interpretations of the tradition.

The Shia branch holds that the leadership should come from my descendants. While they also follow the Qur'an and the Sunna, they have their own sources from the teachings of Ali as well as interpretations by their learned jurists.

There is still another group called the Kharijites. They were rather extreme, insisting that their rulers be sinless and just, or else they should be subjected to violence. There are also the Sufis, who try to emulate my spiritual, mystical side. They emphasize love over obedience and are much like your religious communities who left the world and practiced strict asceticism and devotions. Their great poet Rumi has captured the spirit of my teachings and is a worthy ambassador of my vision for life.

Jesus: Your followers have certainly had their divisions, as have my disciples. Jewish Christians were in conflict with Gentile Christians. Gnostics, Arians, and others were in conflict with the more traditional Christian believers. There were also many other divisions: the Eastern Orthodox Church vs. the Western Roman Catholic Church, Catholic vs. Protestant, and Denominational vs. Non-denominational. Even among Roman Catholics today there are serious divisions between conservatives, progressives, and radicals.

You insisted that Islam is peaceful. Could you tell us something about what your followers are doing for peace?

Muhammad: My revelations showed the common origin of humanity and the equality and solidarity of all people. All humans come from Allah and can return to Allah. We strongly advocate openness, respect, and unity.

Most of my followers condemned the U.S. attacks on 9/11 and at the same time opposed (as did your Pope John Paul II) the invasion of Iraq. Most oppose the killing of innocent people in places like Russia, Syria, Afghanistan, Somalia, Yemen, and Sudan. Syrian Muslims have risked their lives opposing the torture and cruelty in Syrian prisons. Many of my followers have been imprisoned or killed for protesting the abuse of human rights in countries like Egypt, Iran, Yemen, and Israel. They have opposed nuclear weapons in India, Pakistan, and Israel.

These Muslims who oppose violence, torture, and the abuse of human rights are indeed true to my teachings.[8]

Jesus: I know that we both share the creation stories from the Hebrew Bible and honor God as the Creator of all things. I know that my followers have begun to see the sacredness of all things, and now are making strides in sustaining the quality of the air, water, land, and resources, which they have abused for so long. I grew up close to the land and the animals and used the harvest and the birds of the air in my parables. But somehow that message to love and preserve creation got lost until recently.

What do your followers think about the environment?

Muhammad: Well, until recently, many Muslims thought of the environmental crisis as being of Western making. They thought: "They caused it. Let them fix it." Now Muslims have begun to realize that their oil products, industrialization, pollution, consumerism, and waste make them equally part of the problem. Muslims are now beginning to step out into international, national, and local movements to sustain the Earth and its resources.

Khadijah: The Qur'an teaches that the entire universe is from Allah and that the oneness of Allah is reflected in the oneness of humanity with creation. Humans have been mandated to keep balance, harmony, and unity in the world. Unity implies serious collaboration with each other and with the Earth. The serious problems of pollution, degradation, and waste come from human neglect and must be attended to through human consensus and serious efforts to improve the environment. The Qur'an says that humans have been sent by Allah as a mercy. Too often, Muslims, as well as many Christians, have thought they are on the Earth to dominate and manipulate nature. When we were given "dominion," it was to rule as God does, with wisdom, compassion, and care.

---

8. See Winter and Williams, *Understanding Islam and the Muslims.*

We are not masters of the universe, but, rather, benevolent caretakers guided by Allah as to how to preserve and sustain the Earth and its resources. The Qur'an teaches that we will be punished for not fulfilling our God-given responsibilities and for the evils that we perpetrate. Degradation, waste, and pollution are indeed evils.

Jesus: I know that there is much unrest among the women in our religions, so we should talk about this. Khadijah, I know that when Muhammad came along with his revelations, it was a challenge to many Arabs and their traditional views on women.

Khadijah: Indeed. I grew up in an Arab culture where women had few rights. They were often traded from one family to another, much as one would do with property or goods. Women were definitely viewed as much inferior to men, a weak creation. Their primary duty was to serve the men of the family. Fathers married their daughters off young in arranged marriages, with a dowry as part of the marriage agreement. Since females weren't able to work as hard as men, and since they required a dowry, they were considered to be a liability. A male child was welcomed with great joy and celebration. A female child was often killed or left in the countryside to die from the elements.

Muhammad: My revelation teaches that men and women are equal. Both were created by Allah, and both are called to the same final reward. Allah watches over both with the same benevolence. This equality is the bedrock of the Qur'an; there is no place in Islam for abuse or injustice toward women. The "rib story" in Genesis, which many use to indicate that women are derivative and inferior to the male, is not in the Qur'an. Nor does the Qur'an refer to the Fall in the garden, where Eve was seen as succumbing to temptation and alluded to as the male's temptress. Moreover, the Qur'an does not speak of burkas or the veiling of women. It merely says that women should dress modestly. Neither does the Qur'an call for women to be secluded and separate in society. All one has to do is go to Mecca today and see how the women and men dress similarly and walk side by side during the pilgrimage. That is my vision of equality. The separation of women at prayer as well as the horrible practice of stoning women for adultery are not in the Qur'an either and were not part of our original practices. It was the later leaders who introduced these practices of ostracizing women and treating them like inferior servants. Much of this was from culture and not from my revelations.

I treated women with great respect, consulted them, and appointed them as spiritual guides. At home I helped with the domestic chores. In the original places of prayer, I prayed side by side with women. Islam outlawed the killing of female infants. Both male and female infants are bestowed on parents as blessings.

It is true that in the courts a woman's testimony held less weight than a man's, and that inheritance and divorce laws favored men. I have to acknowledge that none of this was in line with my teachings. Like everyone, I was surrounded by cultural practices that were almost impossible to change. You faced the same problems: you preached equality and dignity of women, but could do little to change abuses such as slavery, arranged marriages, and divorce laws slanted against women.[9]

Khadijah: Muhammad can teach the ideals, but it takes many centuries before cultures recognize them. Today many Muslim women are resisting inequality and are making their voices heard to gain the equality that Muhammad's revelations proposed. Muslim women are entering universities and professions and are standing up for their rights with regard to dress and being present in society. Some are being elected to office. We are very proud of the young Pakistani, Malala, who won the Nobel Peace Prize for defending the right of women to be educated.

Jesus: I see your point. Christians are often critical of how Muslim women are treated, but they don't see the plank in their own eye, as it were. My teachings on the dignity of the human person, on the centrality of justice, compassion, and love of neighbor as the self were never compatible with slavery or women's inequality. Yet it has taken almost two thousand years before Christians came to realize the evil of slavery. And it was only in this century that Christians in the United States came to approve the civil rights of African-Americans. The women's rights movement is mostly from recent times, and there is still a long way to go before women will be seen as equal.

Ironically, the churches have been behind modern-day culture where women's rights are concerned. The recent popes have often proclaimed the equality of women, but have left the power in the Roman Catholic Church in the hands of the all-male clergy and hierarchy. Today, Pope Francis urges Catholics to get back to the Gospels. If they do, I think they will find my teachings with regard to women to be very different from the practice we see today.

9. See DeLong-Bas, *The Oxford Encyclopedia of Islam and Women.*

Muhammad: Jesus, your religion came after the great classical cultures of Greece and Rome with their many contributions. What has Christianity contributed to culture?

Jesus: Well, I think of the Gospels, the early writings of the Church Fathers, the magnificent writings of Ambrose and Augustine, and the brilliant synthesis of Christian theology by Thomas Aquinas. There are the great cathedrals in Rome and across Europe, the early art of the catacombs, the magnificent art and sculpture of Michelangelo, Giotto, Raphael, da Vinci, Matisse, and Chagall. The beautiful Russian art of the nineteenth century is often life-size and creatively captures scenes from the Gospels.

The Gregorian chant is quite inspiring. There are the classical music pieces of Palestrina, Mozart, and Beethoven.

Great Prophet, I know there have been many important contributions to culture by Islam.

Muhammad: Indeed. During the so-called Dark Ages of Europe, culture in the Muslim world flourished. In our large cities, caravans from far and wide brought the best goods. Our houses were finely furnished and had running water and sewer systems. Our streets were paved. We had marvelous irrigation systems and were far advanced in agriculture, manufacturing, and medicine.

We established excellent universities and libraries a century before Europe and preserved the classics from Greece and Rome that became the basis of European education, especially in astronomy, mathematics, philosophy, and theology.

We had outstanding scholars, such as Avicenna (d. 1037), Averroes (d. 1198), and al-Ghazali (d. 1111), who greatly influenced the European medieval scholars. In literature we are most proud of the poetry of Omar Khayyam (d. 1131) and Rumi (d. 1273), both of whom are still read today throughout the world.

Our architects designed and built magnificent mosques such as the Dome of the Rock in Jerusalem, the Grand Mosque of Damascus in Syria, the Blue Mosque in Istanbul, and the marvelous mausoleum, the Taj Mahal in Agra, India.

Jesus: Tell me what happened to this great empire.

Muhammad: We lost much of our great Islamic influence during the Crusades in 1095, as well as when we were driven out of Spain in the thirteenth century, and after attacks by the Mongols led by Genghis Khan in the same century. Later, many of our areas came under British control as they built their British Empire.

Jesus: Tell me, Khadijah, about what is going on in the Muslim world today.

Khadijah: As we mentioned before, today the Muslim population totals 1.6 billion and is about one fourth of the world's population. Islam is the second-largest religion. Large numbers of Muslims are in the Middle East, North Africa, and sub-Saharan Africa, with a majority living in parts of the Asia-Pacific region. The number is increasing in Europe.[10]

The Islamic revival started in the beginning of the nineteenth century with Modernist movements to update Islam and resist Western domination. In the 1920s the Muslim Brotherhood was established in Egypt to unite Arabs against the West as well as against the wealthy Arab rulers. Persecuted, the Muslim Brothers fled to Saudi Arabia, a country that was prospering from oil money. They were joined with another fundamentalist group, and Wahhabism was formed. Wahhabis wanted to restore Sunni Islamic purity, which created a situation in which Shia and Sufis were oppressed. The Saudis took control of Mecca and Medina, which coincidentally boosted the region's coffers from the hajj pilgrims.

The Saudi radical group al Qaeda was formed by Osama Bin Laden during the Afghan War in the late 1980s.[11] Bin Laden, a devout Wahhabi Muslim raised in a wealthy Saudi family, turned on the Saudi royals and went to fight with the Afghans against the Russians, supported by his own money—in addition to money and weapons from the United States. Bin Laden later turned on the Americans because of their interference in the Gulf War and began to organize terrorist actions on the U.S. embassies in Africa, on an American ship, and the World Trade Center. His group, al Qaeda, also organized terrorist actions on the Pentagon and the U.S. Capitol on September 11, 2001. Bin Laden was killed by American troops in 2011.

Terrorism is a brutal attack on innocent lives, both Muslim and non-Muslim, and bears no support in my Qur'an. Most Muslims worldwide are peace-loving and respect human life as coming from Allah.

And how is the Christian religion doing today, Jesus?

Jesus: There are about 2.18 billion Christians worldwide, including about 1.2 billion Catholics. The largest Christian population is in the United

10. PewResearch Religion & Public Life Project, "The Future of the Global Muslim Population."

11. See Encyclopaedia Brittanica Online, s.v. "al-Qaeda," http://www.britannica.com.

States. The most significant places of growth are in sub-Saharan Africa and the Asia-Pacific region.[12]

In the early 1960s Catholics held a worldwide Vatican II Council, which opened the doors to significant reform and vigorous ecumenical and interfaith dialogue. Catholics since that time have been divided into progressives and traditionalists. The church's reputation has been damaged by some members of the clergy who sexually abused children, by cover-ups, and by financial corruption in the Vatican. You will never know how much all of this saddens me.

There is a new Roman Catholic pope, Francis, who is dedicated to reforming the church. He teaches about and lives a life of simplicity, generosity, and care for the poor. It is a time of great hope among Catholics. Christians seem to be moving back to the center—living the gospel of love of God, love of self, and love of each other.

Muhammad: Jesus, it has been an honor for me and my wife Kahdijah to be with you and to share insights on our traditions. Our hope is that Muslims and Christians today can come to better understand each other and work together for peace and justice in the world. *Hudafez* (God go with you).

Jesus: Peace be with you both!

SUGGESTED READINGS ON ISLAM

Ahmed, Akbar. *Islam Today.* London: Taurus, 2002.

Kaltmer, John. *Islam.* Minneapolis, Fortress, 2003.

Nasr, Seyyed Hossei. *The Heart of Islam.* San Francisco: Harper San Francisco, 2002.

Shepard, William. *Introducing Islam.* New York: Routledge, 2009.

Yazbeck Haddad, Yvonne and others. *Muslim Women in America.* New York: Oxford University Press, 2006.

---

12. See PewResearch Religion & Public Life Project, "Global Christianity."

Chapter 3

Hinduism

∼ Jesus with Krishna and Radha

Strive constantly to serve the welfare of the world; by devotion to selfless work one attains the supreme goal of life. Do your work with the welfare of others always in mind.

— Krishna, Bhagavad Gita 3:19–20

. . .the Son of Man came not to be served but to serve, and to give his life a ransom for many.

— Matt 20:28

Jesus: Namaste, Krishna and Radha. It is delightful sitting in this beautiful garden where you both once played. I know you are important divine figures in Hinduism, and I am looking forward to learning firsthand about you and your ancient religion. I am aware that its roots began thousands of years before I was born. The only contact I had with your followers was in some of the caravans from the East that passed by my village, Nazareth.

There have been legends that during my "silent years" I studied in India, but I'm afraid I was too busy building things and tending the farm for

49

that. I am proud, though, that my apostle Thomas brought Christianity to your land of India.

Krishna: It is wonderful to meet you, Jesus. Some have compared me to you, so I want to get to know you better and see if there are some similarities.

Radha: Namaste, Jesus. I too am looking forward to our conversation and to learning more about the Christian religion you inspired—even though I understand that you practiced Judaism throughout your life!

Krishna: As you know, I am Krishna, one of the best-known deities in Hinduism. I am an avatar of one of the main gods, Vishnu. An avatar is a deity who descends in bodily form, a god appearing as human. Many Hindus believe that I was a historical person, and so they visit this garden, where we meet today. It is part of the town of Vrindavan, where I lived as a young man. There are many stories about my childhood, my devilish youth, my flute playing, and my dancing and singing with milkmaids as a young cowherd. My heroic actions and my advice to Arjuna, the warrior hero, are described in the Bhagavad Gita, one of the most important Hindu writings.

These stories are favorites among Hindus and have inspired many people across the millennia, including the famous Indian spiritual leader Gandhi. He related that because he was a nonviolent and chaste person, he was, at first, shocked by my violent actions in war and by my sixteen-thousand wives. Then, he became aware that these symbolic stories were created to teach courage amid life's struggles and challenges, as well as to protect women from oppression.

I have been and will always remain an inspirer and protector of my people. That is why my statue is featured in most Hindu temples.

Jesus: I am familiar with avatars. There is a similar notion in Christianity: incarnation. In the Gospel of John, it is said that the Word, which is considered to be the creative aspect of God, became flesh. In the early days of my religion, some thought that I was only divine and merely appeared to be human. It took centuries before Christians defined that I was both human and divine—one person with two natures.

Radha: As you now know, Jesus, my name is Radha. I was one of the *gopis*, or milkmaids, of whom Krishna was so fond. I have always been his close friend and advisor. In some traditions we are portrayed as husband and wife and share in the great love of God.

As a goddess, I enjoy being a symbol of God's beauty and power. It makes me happy that I can inspire people and attract them to the divine.

Jesus: I am honored to be with you, Radha. You remind me of my mother, Mary. She is not a goddess, but she is addressed "full of grace," which means "full of divine life." Her blessedness, humility, courage, and compassion have inspired countless souls. My followers pray that she will be present at their death to take their hand and usher them into the light.

I'm interested in learning more about how your religion started.

Radha: Well, Hinduism is an ancient religion. Its roots are more than five thousand years older than Christianity. Countless people practiced Hinduism long before there ever were Hebrews or Christians. Hinduism can be thought of as more than a religion: it is a cultural tradition, a way of life. More properly, Hinduism is called The Eternal Law (*Sanatana Dharma*). We believe that this law was revealed to our holy men and women and that it applies to all human beings.

Krishna: Unlike most religions, we don't have any specific founder. The traditions that culminated in Hinduism began many millennia ago in the Indus Valley in the lower Himalayas. The word *Hindu*, like the word *India*, is derived from the Indus River of that area. Some historians say that Aryans, a nomadic group from the east, brought with them an advanced culture to the region, including horses, chariots, bronze tools, and their Sanskrit language, which became the classical language of Hinduism.

Radha: The Aryans also had a rich, religious tradition with sacred chants, fire ceremonies, ritual sacrifices of animals by priests, and a fermented drink called soma.[1] These traditions conjoined with beliefs in the gods and goddesses of the Indus Valley, as well as with a fondness in ritual cleansing in the local river. Even today one can see this devotion as Hindus flock to bathe in Mother Ganges and other rivers. After death, Hindus have their ashes scattered in sacred rivers.

Krishna: Many find Hinduism extremely difficult to understand. There are many versions of it, and it is a tradition that is constantly evolving. In addition to having no single founder, it has no organized creed and no single set of scriptures.

1. Griffith, *Hinduism, The Rig Veda*, Vol. 5, 1–45.

Contrary to what many often think, we worship only one God (Brahman), although we do worship many manifestations of this one God. We refer to these manifestations as gods and goddesses. We will have a great deal to discuss on the subject of the deities.

Jesus: You said that Hinduism has no single set of scriptures. That is one area where we differ indeed.

Christians have the Bible, which consists of both the Hebrew and the Christian Scriptures. This Bible is our primary resource. While some think of the Bible as a single book, it is really a library of many different kinds of literature. The Hebrew Bible, also referred to as the Old Testament, contains creation myths, ancient historical stories, laws, prayers, plays, prophetic material, and many other literary forms. The New Testament contains four Gospels, historical stories, early Christian letters, and other genres.

You mentioned your gods and goddesses. The Hebrew Scriptures often focus on the struggle of this ancient people to move away from many gods and be faithful to just one God, Yahweh. Worship of and fidelity to this one God is the bedrock of the Hebrew religion as well as the Christian religion. The stories of the struggles of the Hebrews are often highly imaginative and symbolic. Unfortunately, these stories are often read as literal truth and history; that perception has brought about numerous controversies.

Radha: People of our religion also love to tell faith stories that are highly imaginative and inspiring. Many of our stories seem far-fetched to those not familiar with our religion, but we love to tell them and are lifted up to the divine by them. Isn't that what religion is all about, Jesus—to help us transcend ordinary life and be in touch with the divine?

Your followers have many fanciful stories also. For instance, the parting of the Red Sea by Moses, the story of Noah's ark, or the story where three magicians come to bring exotic gifts to you as a baby are quite far-fetched. But, in fact, they can help people understand how God is a wondrous protector as well as a savior of all nations. I feel sorry for people who take such stories literally, because they often the miss the point of these faith narratives.

Jesus: The Christian Gospels can also be confusing if they are taken literally. These were written decades after my death and can hardly be considered to be biographies. They actually tell little of the first thirty years of my life!

The Gospel stories are based on the things that I said and did, but often they are faith narratives, designed to profess the meaning of my life and teachings rather than give factual accounts of my life. True, they tell of my miracles, teachings, and Crucifixion, but in a very stylized fashion.

Krishna: The history of our tradition is spread over thousands of years and can only be found in our vast collection of sacred texts.

First of all, we have the Sruti, the writings that were "heard." These we consider to be infallible revelations. They come in the form of the Vedas (hymns) and the Upanishads (scriptures). Then there are the Smriti, the writings that are "remembered." These are not infallible revelations, but written codes of conduct, such as the Laws of Manu, and treasured epics—Mahabharata and Ramayana. The popular and influential Bhagavad Gita is contained in the Mahabharata and recounts Lord Krishna's wisdom and advice given to the warrior Arjuna. Finally, there are the Puranas, which largely compose devotional literature.

Radha: The Vedas were written down around the year 1000 BCE. This wonderful collection of hymns was sung at the early sacrifices. The hymns comprise the highest form of revelations given to the original celebrants. They first existed in oral form.

The Rigveda is the oldest of the Vedas and contains more than one thousand hymns. In these hymns you can see our religion developing. Ours is a religion that values nature, so there are hymns to more than thirty deities connected with the natural world. There are Indra, the god of the sky; Rudra, the god of the primitive and the wild; Agni, the god of fire; Surya, the sun god; and Usas, the goddess of the dawn. Here you can see the development of the worship of Vishnu, who will eventually become the prominent god.

Krishna: I fondly remember those great sacrificial celebrations, with thousands standing around a blazing fire near an enormous altar, encircled by priests dressed in elaborate robes. Our people prayed for good harvests and strong health. They drank the soma, which stimulated everyone, and they sang with great emotion throughout the night.

With great ardor, they worshiped the impersonal ultimate reality called Brahman and grew to believe that Brahman was the creator of all things.

As the Indo-Aryan culture moved south to the Ganges, our religion went beyond the Vedas. It went beyond a preoccupation with nature and material questions. In the amazing Axial Age (800–200 BCE), there was an unprecedented explosion of philosophical and religious thought! Just think of it—Greek thought, the Jewish prophets, Buddhism and Jainism in India, and Confucianism and Taoism in China. It was during this incredible period that Hinduism gained a new maturity and began to dwell on the nature of the divine, the meaning of life and death, and the problem of evils—both natural and human.

Jesus: I observed a similar evolution in the Hebrew tradition. One Genesis story begins with the creation of the material world and only toward the end considers the creation of human beings. The other creation story is concerned with temptation, sinful disobedience against the law of God, violence, wickedness, and judgment. Then, during the Axial Age, our Jewish prophets turned to serious issues of human purpose and justice.

Krishna: The Upanishads, which appeared in the Axial Age, turned to the more ultimate questions such as: Who is God? Is God both within all and beyond all? Our religion faced the fact that everything is impermanent and observed the endless cycle of life, death, and rebirth. The notion of reincarnation, which the Greek philosophers had explored, was adopted by Hindus.[2] We also began to make the connection between karma (how one lives one's life), and the rewards and punishments after death, especially in terms of one's rebirth up or down the scale of living things. Hindus came to believe that they could become masters of their own fate, no longer at the mercy of the gods.

Once we saw that Brahman was the ultimate reality, we began to question the realities of the material world. Could all that we see and feel be a mere illusion? Might it be that only in freeing ourselves from attachment to material things (moksha) that we could be free to be one with the ultimate reality? Liberation from all attachment to illusory material things as the way to ultimate happiness became the foundation for Hinduism and later for Buddhism.

The Vedic period focused on praising and petitioning the gods. The Axial period shifted the focus to personally relating to divinity. Brahman was now viewed as being within all. The shift now moved to the inner self—the atman, or soul—and the inner experience of the divine. The realization arose that the human can be united with the divine. Our treasured mantra became "thou art that" (tat tvam asi)—a way of saying that you are the divine reality. At the same time, Brahman, the ultimate reality, remained an impersonal mystery beyond all understanding. Yet because Brahman is consciousness, knowledge, and light, Brahman can be one with the true self, or the atman.

---

2. Limaye and Vadekar, *Eighteen Principal Upanishads,* Katha Upanishad, 5:6–8.

Jesus: I have seen the same development in Judaism. In the days of temple worship and sacrifice, the focus was on praise and petition to the distant Yahweh—the nameless, all-powerful, all-knowing God. In Rabbinic Judaism and later Jewish mysticism, there was more emphasis placed on relating to God. There was a shift from an "outside God" to an "inside God," from transcendence to immanence.

With my birth, the divine was born as a human being. God was now revealed as one with the human and could be intimately related to all humankind. I told my followers that they could call me "friend," and I promised them that I would be with them all days. I prayed that they would be one with me and with each other. In Eucharist I come to them in spirit in the intimacy of eating a shared meal. They know that they are in me, and I am in them. My prayer at my last supper with them was: "that they may all be one. As you, Father, are in me and I am in You, may they also be in us. . ." (John 17:21).

Radha: It makes me sad that neither your people nor ours can be nourished by each other's revelations. Our great epics have so much to teach on the human search for the divine.

In the epic Ramayana (c. 800 BCE), the great god Rama is in exile, but he rescues his wife Sita from the demon king Ravana and brings her home. There, Rama reigns as a benevolent king. This is an inspiring allegory about God freeing the soul from the body. It is about the divine rescue of souls from sin and establishing them in the land of peace: "in the happy land no diseases knew. . . no harvest failed, no children died. Unknown were want, disease, and crime; so calm, so happy was the time."[3] It is the great longing that all people have—eternal life after death.

Jesus: Indeed, we each have a great deal to share. My Gospel tradition recounts how I bring salvation to the world through my life, death, and Resurrection. The inspiring letters of my apostle Paul to the early Christian communities proclaim how God has expressed love, compassion, and forgiveness through me.

Radha: One of my favorite religious writings is the Bhagavad Gita. It can fit into a small book that is just over one-hundred pages, but it has shown the way to ultimate happiness for countless souls throughout the world. These stories tell how God and humans dwell within each other. It proclaims that salvation comes through love and devotion to the one God. The

3. Griffith, *The Ramayana*, Canto, 130.

Gita proclaims: "They, who with devotions worship me, are in me and I in them."[4]

My beloved Krishna plays a major role in this epic, which is framed around an epic battle over the throne. He accompanies Prince Arjuna into battle and advises him how to fight. He tells Arjuna that he must fight because it is his duty as a warrior; his obligations should be carried out because of the rightness and justice of his cause and not for personal success or material gain. The battlefield is the human struggle, and Arjuna represents humanity discovering the divine, self-instructing him from within. Krishna tells him that God is his friend. God sends avatars like Krishna to reveal the truth to him and to protect him.

Here Krishna teaches Arjuna the ultimate lessons of life: the need for love of all, devotion to God, and the attainment of eternal happiness through divine grace. In the Gita an amazing truth is revealed—the soul is "God's spirit," and is, therefore, infinite and immortal. Soul exists in every living thing, thus there is a universal equality among all living things. It follows that inner peace comes from detachment from all material things and by focusing on the inner realities of spirit.

Jesus: Our tradition differs from this in part. We believe that all things of creation are good and blessed, but that eternal souls only exist in humans. All humans have been created by God and are equal. Only humans will be given eternal life should they choose to accept it. Only humans are graced with divine life. It can be truly said that we are all in God, and God is in us all. As I have taught: "Those who love me will keep my word, and my Father will love them, and we will come to them and make our home with them" (John 14:23).

Radha: Lord Jesus, I also want to mention the Puranas, which were written during a period before and after your birth. These repeat Hindu traditions from the past, but interestingly focus on the worship of three gods: Vishnu, Shiva, and Brahma. There are different characteristics of these gods. Commonly, Brahma is viewed as creator; Vishnu, the preserver; and Shiva, the destroyer or transformer. At the same time, the tradition holds that there is but one God, Brahman.

Jesus: Some have compared these three gods to the Trinity in Christianity, but the notions are quite different. In Christianity, the Father is the creator, and the Son and the Holy Spirit are the inspirers and the enablers. We agree

---

4. Mascaro, *The Bhagavad Gita,* 11:29.

with you that there is but one God. While Christians have three manifestations of God, yours seem to be countless.

Radha: It is important to point out another difference we have with regard to divinity. In Hinduism, many gods have a feminine partner. As you already have learned, I am Krishna's partner; Shiva has Devi, sometimes known as Durga, Kali, or Parvati; and Brahma has Saraswati, who is also known by other names. Hinduism tries to honor the feminine aspects of the divine. But our one God, Brahman, is without gender and is impersonal. I am aware that your God is personal and seems to have personal attributes such as intellect, emotions, and will. Your God seems to be male and is often called Father.

Jesus: Yes, we give human and personal attributes to God. We believe that God is ultimately a mystery, beyond understanding. At the same time we do attempt to understand this mystery by using human imagery and names. My Jewish people have called God: El Shaddai, Yahweh, Adonai, King, Shepherd, and many other names. Christians usually use images such as Father, Lord God, Creator, or even Rock.

Our Bible reveals feminine images for God, which often have gone unnoticed in patriarchal cultures. The word *spirit* is often used throughout the Bible. The Hebrew word for spirit is *ruah*, which is a feminine noun. The very act of creation is described as the spirit (*ruah*) sweeping over the waters (Gen 1:2). In Deuteronomy, God is described as a mother eagle who hovers over her brood and bears them aloft on her pinions (Deut 32:11), and as a mother bear robbed of her cubs (Hos 13:5–8). Israel is rebuked for forgetting "the God who gave you birth" (Deut 32:18). At times God is portrayed as a mother: "When Israel was a child, I loved him. . . I was to them like those who lift infants to their cheeks. I bent down to them and fed them" (Hos 11:1–4).

In my own teaching I used feminine images of God. I once described my God as a woman sweeping her house looking for a lost coin in order to show how God searches for lost souls (Luke 15:8–10). At another time, in my lament over Jerusalem, I said, "How often have I desired to gather your children together as a hen gathers her brood under her wings, but you were not willing!" (Luke 13:34).

Krishna: It seems like both of our traditions have made efforts to note the feminine dimensions of the divine. Unfortunately, patriarchy has so often prevailed over our efforts.

Now let us tell you about some of our gods and goddesses, all of whom are manifestations of Brahman. There are many teaching stories featuring these deities that Hindus cherish.

One of the most popular stories focuses on Ganesha. You can't miss his statue in the temple because he has the head of an elephant! Ganesha is the son of Shiva, who apparently cut off Ganesha's head, thinking he was an intruder in the house. One story says that the father sent his servants to the forest to bring back the head of any sleeping creature facing north (a sign of wisdom). When they brought back the head of an elephant, the father grafted it on to his son's body and revived the boy. Since then Ganesha has been honored as wise and clever, a god who can help a person pass an exam or get a job. Ganesha is portrayed with four arms, a symbol of his power. He stands on a mouse, showing his power to help people get rid of bothersome things in their lives. Children love to hear the many stories about his antics.

Radha: Many Hindus honor Mother Durga, the partner of Shiva. She is portrayed as a beautiful woman dressed in regal garments. She has eight hands and sits astride a lion, all symbols of the great power of women. One can turn to Durga to seek strength and courage during difficult times.

Krishna: Another fascinating god is Hanuman, who has a human body but the face of a monkey. In the great epic Ramayana, he is a devoted and talented chief of the army, a great fighter who brings many blessings to his people. It is thought that he was given the monkey face to show how leaders can be led astray by material gain. Hanuman is the exception because he was always faithful to his duties. He can help devotees be faithful too. These are but a few of the most notable among our countless gods and goddesses.

Jesus: These gods and goddesses remind me of our Christian saints. We don't call them gods, but we honor them because their lives were godly and filled with the graced life of God. Some of the stories that have grown up about them are also somewhat far-fetched.

My mother, Mary, is venerated as the Mother of God by Catholic Christians because she was so "full of grace" (God's life) that she was able to bear me, the Son of God, as her own flesh and blood.

Catholics have statues and paintings of my mother and many other saints. The Eastern churches have produced marvelous icons of them. They all honor these saints as exemplary role models for various aspects of Gospel living.

These role models include St. Francis, who so fervently followed my Gospel teachings on poverty and service to the needy; St. Teresa of Ávila, who was a great teacher of contemplation and mystical prayer; and St. Thérèse of Lisieux, who was exemplary in finding God in the simple tasks of life. Her "little way" has inspired many of my disciples. Recently, two great popes have been declared saints: John XXIII, who brought profound renewal to the church, and John Paul II, who fought communism and promoted social justice and interreligious dialogue.

Krishna: Jesus, there are many other areas of our extremely diverse and complicated religion that we can discuss.

There is our caste system, which is quite controversial, especially in this age of equality and democracy. Legend tells us of its origins. There is a story that a cosmic being was dismembered and separated into four classes or castes: priests, warriors, farmers and merchants, and servants. In addition, there were those who had no caste: the outcastes or untouchables (Dalits).[5] These individuals were to be shunned and given the most menial jobs, like cleaning the latrines. Each person is born into a caste, and one's caste determines who the marriage partner will be, as well as social status and even employment.

Through the efforts of Gandhi, the outcaste status was banned in India, but culturally it still exists. Today the caste system might be apparent in the different castes and sub-castes represented in various professions, in locales, in language, and in kinship. The entire caste system still deeply affects marriage and social status in India. In the big, modern cities, these classifications are more flexible and not viable in the corporate and social areas of urban life. Amazingly, a Dalit was actually elected president of India in 1997.

Jesus: All societies seem to have a caste system, either official or unofficial. Christian churches have their own pecking order. For many centuries Catholics have had a hierarchical structure. It is a triangular model, from top down. It consists of the pope, then bishops, priests, sisters, and then laity. Largely, it has been a "church of unequals." The medieval canonists strictly divided the clerics, who were called by God for exclusive service in the church, from the laity, who were allowed to marry and own property. This often lent an unwarranted air of superiority to the clergy. This was a far cry from my teaching: "Whoever wants to be first must be last of all and servant of all" (Mark 9:35).

In the 1960s a Vatican council was convened. It proclaimed that the church was "the people of god." Since that time, the laity has made great

5. Flood, *The Blackwell Companion to Hinduism*, 497.

progress with many women insisting on equality, though there is still a hierarchy in the Catholic Church. Some women advocate for the ordination to the diaconate and the priesthood.

Radha: Let's talk about the goals of the Hindu religion. Traditionally, there have been four goals: duty (*dharma*), prosperity (*artha*), freedom from attachment (*moksha*), and sensual pleasure (*kama*). Consequently, the Indian people stress rigorous education, hard work, and enjoyment of the pleasures of life.

Krishna: The laws that guide Hindus in their effort to achieve these goals are contained in the ancient Laws of Manu. This document also speaks of four stages of life: the student, the married householder, the retired person dedicated to the spiritual life, and the elderly person seeking liberation. In regard to this last stage, we often see the elderly *sadhus* (ascetics) sitting by the Ganges or the roadside, detached from material things and dedicated to self-liberation and the mentoring of others. On the whole, Hindus are usually very seriously dedicated to the duties of each stage.

Jesus: There are no neatly delineated stages in Christianity, since my religion has taken root in so many different cultures where the stages vary. An elder in Africa might be fifty years old, while in the West the elder might be ninety. In some cultures the young have few educational opportunities, start to work early in life, and marry quite young. In the West, schooling can take so long that many individuals marry and start to work at a later age. No matter what the stage, the spiritual path needs to be followed intensely.

Krishna: Besides our specific goals and stages of life, we recognize three paths of salvation: knowledge, works, and devotion. We have many forms of Hindu beliefs and practices, but the faithful, in one way or another, follow these paths.

The knowledge path is usually led by gurus who teach people about the scriptures, meditation, and yoga. Gurus are our teachers. The word guru is derived from two words: *gu*, which means darkness and *ru*, which means light. The guru is one who brings light into the darkness—enlightenment for those who are searchers for truth.

Our gurus help Hindus encounter the ultimate reality, Brahman. They help people to understand our tradition, to realize that everything is connected, and to experience that the absolute can be manifested within the self.[6]

Our teachers and priests help individuals to meditate, to go inward and separate the false self from the true self, and to separate illusions from the truth—the unreal from the real. Our teachers also lead us in devotions to the gods and goddesses, tell us their ancient stories, and seek favors from them in our daily lives.

Part of the knowledge path is instruction on the atman, the self or the soul, which is the "deathless" ground of the person.[7] The soul comes from the creator god and has the capacity of being united with Brahman, the ultimate reality, who dwells within each individual. In discovering the depth of self, one can discover the mystery of the supreme person. Then, the self can be discovered as one with the divine. Of course, many years of discipline and meditation are needed to discover this.

Jesus: My tradition also teaches that God dwells within each person. The true self is where this divine indwelling can be discovered. Regular meditation and contemplation are the paths to this inner self. Today the term "centering prayer" is used for a type of prayer that seeks the center of the person. It involves putting aside all roles, masks, and false selves and going to the place where the person meets God, the place where all are made in the image and likeness of God. We have a strong mystical tradition with instruction on how to pursue this path. Both the Carmelites and Trappist religious orders have made valuable contributions in this area.

Radha: Do you know of karma, Jesus? Our Hindu path of knowledge also includes attending to our karma. Karma refers to our personal actions that bring consequences or results into our lives. Karma follows each person after death. The Upanishads say: "as one acts and as one behaves, so one becomes."[8] Dharma, or teaching, tells us what is required, while karma is what we actually do. Our karma determines our rebirth after death.

Rebirth (samsara) is central to the Hindu faith. We believe that each soul is reborn a number of times, depending on the quality of that soul's karma. Since no one wants to be caught up in an endless series of rebirths, we are motivated to live good lives and seek oneness with God.

6. Klostermaier, A Survey of Hinduism, 165.

7. Sharma, Classical Hindu Thought, 92.

8. Muller, The Upanishads, IV, 4:1–7.

Jesus: There is a notable difference here between our two religions. It is true that some of the early Christian Gnostic communities believed in reincarnation and even interpreted my Resurrection as reincarnation. Even Origen, a learned second century theologian, accepted reincarnation. However, these views of the Gnostics and Origen were rejected by mainline Christianity.

Christians do have a belief similar to karma. I taught that actions determine what happens to individuals after death. In my parable on the last judgment, I use the image of the sheep being separated from the goats, and afterlife is determined by how individuals have served the needy. A person's love for God, self, and others signals that person's choice to be with God or to be separated from God for all eternity.

Krishna, please help me understand more about your tradition on afterlife.

Krishna: Our traditions on afterlife have evolved and have been diverse. The teaching in the early Vedic period was rather vague but gained clarity in the Upanishads. Some traditions speak of various kinds of hells, with darkness or fire, and of different kinds of heavens, such as a paradise with God. None of the texts speak clearly about the times in between rebirths, but some refer to stopping places to meet the spirits of ancestors and others.

Jesus: Our beliefs about afterlife vary also. There are popular notions of "pearly gates" and an interview with St. Peter. There is an idea of a burning hell ruled by Satan, who tortures the condemned. In my Gospels, I often refer to evil people being sent to Gehenna, a cursed valley outside of Jerusalem where in ancient times pagans burned children in sacrifice, or where in later times bodies were cremated. I use the horrors of this place as an image for an evil person's separation from God.

Catholic Christians also had to deal with financial scandals around the practice of "indulgences," which at one time were understood as promising donors that they could lessen their time in purgatory for themselves and their loved ones. Abuses crept into the system in the Middle Ages, but these were later resolved.

Christians believe in the resurrection of the dead, because that is what I demonstrated in my own life and promised my faithful followers. Just when this takes place is ambiguous in the Christian tradition. At funerals there is the understanding of immediate resurrection, but there are also prayers indicating that this takes place at the end-time.

Many of my followers leave what happens after death in mystery. The apostle Paul put it this way: "What no eye has seen, nor ear heard, nor the human heart conceived, what God has prepared for those who love him" (1 Cor 2:9).

Radha: It sounds to me that your followers believe that heaven or eternal life is the culmination of a good and loving life. In part, it seems to be a reward for good deeds. For Hindus, heaven is a liberation from karma altogether. Karma is viewed as finite. It clings to the individual. We keep getting reborn because our desires and actions are finite. Only when one is free of desires and free of karma is one free to become one with the infinite.

Jesus: Christians have, at times, been divided over the role of good deeds in justification before God. This was a main issue of controversy during the Protestant Reformation. I have been pleased to see the Lutherans and Catholics recently agree that eternal life is a free gift from God and that good deeds dispose us to accept this gift.

With regard to hell, there seems to be a movement away from seeing this as a punishment from an angry God and toward seeing this as a decision on the part of the person to reject a loving life and eternal life with a loving God.

I lived and taught the importance of love. I promised those who followed me that they would have eternal life or salvation. I said, "Just as I have loved you, you also should love one another" (John 13:34).

Krishna: Hindus don't speak of salvation, but of liberation, or *moksha*. Liberation means being free from desires for things or from attachments to the finite world. The virtuous life is filled with effort to detach from the finite so that the soul can be free to be in union with the infinite, with Brahman.

We see life as a struggle, with many setbacks, tragedies, and failures, which teach us the limitations of the finite and gradually turn us toward the infinite, the ultimate. The goal here is to free ourselves from ignorance, desires, and evils that hold us back, cause rebirths, and lead us away from fulfillment and liberation, keeping us stuck in the cycle of death and rebirth.

Jesus: My followers also use the term liberation and have indeed built a whole theology around it. This way of thinking can lead Christians to free themselves not only from desires but also from oppression and injustice. They want church leaders to be on the side of the poor and the needy. They want church leaders to struggle against political and social movements that offend human dignity and unjustly oppress people, especially the poor who have just desires for shelter, food, and water, but who are deprived of these rights. They see me as their liberator, one who powerfully supports them in their heroic efforts to gain justice and peace.

Those who profess these liberating views do not urge a detachment from the world. Rather, they plunge into the world and confront society with a passionate commitment to my Gospel teachings for social justice as a defense of human rights. This is not a detachment from action, but instead a strong commitment to action for the liberation of the oppressed. They recognize that I was a rebel against religious and political corruption, prepared to give my life for the poor and oppressed.

Radha: As we speak of liberation, I should emphasize that yoga can liberate our followers for virtuous living and ultimately union with the divine. It is another important practice along the path of knowledge. Yoga can help our people gain self-control of the senses, body, mind, and spirit. Hatha yoga, one of the most common practices, attempts to balance the mind and body through various physical postures, breathing and relaxation exercises, and meditations. One goal is external control of the body and senses so that the person will refrain from doing harm to others through deceit, lying, stealing, or abusing sex. Another goal is internal control, which leads to serenity and purity.

Yoga aims at concentration, focusing and centering the self, opening the self, and freeing the self for union with the divine. More advanced yoga is concerned with awakening energy sources from centers in the body called chakras, so that one can move along the path toward union with the divine.[9]

Jesus: Many of my followers practice yoga—some only for exercise and good health, others as a means of aiding meditation and contemplation. It is a good example of how ancient traditions from other religions can be valuable assets to my disciples.

Krishna: Let me tell you a bit about the path of good works. In the early days of the tradition, the works of the gods were front and center, and the people tried to participate in these divine works through their elaborate sacrifices of animals and rituals. These special fire sacrifices are rarely carried out today except at the death of a beloved priest or at some outstanding anniversary.

Hindus no longer offer sacrifices of animals. Instead, they offer objects such as rice, fruits, and flowers in temple services. More important than the type of offering is the good heart and love with which it is offered. The daily sacrifices, or puja, at home are important to devout Hindus. Several times a

9. Mascaro, *The Bhagavad Gita*, 39–40.

day, families will gather and make offerings of flowers and food, often along with incense. They will also read from the sacred texts.[10]

Jesus: My Jewish people also sacrificed animals in the Temple. When the Romans destroyed the Temple in 70 CE, this practice ceased. My Catholic followers speak of the Mass as a sacrifice because it commemorates my sacrifice on the cross for them. Catholics also practice devotions, such as "the way of cross" and the rosary. It is common for Christians to pray before meals and upon rising or going to bed.

Krishna: Another part of the path of works is the purification of the mind. Keeping the mind free of toxic thoughts leads to a better understanding of the self and world. Efforts to open and purify the mind enable us to meditate, which is a way toward union with God. Doing other important works, bathing regularly in sacred waters, going on pilgrimages, worshiping at home and temple, and the use of mantras to pray are all means of gaining merit with the divine.

Radha: The path of works includes the renunciation of sin and the performing of penance for sin. A basis of sin is delusion, which leads to bad judgment and is often connected with anger and greed. Desires lead to sinful excesses in sex and other pleasures. Murder, stealing, and adultery are among the most serious sins for Hindus. We avoid alcohol, which so often leads to addiction and sin. We are taught to avoid ignorance and laziness, and we are encouraged to be good in our lives, for goodness draws us toward the divine.

You will find that certain virtues are important to our people: compassion, dutifulness, hospitality, honesty, and detachment. For us, it is important to follow one's conscience and to have good intentions. You will generally find that Hindus are not legalistic about morality. Virtue is preferred to the law.

Krishna: Penance for sin is important for my people. They will cut back on food and drink or on some other pleasure or entertainment in order to discipline themselves and make up for excesses. Pilgrimages, retreats, and giving alms to the poor are also means of atonement.

Jesus: Christians have strong traditions on morality. For some, the Ten Commandments are the foundation; the commandments forbid such sins

10. Doniger, *The Hindus*, 256–57.

as stealing, lying, killing, and adultery. There has been a tendency among Catholics to be extremely legalistic toward morality; their focus has often been on sexual sin. Would you believe that in the recent past the most serious sins for Catholics were missing Mass on Sunday, eating meat on Friday, or any kind of sin with regard to sex?

Fortunately, there has been a shift from focusing on the laws to focusing on the Gospel as the basis of Christian morality. Love of God, love of self, and love of neighbor are at the center. Social justice, nonviolence, and concern for the poor have once again come to the fore.

Many Christians also value pilgrimages to holy places, such as the area where I lived and died in Israel. Catholics visit Lourdes, where my mother Mary appeared, and Assisi, the area where St. Francis lived. Christians also fast, especially in Lent, the period before the commemoration of my death and Resurrection.

Krishna: Most religions have treasured rituals to mark certain rites of passage. In our tradition, at birth, babies are ritually washed; sacred texts are whispered in the ear; and Om, our sacred sound, is traced on the tongue with honey. Twelve days after the birth, there is a naming ceremony with singing and the marking of the horoscope. There are rituals for the first time the infant is taken outside, for the first feeding of solid food, and even the first haircut. We surround our children with blessing! For boys, there is a sacred thread ceremony around age eight when they are introduced to the notion of Brahman, our God. That is repeated every few years with singing, dancing, and eating. The three strands in the thread represent his speech, mind, and body.

Radha: Our weddings are elaborate. They last for a week or more, with much celebration and eating. Marriages are usually arranged by families according to caste and class background.[11]

We have unique death rites. The body is washed and dressed. Chants are sung as it is carried to the place of cremation. We believe that cremation frees the body from the soul. Cremation is carried out by untouchables, but presided over by the deceased's eldest son, who has his head shaved and wears a white robe. Rites are done very carefully so that the deceased will properly migrate to his or her ancestors. Other ceremonies are performed for the next twelve days. Then, all the male relatives cut their hair, and the house is thoroughly cleaned to free it from the pollution of death. When the

11. See Fowler, *Hinduism*.

death period ends, a special meal is prepared for the family, as well as for the spirit of the deceased.

Jesus: My followers also have a number of sacraments and rituals to mark life's stages or states in life. Catholics have seven sacraments, while other Christian communities have only two.

Catholics, aside from converts, celebrate baptism soon after birth. Other Christian churches will not baptize infants. They baptize only those who can choose the sacrament. Confirmation was originally part of the baptism ceremony, but in time became a separate ritual. Catholics now see this sacrament as a completion of baptism. Protestant churches attach a variety of meanings to confirmation and some churches do not celebrate it.

Marriage for all Christians is sacred. Catholics hold it to be a sacrament and do not allow for divorce and remarriage without an annulment. Catholics also hold ordination to the priesthood to be a sacrament, as well as penance, or reconciliation, and the anointing of the sick. Most Christian churches believe in the sacrament of the Eucharist, but there is a wide range as to how this is interpreted. Some churches believe in my real presence in Eucharist, while others see my presence as only symbolic.

Radha: Our final path is that of devotion. This includes our prayers at home and temple, as well as our festive celebrations. The object is to develop a devout and loving heart that will be open to God and all of God's children.

Krishna: Allow me, Lord Jesus, to describe our main festivals. Holi is our spring festival. It can last for sixteen days. There are many ceremonies, huge fires, and great family reunions and meals together. Navaratri is our fall festival. We especially honor our great goddess Durga; Saraswati, the goddess of learning; and Lakshmi, the goddess of good fortune. Dipavali (Diwali) is a five-day celebration of the new moon in the fall. Our people prepare special meals, wear new clothes, and exchange presents. The Hindu New Year is celebrated at the onset of spring.

Jesus: It seems that all of the world's religions are attempting to make a difference in regard to the crucial issues of the modern world. I know Christians worldwide are concerned about poverty, the environment, peace, and women's issues.

I see Christians turning to their beliefs and connecting them to these issues. We believe that all creation somehow finds its origins in God. In Genesis, God tells us creation is all good, and in Psalm 24 there is the profound statement that "The Earth is the Lord's." The book of Wisdom proclaims that the spirit of the Lord has filled the world (Wis 1:7).

In my own mission I stressed that God is loving and cares for his children as well as the lilies of the field and the birds of the air. I constantly expressed God's compassion for the poor, the sick, and the disabled. Christians are coming to realize that they are stewards, indeed co-creators, of the Earth. They are waking up to the fact that humans are responsible for the extreme weather that shocks the Earth and often causes shortages of good water and food.

Radha: Hindus are also studying the Eternal Law that has been entrusted to them and are applying it to ecological concerns. As we said earlier, we believe that divinity is in all things. If we really believe that, we must stop polluting our air, water, and land. Our belief in the interconnection of all things demands that we stop our destruction of the world's resources, with the resulting damage to the poor. *Ahimsa* (do no harm) commands that we lessen our carbon footprint, recycle, stop wasting our resources, and protect our species from extinction.

Jesus: Wars, revolutions, terrorism, and neighborhood and domestic violence seem to be widespread. I was quite clear in teaching that we should turn the other cheek, love our enemies, and pray for those who oppress us. Those who have ears should listen: our human life is sacred. My Gospel teaching vehemently opposes violence of any kind. War kills people by the millions. Guns spread through the United States like a demonic plague, yet lawmakers seem to be too paralyzed to do anything about it. The capacity for nuclear destruction spreads, and yet nations seem to be unable to stop it.

Radha: Of all religions, we should be qualified to work for peace. We too believe that God is the creator of all things and that everything is sacred. My beloved Krishna has said: "And when a person sees that the God that is in himself is the same God that is in all that is, he hurts himself by hurting others" (Gita 13:27–29).

It was our esteemed Gandhi who extended the ancient value of *ahimsa* (nonviolence) from a practice of ascetics to a universal force against justice and violence. As you know, your great nonviolent advocates Martin Luther King Jr. and Cesar Chavez were both deeply influenced by Gandhi.

Krishna: Earlier we talked of liberation, Jesus. That is one of our greatest values—liberation from all attachment and self-deception, so that we can sacrifice ourselves for others. The Gita says that the Hindu holy person is "free from all bonds, his mind has found peace in wisdom, and his work is a holy sacrifice."[12]

Jesus: Both of our religions need renewal when it comes to honoring the dignity and equality of women. During my life I attacked the patriarchal structures of Judaism. I was critical of the unjust divorce laws that favored men, the stoning of women, the laws that prevented the religious education and schooling of women, and the prohibitions of even talking with them in public. I protected women, taught them, sat at table with them, and even called them to be my disciples.

Sadly, women have lost ground in Christianity. They lost ground throughout the ages and again were characterized as weak, inferior, and emotionally unstable. Today they still suffer from inequality in most of my churches. Don't religious leaders know that women are also created in the image and likeness of God? Don't they see that there is enormous loss in ministry if women are pushed to the background? Of all the reforms needed in my church, this is the most urgent!

Radha: As in your religion, women have had their periods of recognition as well as degradation. In the early Vedic period, women were free to be educated, participate in rituals, and even write our sacred documents. At the time, the goddesses were held in high esteem. During the Brahman period, men took privilege away from women, said that they were impure because of menstruation and childbirth, and classified them as slaves and servants to their husbands. Women lost their legal rights. Later, they regained their rights and privileges and became leaders and even warriors. In the Middle Ages, some became great poets and gurus.

In the modern period, laws forbade child marriage and sati, a practice where a wife was expected to throw herself on her dead husband's cremation fire. Yet, still today, there is widespread prostitution and sex trafficking among Hindus in India, as well as honor killing, where women are killed for disgracing their families.

Much reform is needed among modern Hindus. The goddesses must be studied and held up as role models. They are the embodiment of the divine feminine. On the other hand, Brahman, our one God, is the very ground of being and is beyond gender, teaching us that gender is not grounds for discrimination. We must be reminded that mothers give life and nurture life. They should be honored for their unique gifts to build community, reach out with compassion, and serve others with courage and strength.

12. Merton, *Gandhi on Non-Violence*, 23.

Krishna: What a joy it has been, Jesus, to have you with us in this beautiful Indian garden. We have learned so much from each other. I think we agree that there are major differences in some of our beliefs, and yet we share much in common. Our mutual respect and love for each other demonstrate that together our people could be a force in the world today for peace and justice.

SUGGESTED READINGS ON HINDUISM

Berry, Thomas. *Religions of India*. Beverly Hills: Benzinger, 1971.

Chapple, Christopher Key and Mary Evelyn Tucker, eds. *Hinduism and Ecology*. Cambridge, MA: Harvard University Press, 2000.

Haker, Hille and others, eds. *Women's Voices in World Religions*. London: SCM, 2010.

Hooper, Richard. *Jesus, Buddha, Krishna, and Lao Tzu: The Parallel Sayings*. Charlottesville: Hampton Roads, 2012.

Michaels, Axel. *Hinduism: Past and Present*. Princeton, NJ: Princeton University Press, 2004.

Chapter 4

Buddhism

∼∽ Jesus with Buddha and Kuan Yin

The middle path. . . produces insight and knowledge, and conduces to tranquility, to transcendent knowledge, to complete enlightenment, to Nirvana.

—DISCOURSE OF SETTING IN MOTION THE WHEEL OF THE DOCTRINE[1]

Blessed are the poor in spirit, for theirs is the kingdom of heaven.
Blessed are those who mourn, for they will be comforted.
Blessed are the meek, for they will inherit the earth.
Blessed are those who hunger and thirst for righteousness, for they will be filled.
Blessed are the merciful, for they will receive mercy.
Blessed are the pure in heart, for they will see God.
Blessed are the peacemakers, for they will be called children of God.
Blessed are those who are persecuted for righteousness' sake,
for theirs is the kingdom of heaven.
Blessed are you when people revile you and persecute you and utter all kinds
of evil against you falsely on my account. Rejoice and be glad, for your reward
is great in heaven, for in the same way they persecuted the prophets who were
before you.

—MATT 5:3–12

1. See Lao Tzu, *Tao Te Ching*, http://www.sacred-texts.

Buddha: Namaste, Jesus. It is pleasant sitting with you under this Bodhi tree, a tree similar to the one where I was first enlightened. Even though I was born 450 years before you, Jesus, my followers have often crossed paths with yours, and I have always wanted to meet you. It is truly an honor.

Jesus: Thank you, Lord Buddha. We have so much to learn from each other. I am pleased that Kuan Yin has accompanied you. She is revered throughout the world. Please tell me about yourself, Kuan Yin.

Kuan Yin: Yes, Jesus, by reputation I am honored as a model of compassion. In many areas of the East I am viewed as the embodiment of the divine feminine.[2] Some call me "Lady Buddha." I represent values that are familiar to you: love of God, self, and neighbor. Many people call upon me for protection, healing, and liberation.

The Buddhist monks, who are the leaders in Buddhism, have for centuries been males. Our women's voices have not been heard until just recently. I am delighted to be part of this conversation so that I can present a feminine perspective.

Jesus: You remind me of my mother, Kuan Yin. She too is very compassionate and loving. So many of my values and ideals come from her. She was never afraid to speak up, and she knew how to put me in my place.

Kuan Yin: Your mother, Mary, truly embodies the divine feminine, and the very purposes for which women were created: to provide wisdom and creativity, to bring forth life, to offer their children wings to go on their own, and to uniquely bring people together in love, protection, and healing.

Jesus: My mother is not called a goddess, but she is referred to as the "Mother of God" because she gave birth to me, and I am called "the Son of God." Many of my followers have great devotion to her, ask her for healing, and pray to her at the hour of death.

Kuan Yin: I will be eager to talk more with you Jesus about the feminine dimension of Buddhism and share my perspective.

Jesus: Lord Buddha, I have heard of you and your teaching from some on the caravans from the East that passed near my village, Nazareth. Other Eastern

2. Kuan Yin is at times portrayed as a male figure. Here we are featuring the more common feminine representations.

religions have always sounded exotic to me. In modern times my disciples around the world have integrated your teaching into their spirituality. One of your teachers, Thich Nhat Hanh, wrote an amazing discourse entitled *Living Buddha, Living Christ* and perhaps you have read Paul Knitter's book: *Without Buddhism, I Wouldn't Be A Christian.*

But please give me some more background.

Buddha: Well, Buddha is not my name, but rather a title, which means *the enlightened one.* My real name is Siddhartha Gotama. I was born about 450 years before you in a small village near the border of India and Nepal.

There are many legends about my life, most of which appeared after my death. These legends tend to be more symbolic than factual. One common theme is that I was born into wealth and that my father was a warrior leader of a small kingdom. There are a number of magical stories about my birth. One tells of my mother conceiving me in a dream where a magnificent white elephant carrying a lotus flower entered her side. Some legends say that I was born under a lovely tree in a grove filled with birds singing. It is said that at my birth I actually stood up and spoke about my noble destiny. (I must have been quite the infant!) Some stories tell of wise men predicting that I would be a ruling emperor, while others prophesied that I would be a wandering ascetic.[3]

Jesus: How fascinating! There are also many stories that surround my birth and life. They are often more about the meaning of my life and teachings than about the actual facts. There are stories about my being miraculously conceived, being born in a barn, and about a visit from three Magi from your area.

Buddha: Apparently my father heard of the latter two prophecies and wanted to make sure that I became an emperor rather than a poor, skinny monk. He kept me in idyllic isolation, surrounded by every luxury, beautiful women, and sumptuous living. He matched me with a wonderful wife, who bore me a son. He did everything to prevent me from seeing the real world of suffering that existed outside.

Jesus: My childhood was quite different from yours. I was born into a poor Jewish family in a mountainous and rural area of Galilee in northern Palestine. We lived simply in a small house made of clay. Our land was poor, because when the Romans took over they confiscated the best land and drove

3. Harvey, *An Introduction to Buddhism*, 16–17.

us peasants to the north where we had to rent land from the wealthy people in big cities like Jerusalem.

My father Joseph was an experienced builder. He taught me how to work with wood and stone. We built houses, made furniture, and did all kinds of repairs for our neighbors. My mother was a humble peasant girl. She was bright and vivacious—very generous and loving. She was hard-working and quite devout.

We had a small farm. Along with my brothers and sisters, we plowed the land, grew vegetables, and tended our goats and sheep, which provided us with food and clothing. We made a modest income from what we could sell at the marketplace or to passing caravans.

At times, the people in nearby Sepphoris called my father and me to help with the city's reconstruction. (Laborers were needed to rebuild the town from a Roman crackdown on an earlier rebellion.) Occasionally we would join a caravan to Jerusalem to celebrate feasts. Sometimes Joseph and I helped with the work on the temple that Herod was building. At first, Jerusalem startled me with its wild animal shows, camels laden with beautiful items such as silk and gold, lovely young women, and prostitutes waving their spangled scarves and bells at me. I saw the rich, religious leaders strutting with their bejeweled outfits and shoving the peasants aside in the streets. It was all pretty amazing for a country boy like me. I began to see that there was corruption in my own religion also. I thought that my religion needed to be changed.

Buddha: Jesus, You had a much more difficult youth than I. I was really pampered and protected. Were you sheltered from the sight of serious suffering the way I was?

Jesus: Actually, Buddha, that was not my experience. We were exposed to poverty, crippling diseases, the hardships of old age, and death. We always looked after our family members and neighbors. Many women died bearing children, so we often took in their babies. There was also much brutality around us. We were highly taxed for the land we leased. If we did not pay those taxes, we could be thrown off our land and even sold into slavery.

The rebellion in Sepphoris that I mentioned earlier happened about the time I was born. I remember hearing stories about how the Roman soldiers came in, leveled the city, and crucified thousands along our roads. Yes, I learned early on about suffering. I was well aware of how dangerous it was to stand out as a troublemaker.

But please tell me how you managed to break out of your isolation and observe how people suffered.

Buddha: Well, after several clandestine forays outside the palace, my eyes were opened to death, disease, and old age. I now knew that I needed to explore the real world in order to discover the truth, so I left my family and became an ascetic. I soon found that extreme fasting and exposure to the elements brought me suffering, an emaciated body, and little insight.

I decided to enter a long meditation under a Bodhi tree. Soon, I was deeply moved by an enlightenment that changed my life and set me off on many years of teaching. I was now determined to reform the religion of my youth.[4]

Jesus: And what was the religion that you wanted to reform?

Buddha: I was born into the Hindu religion, and early on was disturbed by its beliefs. The many gods and goddesses, the long empty rituals, and the unjust division of people into castes bothered me.

My enlightenment taught me to avoid all the endless and confusing god talk of Hinduism and to follow simple rituals. I wanted to view all peoples as equal. My enlightenment taught me to live a simple and detached life. I learned that clinging to things only brings suffering and "letting go" can transform suffering into love and compassion. I set out to teach a simple, religious life, free from superstition and legalism, a life focused on the present. I diligently pursued my mission to spread this vision until my death at age eighty.

Jesus: I am inspired by your teachings on suffering and "letting go." My own path was quite different since my family members were all devout Jews. We celebrated Sabbath and the Jewish feasts such as Passover at home. We gathered in our small, local house synagogue for readings and prayer. We were a hardworking, gracious, and peace-loving family. We took care of each other. As Jews, we loved God as well as our neighbors—especially the poor, sick, or troubled in our community. Early on I learned that I could bring healing to them.

As I grew older it became clear to me that my religion was also in need of reform. Some of the leaders in Jerusalem had become greedy and cooperated with our oppressors, the Romans. Others had become hypocrites, teaching one thing but doing another. Legalism was widespread. The poor and disabled were seen as cursed by God. The Temple in Jerusalem had become a money-making marketplace; the Sanhedrin Court unjustly

4. Berry, *Buddhism*, 13.

and harshly punished the poor for minor offenses and even stoned to death people whom they judged to be sinful.

As time went on, I came to treasure the authentic Jewish ideals my parents taught me: a strong faith in God; a fervent love of God, self, and neighbor; prayerfulness; compassion for the sick and the poor; forgiveness; and hope in eternal life. I am feeling a kinship with you now as we talk.

Buddha: I told you that I left my home and family to find out what real life was about. What caused you to leave home, Jesus?

Jesus: Well, around age thirty, I felt a call. My enlightenment did not come all at once the way yours did. Mine came gradually and had its peak moments. Even at age twelve, I began to feel a strong call to speak for my Father about the divine presence and power in the world. On a trip to Jerusalem, I stayed behind to discuss my beliefs with the elders. My distraught parents had to come back for me. On another occasion, as an adult lector in the synagogue, I read a prophecy by the prophet Isaiah and proclaimed that I was also a prophet. The locals were not happy with that; they threatened to kill me.

At my baptism and once on a mountaintop with my disciples, my Father told me that he was pleased with me and that I was his beloved son. It slowly dawned on me that I shared a unique intimacy with God—that he was giving me a mission to speak for him.

Buddha: I was wondering if you had any mentors who helped you understand your true identity? I know that in my case, there was a servant who secretly took me out of the palace into the real world, where I discovered human suffering in the forms of old age, sickness, and death.

Jesus: I would have to say that I learned a great deal about my true self from my mother, Mary. She was an amazing role model for how to live a godly life. Later, John the Baptist became my mentor. He taught me much about God's presence, and he baptized me in the Jordan River.

After my baptism, I followed John's example and retreated to the desert for prayer and fasting. There, nearly overcome with hunger and thirst, I experienced the power of evil tempting me to pride, power and evil ways.

Buddha: I can relate to that Jesus. I had to wrestle with Mara in order to conquer the forces of evil within me.

Jesus: So you understand my struggle and how I needed to lean on John who taught me the importance of resisting evil. It was then that I felt called to begin my mission—not as a desert hermit like John, but as a teacher and healer among the people. I used John's message: "Repent, the kingdom of God is at hand."

Buddha: How interesting it is that we both chose a middle way between strict asceticism and affluence.

Jesus: After John's execution by Herod, I decided that it was time to begin my own mission. This was very hard on my mother and my family. They actually thought I was losing my mind. On one occasion they came after me, hoping to bring me back home.

Buddha: It sounds like both of our families were bewildered by our choices. Why would your family think that you were losing your mind?

Jesus: Well, until age thirty I had led a rather quiet life in the shelter of my family. Suddenly, I became a public figure through preaching and healing. I was drawing attention, especially among the poor and oppressed. That was seen as threatening to the Roman authorities, as well as to our religious leaders, many of whom were nothing but Roman puppets. I was teaching on my own authority. I healed people on the Sabbath, ignoring religious laws, and I was challenging the religious leaders and their corruption. My family knew that I was choosing a dangerous path by gathering disciples and training them to spread my teachings. They thought that I was putting my life and the life of my followers in peril.

Buddha: After my enlightenment I also felt moved to teach what I had learned to the community of followers around me. Their numbers increased rapidly.

Unlike your experience, I did not find that my life was in danger or that my message was threatening to others. On the contrary, many people were open to the simplicity of our lifestyle and the clarity of our message.

Tell me more about the community that you gathered around you.

Jesus: Like you, Lord Buddha, I gathered a small community of followers. Most were simple folk—rugged fishermen like Peter and Andrew and hard-working farmers. Some, such as Simon and Judas had led violent lives, in opposition to the Romans. Another, Matthew, had worked as a tax collector for the Romans, despised by our own people.

Unlike any other rabbi, I also chose female disciples. Mary, my mother, once she came to understand my calling, stayed close to us, offering wisdom and inspiration. One of my favorites was Mary of Magdala, a woman of means recovering from a serious disease, who helped our group by supplying money for food and clothing. There also was Joanna, who had lived in the court of Herod where her husband was the minister of finance. She also supported us financially. I was very close to Mary and Martha of Bethany too.

Kuan Yin: It has been heartening in modern times to experience the voice of women in leadership and service becoming more prominent. The feminine dimension of Buddhism is gaining more attention. Many of our Buddhist women are calling for equality and are doing so much in service and education that they present a challenge to many of our monks.[5] They are calling for the ordination of nuns.

Jesus: Let me come back to this topic, Kuan Yin. There are many Christian and Jewish women who are eager to dialogue with you.
    But first, Lord Buddha, tell me more about your signature teachings.

Buddha: People often call me Buddha, but as I mentioned earlier, that is not my name. Buddha is a title. It means *enlightened one,* or *one who woke up.* I woke up to the truth about human life and how suffering can be turned into compassion and love. I woke up to four noble truths. My first truth is that suffering is universal. Suffering, or what I call *dukkha,* means many things: impermanence (nothing lasts), the process of being born, old age, illness, death, grief from the loss of loved ones, the presence of things we hate, even not being able to get what we want.[6]

Jesus: I must say that I saw suffering everywhere also. As I mentioned earlier, many suffered in my village of Nazareth: there was hunger, lack of good water, and disease. Many of the young mothers died giving birth. It was common for those who did not pay their rent to be exiled or sold into slavery. Resistance to Roman authority could lead to crucifixion.
    Then once I left home, I was overwhelmed by the suffering of so many from hunger, blindness, leprosy, disease, poverty, and death. I was saddened by the plight of the poor and the homeless along the roadsides.

5. See Tsomo, *Innovative Buddhist Women.*
6. Van de Weyer, *366 Readings from Buddhism,* 1/25.

Buddha: I found the very same widespread suffering in my time. I have heard that you once said: "The poor you will always have with you."

Some say that with all my talk of suffering I am a pessimist. But I am quite the optimist because I believe that we can be liberated from the grip of suffering. We all have the power within to break suffering's hold on us and become loving and compassionate people. It is not that suffering ever stops, but we have the power to be free of its domination. I have always said: "Suffering I teach—and the way out of suffering."[7]

Kuan Yin: Indeed, Jesus. Our path is a way out of suffering. We believe that we can break free from the bonds of impermanence, even the impermanence of the self and everything around us, and experience the inner peace of the now and our eternal connection to each other and to all things.

Jesus: I too taught the notion of impermanence, urging my followers not to lay up treasures on earth, where moths and rust and thieves can ruin.

Kuan Yin: Our second noble truth focuses on the cause of suffering. It states that cravings and desires are the cause of our suffering. We often try to hold onto things, not realizing that everything is impermanent. We try to hold on to money, power, fame, youth, our loved ones, even life itself. But everything slips from our grasp. We are like apes bounding through the forest, clinging to one branch and then another.

Suffering is especially brought on by attempting to cling to negative feelings like hatred, greed, or anger.

Jesus: I have a different understanding of suffering. For me there are various kinds of suffering: loss, sickness, betrayal, oppression, even death. I don't think we can eliminate suffering, but I do believe that suffering can help us turn to God for strength. I believe that suffering can strengthen us; it can be a means toward growth. I taught that there can be a saving power in suffering. At the same time, I tried to alleviate the suffering of many by healing them through the power of God.

For me, the noblest suffering is to give yourself for another. That's why I was able to offer my suffering and death for the salvation of the world. My suffering was brought on by refusing to give up my mission and by my willingness to face the hatred of my enemies with love and forgiveness. My suffering was transformed into an act of love.

---

7. Farrer-Halls, *The Illustrated Encyclopedia of Buddhist Wisdom*, 14.

Buddha: It would seem that my message is to eliminate suffering, while yours is to embrace it and offer it as a way toward salvation. However, we might be interpreting suffering in two different ways. Suffering for me comes from trying to hold on to things when they are, in fact, impermanent. For you, suffering seems to come from different mental, physical, or emotional setbacks.

Jesus: Yes, and we both seem to believe that suffering can be transformative, that as we "let go" and forgive or accept, any bitterness or anger can be healed.

Kuan Yin: Our third noble truth is concerned with becoming free from suffering. Simply put, this truth states that one can be liberated from suffering by eliminating cravings or desires. Our goal is spiritual freedom. We teach people that "you are to be lamps unto yourselves."[8] Each person has the power within to become free, to become loving, and to become compassionate. Unlike you, we do not believe that help from a god is needed to gain liberation.

Jesus: This is a major difference in our teachings. I teach my followers to ask God for assistance. I teach my disciples that I am the way, the truth, and the life, and that "I am the light of the world." Since I am the Son of God, if they become one with me, they become one with God.[9]

Buddha: I see how we differ here. I teach self-reliance, whereas you teach reliance on God. At the same time, I do encourage my disciples to take refuge in the Buddha, the teaching, and the community, but for me that does not imply dependence on God.

The fourth noble truth teaches how one can eliminate cravings and desires. It states that these can be eliminated by following the eightfold path of right, or good, living. The first three paths pertain to wisdom. They include good views on life, which rule out hatred, anger, and ignorance. They also include following the paths of good thoughts and good speech.

The next two paths are concerned with morality. They pertain to one's actions (no killing, stealing, lying, or sexual misconduct), as well as one's choice of a good trade or profession.

---

8. See Swinson, P., "Be A Light Unto Yourself," *Mahaparinibbana Sutta*.
9. John 14:6; 8:12.

Jesus: I can see so many similarities here with our Beatitudes and commandments.

Kuan Yin: The final three paths of Buddhism are right effort, mindfulness, and concentration. All three of these paths are related to meditation. Mindfulness is key. It gives us the capacity to be fully present, completely alive, deeply understanding, and ardently loving. Mindfulness sheds a light on everything you do.[10]

Jesus: In all my conversations with other religious founders and leaders, there is frequently a common understanding. In modern times, mindfulness is recognized not only as a form of meditation but as a way to reduce stress, to handle depression, or to improve parenting or workplace dialogue. The stress of life is calling us back to deeper reflection and presence in the NOW. We have learned so much from you, Lord Buddha.

Kuan Yin: Please allow me to sum up the good life for a Buddhist. It is a life of love and compassion, characterized by sound wisdom and good morality. Such a life requires mindfulness, meditation, and effort. It can be achieved on one's own, without any divine assistance.

Jesus: I find all this to be very inspiring. I see some similarities with my teaching on compassion and righteous living. But our major difference is with regard to God, who is at the center of my religion. As I said earlier, my people believe that they can turn to God for grace, divine assistance, healing, and forgiveness. At the same time, they have to do their part to deal with suffering. One of my saints, Ignatius of Loyola, said: "Act as if everything depended on you; trust as if everything depended on God."

Kuan Yin: Trust in God is quite foreign to our tradition. We depend only on the inner strength within to rid ourselves of those things that bring us suffering.

Jesus: It is so foreign to me to eliminate God from a religious tradition. Earlier I pointed out that my teaching mission opened with a declaration that the kingdom of God was at hand. In other words, God's loving and saving presence reigns supreme in the world and in all God's children. We begin with the basic belief in God as the divine creator of all. You seem to begin with the human and don't mention God at all. Do you not believe in God?

10. Byrom, *The Dhammapada*, 20ff.

Buddha: We get asked that question a great deal. I would not say that I am an atheist. As I mentioned earlier, my native Hinduism was preoccupied with countless gods and goddesses. I felt that all this distracted from a sound interest in understanding human life. I needed to back off and let the divine remain in mystery. I don't deny the divine: I bypass it because it is beyond all description and understanding. I ask my followers to set God aside and focus on transforming themselves. I believe that they can do this on their own, without the help of God's grace. I can see that we differ a great deal on this point.

Kuan Yin: Even though we encourage our followers to be independent, that does not mean that we want them to be loners. We Buddhists believe that all things are connected. When you are truly in touch with the depth of people and things, you are in touch with the ultimate. The deeper one goes into reality, the closer you come to the ultimate.

Jesus: I can see how we are coming at this from different angles and that Truth embraces many points of view.

Kuan Yin: We want our disciples to have "an all embracing love for all the universe for all its heights and depths."[11] I think that might be similar to your notion of the kingdom of God present in all things.

   I should add that later forms of Buddhism developed around the time that you were born, Jesus. These followers consider the Buddha to be divine and believe that each person has Buddhahood within, which helps him or her to enter into Buddha's heart. I will tell you more about this and will discuss the many traditions of Buddhism later on.

Buddha: Kuan Yin and I are eager to hear your teachings about God and to learn how one can be faithful to this God.

Jesus: My teaching about God is from my Jewish faith and from what I have personally learned from my God. It centers on faith in only one God, the Creator and Savior of all. Our God commands that we love God with our whole heart, mind, and soul and that we love our neighbor as we do ourselves. The kingdom of this God is present to the entire creation, and every person is a child of God, loved unconditionally.

---

11. Chalmers, *Buddha's Teaching,* Book 1, Sutta 8:150.

Kuan Yin: We told you about our four noble truths and the eightfold path to end rebirths and reach the fulfillment of nirvana. Please tell us about your way to a good life.

Jesus: My teachings on the virtuous life have been distilled into eight Beatitudes. These are eight signs, if you will, of knowing if one shares in the holy and joyful happiness of God's life.

First of all, the poor often have a unique experience of the divine in their lives because they have nowhere else to turn. But even those who have security and money can experience the kingdom of heaven if they are detached and generous in their sharing with others. They can be poor in spirit. Blessed are the poor.

Kuan Yin: Poverty is also important for us and is especially important in the lives of our monks and nuns. By poverty, we mean detachment from all things, letting go of all so that we can be utterly free or liberated, something we call *moksha*.

Jesus: My second beatitude points to the blessedness of those who mourn the loss of friends or loved ones or who see their own death approaching. Such mourning can bring us to the awareness of the presence of God in our lives. Those that mourn with others in their loss can be instruments of God's blessedness and healing power.

Kuan Yin: Mourning the dead is also important to Buddhists. Death is a stark reminder of the impermanence of everything, especially the lives of our loved ones. When someone dies, we spend long periods of time performing rituals, recalling the good karma of our deceased, and preparing him or her for the next stage of rebirth. Death reminds us of our own impermanence and motivates us to practice good actions, to be more loving and compassionate to others.

Jesus: We also characterize the meek as blessed: those who are humble, nonviolent, and gracious, those who are in touch with their true selves rather than some false self constructed from greed, anger, or pride. These will inherit the land; that is, they will experience the kingdom here and hereafter because they are gentle, kind, and respectful.

Buddha: We also instruct our followers to be meek and humble and to be in touch with the no-self—or, as you might say, the "unselfish self." I teach: "Let him pluck out obsession's root—the craving, 'I am.'"[12] (The craving to please only the self is the root of suffering).

Jesus: God also blesses those who hunger and thirst for justice for all. Those who follow me in standing up against oppression, prejudice, and inequality walk with God. They will ultimately prevail even if they have to suffer and die for God's cause. Another way of being blessed, or one with the divine, is to be merciful and forgiving. This acceptance and understanding of others with all their faults and failings puts one in touch with how God accepts and loves each one of us unconditionally.

Buddha: This is a strong conviction of ours as well. We recognize how hard it is to soften one's heart when there has been betrayal, insult, or physical harm. But ultimately letting go of revengeful desires or clinging to hateful feelings is essential to full awakening.

Jesus: The pure of heart—those who are free from sinning against the self or others—also experience the very life of God and can share that with others. As I heard you say, meditation helps us to overcome negativity and toxic thoughts and purifies our hearts.

As I do this reflection, I am experiencing more synchronicity with you, Lord Buddha.

We also bless our peacemakers, or those who oppose violence, revenge, anger, and war. They never give up their mission of love and forgiveness, even in the face of death. These are people such as Francis of Assisi, Dorothy Day, and Dorothy Stang, as well as the millions of nameless spirits who throughout history were willing to give their all in the name of peace.

Buddha: Yes, I'm sure as you observe our shrines, you notice the calm and serene position in which I am depicted.

Jesus: That is very true. Sometimes I am acutely aware of this image when I realize that more often in our churches, I am imaged as the crucified one on the cross, which does, in fact, lead me to the final beatitude: those who are persecuted for the sake of justice will come to know they are one with the kingdom of heaven. These are the many martyrs who were willing to suffer and die rather than give up their struggle for justice for all of God's children: people such as Mohandas Gandhi, Oscar Romero, and Martin Luther King Jr.

12. Ibid., Book 4, Sutta 14:916.

Buddha: Lord Jesus, it seems to me that both of us have a similar goal: teaching people to be loving and compassionate toward others. But, again, I do see some differences in how we approach suffering. As I mentioned earlier, suffering is everywhere: in sickness, in aging, and in death. I want to free people from suffering by teaching them to stop clinging and to lead a good life. You seem to view suffering differently and to encourage your disciples to suffer for a cause.

Jesus: You are right, Gotama, I do have my own unique perspective on suffering. My Jewish tradition has taught me that suffering comes from sin—disobeying the laws of God. So much suffering is brought about by the sins of betrayal, violence, hatred, greed, and selfishness. All of these are opposed to God's laws.

My mission was to heal suffering. That's why I spent so much time curing the sick, healing blindness, and even raising the dead. I did not believe, as so many of my fellow Jews did, that suffering was a punishment from God. My Father is a merciful and healing God, not an angry punisher. I carried out God's mission of healing, even on the Sabbath, and I was condemned for that.

Buddha: So detachment and leading a good life can help a person deal with suffering.

Jesus: Yes, indeed. We share that conviction, but from my perspective, only the power of God can provide the strength to cope with suffering and give it meaning. I ask my followers to have the virtue of long-suffering—meaning that they are willing to make sacrifices for a cause, knowing that God will give them the courage and strength to bear the suffering. I tried to be a role model for this when I was willing to suffer torture and death rather than give up my mission or my message of divine love.

Kuan Yin: I can see that all three of us have tried to deal with the perennial problem of evil. Our followers have proposed numerous answers. Many have used prayer wheels, long hours of chanting, and extreme fasting in order to conquer evil. Our monks live in poverty, beg for their food, and live celibate lives in order to stop the kind of clinging to things that brings suffering. Nevertheless, we are still stuck with the reality that bad things happen to good people. How do your people deal with this enigma?

Jesus: At times my Jewish Scriptures wrestle with the problem of evil. The book of Ecclesiastes is rather fatalistic about it and says, "eat, drink and be merry" so that at least you will have some enjoyment amid all the toil. The book of Job explores the possibilities that God sends us evil to test us or to punish us for our sins. The god in that story is certainly not the God I know. The God I preached about is a God of love, healing, and forgiveness.

Kuan Yin: I am better appreciating your point of view. We look around and see that everyone suffers, some so very much more than others. It seems unfair that some suffer so much more than others.

Jesus: Sadly, that is true. My life and death underlines that often suffering is not deserved. But I want to emphasize that there can be a saving power in suffering. I point to my Crucifixion and death, along with my life and Resurrection as a means of salvation to the world. I sacrificed myself for my people, the children of God. That is not to say, as some do, that God wanted me to suffer in order to make up for the sins of humans. My suffering and death were not from the will of God, but rather from the will of those who hated me and tried to stop my mission of healing and love. I loved my people too much to abandon them. I refused to turn back, and I had to pay the price. I chose life—the life of love, compassion, healing, and forgiveness. My enemies chose death for me.

Kuan Yin: That is a helpful clarification. So many have the idea that your God sent you to suffer so that heaven could be opened.

Jesus: That presents such a cruel and punitive idea of God. On the contrary, God accepted my suffering as an act of love for everyone. As a result, to this day, many call me their savior because my life, death, and Resurrection have given so many countless others the inspiration and power to be saved from sin and to prepare for eternal life.

Buddha: You speak of people preparing for the afterlife. Your notion of afterlife seems to differ from ours, Jesus. I was brought up in the Eastern tradition, which generally believes in reincarnation. For the Hindus, reincarnation, or rebirth, means that one returns many times either up or down the scale of living things, depending on one's karma or merits. Karma refers to the truth that "we reap what we sow." I teach that "No man's deeds are blotted out; each deed comes home; the doer finds it waiting for him in worlds to come."[13]

Jesus: One often hears the expression today: "What goes around comes around." For us, our lives continue into eternity and our theologians theorize about how that occurs.

Buddha: Well, for us, the final or ultimate goal is Nirvana, or liberation from suffering and sin. Reaching Nirvana, one has come to the very ground of being, where there is no birth or death, no coming or going. That is what I mean by emptiness, the condition where there is no self. Nirvana puts aside discrimination, desires, thoughts, and the passions. It is egoless. Nirvana is "transformation at the deepest level of consciousness leading to realization. Nirvana is where perfect wisdom is manifest and perfect love is expressed."[14]

Kuan Yin: Lord Buddha became impatient, early on, with the Hindu notion of individuals having to go through endless cycles of rebirth before reaching the goal of Nirvana. His enlightenment revealed that it is possible for a person to achieve Nirvana, or ultimate happiness, in one's own lifetime. At the same time, it is true that some require a number of rebirths before they can reach Nirvana. We believe that attachment to either eternal life or annihilation after death are examples of the very kind of clinging that prevents us from being free from the wheel of birth, death, and rebirth and that keeps us from achieving Nirvana.

Jesus: This is such an interesting discussion because Christians struggle with how purification of spirit occurs after death, since few people at their death have achieved what you call full awakening or enlightenment.

Buddha: Well, for us, Nirvana is not a state of being. It is an attainment of freedom from suffering, the achievement of enlightenment.[15] The Buddha teaches that Nirvana is a condition "where there is serenity, and there is no coming or going; and there is no being born or dying; there is neither here nor elsewhere. In this condition, there is cessation of all suffering."[16] For you, Nirvana seems to be eternal life or eternal happiness for each individual soul with God. If I understand you correctly, each human soul gets

13. Ibid., Sutta 3:666.

14. Van de Weyer, *366 Readings from Buddhism*, 8/10.

15. Lamotte, *Samdhinirmocana*, Book 4:37.

16. Van de Weyer, *366 Readings from Buddhism*, 2/28.

only one chance to reach ultimate happiness. That scares me—to think that I get only one chance!

Jesus: Well, it is just as scary for me to think that one has to come back as another creature like a bug or an animal! You are right, I do not teach reincarnation. And for me, rebirth occurs in baptism or when one experiences conversion, then the person is cleansed of sin and begins a new way of life. I teach repentance, or the turning of one's life from sin to holiness. Each person has his or her own individual spirit and can choose to live in the light with God for all eternity or to live in the darkness, cut off from life with God by one's own choice.

Buddha: Conversion of heart, or awakening, was essential in my life as well, and then a journey toward more insight and understanding until death.

Jesus: In my Jewish tradition there are various teachings on afterlife. One is the teaching of Sheol, a kind of half-life that the dead live until the final judgment. Only toward the end of the Jewish Scriptures is there talk of praying for the dead and of being with God after death. This belief finally came to fruition when God raised me from the dead and through me revealed eternal life to my disciples. From then on, resurrection was central to Christian faith. This is the experience of eternal life that characterizes the salvation that I promised my disciples.

Buddha: In my tradition we don't speak about salvation. We "take refuge in." My followers say: "I take refuge in the Buddha; I take refuge in the dharma; I take refuge in the sangha." My disciples take refuge in me as the enlightened one, the one who shares enlightenment with them and guides their lives. I have been described as an energy, a "Buddhahood" that is in each one of my followers.

Jesus: I can relate to much of what you say, Lord Buddha. I too ask my followers to be close to me—in union with me. I told them that by being one with me, they would be one with God. I live within them through the divine grace, the very life of God, perhaps similar to what you describe as an energy of "Buddhahood."

Buddha: Yes, our followers have a unique relationship with each of us. For a guide, there is the dharma or teaching, summed up in the four noble truths and the eightfold path. The dharma is not a set of rules or practices. Rather, it is a way of understanding, a way of life, a walking mindfulness of the depths of reality. It is taking on the suffering of others, even enemies, so that you can love them and have compassion on them. For me, there is no such person as an enemy. The sangha is the community of others, being one with each other, intimately connected. The sangha includes your ancestors, those who went on before you, your family, and your roots.

Jesus: My "dharma" is my Gospel teaching, which was revealed to me by God and was passed on to my followers. It is a message of entering into the suffering of others (even enemies!) with love and compassion. My teaching is also not merely a set of rules. It is a way of life. I taught my followers that I was "the way, the truth, and the life." My dharma is a way of self-sacrifice— what you might call "the no-self." It is a way characterized by a deep faith in me and in God, a strong hope, and a fervent love.

As for a "sangha," I am strongly dedicated to family and community. I want my followers to believe that all people are the children of God and to let go of their prejudices. Tragically, there is so much division in families, religions, and nations today. My prayer is still "that they may be one." I also want followers to be closer to their ancestors— those who went before them. We call them "the communion of saints."

Kuan Yin: As long we are talking about unity in our communities, I would like to discuss the role of women in our traditions. It seems to me that there has always been a prejudice toward women. They are seen as being inferior.

Buddha taught the equality of all, but his original monks were exclusively males. They took vows to be celibate, often viewing women as being seductive. Only reluctantly did Lord Buddha ordain women as nuns. This came about when Buddha's Aunt Mahapajapati Gotami, who raised him after his mother died, led a protest for the women. Buddha finally agreed to ordain women to the nun's level. But even then he insisted that the nuns follow stricter rules than the men followed. These nuns were called bhikkhunis (males were called bhikkhus). This movement did not last for long, however, and the ordination of women all but disappeared for thousands of years.

In the twenty-first century women began to point to this earlier time when Buddha ordained women; they wanted the practice to be restored. Soon women were ordained again, but only among the more progressive Mahayana Buddhists and not among the more traditional Theravada Buddhists. Now there are thousands of ordained Buddhist nuns in many parts of the world.

What is happening with regard to women in your communities, Lord Jesus?

Jesus: Actually, at present there is much controversy about the role of women in my churches. Most Christian leaders will say that men and women are created in the image and likeness of God and are therefore equal, but their attitudes and practices often belie this position.

In Catholic churches women are not allowed into the diaconate or priesthood, nor are they allowed to preach, baptize, confirm, preside at marriages, or administer the sacraments of healing or penance. Most of the positions of authority in Rome are held by males. Catholic women have little authority in the church because one must be ordained to hold a position of authority. Yet, ironically, it is the Catholic women who do much of the pastoral work in the church.

Kuan Yin: Sometimes Catholic/Christian women attend our International Buddhist conferences, and the solidarity among the women is remarkable. There is progress in some levels, and, for us, in some countries, but the women still report that there is such a long way to go in the achievement of equality.

Jesus: I personally have always taught that everyone is a child of God and equal in all respects. It is true that I chose twelve male apostles, but that was largely symbolic of the twelve tribes of Israel. The followers whom I sent out on mission, both during my life and after my death, were men and women. There were a number of women who were my prominent disciples. The apostle Paul mentions a number of key ministers in the early Christian communities, including Phoebe, Priscilla, Junia, Tryphosa, and Julia. In the earliest Christian communities, women were referred to as apostles and equally carried out my mission of preaching the Gospel. They even led the Eucharistic meals when they hosted the community in their house churches. For many centuries, women served as deaconesses in my church.

Kuan Yin: So why is it that your followers have strayed so far from your ideals?

Jesus: I think that culturally there was little acceptance of women, and, until recently, the Scriptures were only interpreted by men. Our women theologians have opened the eyes of many to Scripture insights that were present in the text all along. As for ordaining women to the priesthood, that is a question that has arisen only in recent times. As I mentioned earlier, I was a Jew, but not a member of the tribe of Levi, so I was not eligible to be a priest. Neither were my apostles or disciples eligible. For the record, I did not ordain anyone, either male or female. It was only some years after my death that the priesthood evolved in my churches. This priesthood was originally modeled after the Jewish priesthood, which was male. (Ironically, the Jews have women rabbis today.)

Kuan Yin: Well, since your authorities can't point to your practice with regard the priesthood, what are some of the arguments for and against the ordination of women?

Jesus: My churches today have been divided on this question. In many Christian churches, they see no reason in the Scriptures to prevent the ordination of women. There are even women bishops in some of these churches. The Roman Catholic Church and the Eastern churches have taken strong positions against the ordination of women to the priesthood and diaconate.

Catholic church leaders look to my selection of male apostles and to the male bishops, who are considered to be the successors of the apostles and the preservers of the priesthood to support their position that women never have been ordained and never should be.

Proponents of the ordination of women maintain that the apostolic succession is extremely difficult to trace. At the same time, leading biblical scholars have pointed out that there is nothing in the New Testament to rule out the ordination of women. The question is seriously dividing Catholics, and my fear is that many young women disciples are leaving over this issue. Perhaps it needs to be studied further and more openly debated.

Kuan Yin: Well, this debate over the ordination of women nuns has certainly shaken our communities. The more traditional Buddhists still refuse to ordain women, but the later and more progressive communities see no problem with ordaining women nuns and are moving along with such ordinations.

Buddha: Well, Jesus, I hope we can anticipate much more dialogue and progress with regard our women. Maybe we could move to another topic now, that of violence. There is so much violence in the world today; the media and films seem to be filled with violence. All this must discourage you, Jesus, since you have always been known as a nonviolent person. You once described yourself as meek and humble of heart.

Jesus: I have always stood firmly against violence. The only time I gave into it in my own life was when I saw how the sellers and money changers were turning the Temple in Jerusalem into a den of thieves. But even then I only turned over their tables and drove them out. I was careful not to harm anyone. I was firm in my teachings that one must turn the other cheek when struck and not strike back, and I urged my disciples to love their enemy, to refrain from judging others, and to always be forgiving.

Buddha: We are similar in this regard. The Buddhist monk Thich Nhat Hanh was expelled from Vietnam for protesting the war, and he and the Buddhist nun Pema Chodron have written extensively on being peace ourselves so as to impact the larger world.

Jesus: We have many strong advocates as well, but, unfortunately, many Christians have not followed my teachings on nonviolence. Early on, when Christianity became the official religion of the Roman Empire in the fourth century, Christians persecuted non-Christians. Throughout history, Christians carried out Crusades against Jews and Muslims, tortured and killed "heretics," and fought horrible wars among themselves and against others. The maltreatment of Jews has been an egregious sin on the part of some Christians, especially the Nazis during WWII.

Buddha: Yes, Jesus, that is true, but we are also aware of other disciples who have followed your teaching on nonviolence.

Jesus: Thank you, Lord Buddha. During the Middle Ages, St. Francis of Assisi risked his life to speak of peace with a sultan. In modern times, Dorothy Day stood firmly against violence and war, and Martin Luther King Jr. led a nonviolent struggle for civil rights for African-Americans influenced in part by a Hindu, Mohandas Gandhi, who was, in turn, influenced by my teaching on nonviolence. And, of course, your great Buddhist leader, the Dalai Lama, has always preached "inner disarmament" and has been a powerful peacemaker.

Kuan Yin: Both of us have always taught nonviolence. Buddha's Hindu background taught him to "do no harm," and his enlightenment more deeply revealed to him that we are all connected and should do no harm to anything living. He has said that it is better to conquer yourself than to win a thousand battles.

Buddha: I must admit that there have been times when my followers have also chosen the path of violence. In Japan, during the feudal age, there were warrior monks and shogun fighters. In modern times, many Japanese Buddhists supported imperialism and brutal warfare. Many Buddhists supported war in modern Southeast Asia. It was only recently that the Buddhists ended their long years of wars with the Hindu Tamils in Sri Lanka.

On the other hand, during the Vietnam War many of my monks continually protested the violence. The Dalai Lama has constantly warned his young monks and followers in Tibet not to resort to violence against the Chinese, who have been so oppressive toward the Tibetan nation and its people. He wisely says, "Violence begets violence. And violence means only one thing: suffering."[17]

Jesus: You must be pleased that Buddhist women are taking the lead toward a more peaceful world. Some headliners are the Vietnamese Buddhist nun Chan Khong, who works for peace and human rights, and Aung San Suu Kyi in Myanmar, a winner of the Nobel Peace Prize.

Buddha: Yes, we are indeed very proud of these women. I teach that anger, hatred, and greed cause violence and are unacceptable in the human psyche. True holiness renounces killing and violence, which arise from a false view of reality, a self-centered ego, and a disordered love of self. This has been proven throughout human history. I encourage my followers to live in harmony and peace and to renounce bitterness and self-pity. Hateful grudges and desires for revenge lead to violence. Hate does not overcome hate. Only love can do that.

Jesus: One thing I have always admired about Buddhists is their commitment to a simple lifestyle. Today we live in such a materialistic period, and I would like my followers to learn from you and Kuan Yin about poverty of spirit. When I started my mission I had no place to lay my head and possessed only the robes on my back and the sandals on my feet. I encouraged my followers to leave everything and to carry nothing extra when I sent them out on missions. We shared what we had and often slept on the ground. I remember one young, rich man who wanted to join us, but he could not because it was difficult for him to give up his wealth.

Buddha: My enlightenment gave me key insights: to value simplicity and to practice detachment from things. As I mentioned earlier, trying to cling to money and luxuries can only bring suffering into one's life. Remember when I spoke of leaving my family's wealthy lifestyle in the palace because it was like living in a bubble, protected from all the realities of life? I wanted to strip myself of all my titles and possessions and find my true self, or what

17. Dalai Lama, *Ethics for the New Millennium*, 201.

I refer to as the *no-self*. The no-self is the self, stripped of all pretentions—masks, roles, and fake selves. It is the self, denied and joined to all other things in a unity and oneness.

Jesus: We both had similar ideas here. The Gospel way is this: the poor serving the poor with compassion and love. During my public life, I constantly reached out to the poor, the homeless, and the outcasts, such as the lepers, the blind, and the crippled.

This simplicity and sharing were embraced by my earliest communities. My disciples shared their things, helped each other, and were attentive to the needy and the poor. Yet everyone who could work was required to do so and to be self-sufficient. One of my hardest working apostles, Paul, who spread the good news to non-Jews, made tents and leather goods. He was careful not to be a financial burden to the communities he served.

Buddha: Yes, Jesus, we both adopted the style of itinerant preaching and reached out to those who longed for more meaning and for a better life for all.

Jesus: I taught that we will always have the extremely poor among us—abandoned children, widows, the elderly, the disabled, and people who have few skills. It is always necessary to look after these people and to kindly share what we have with them. Wealth need not be sinful, but the wealthy are always required to share what they have with the less fortunate. They also have to make sure that their wealth is not acquired unjustly. It is extremely difficult for the rich to enter the kingdom of God.

Buddha: Yes, Jesus, clinging has become a hallmark of modern living. And today addictions have caused so many to go down a path of destruction.

Jesus: Sadly, these Gospel ideals have not always been followed. Religious leaders have often grown wealthy off the donations of their flocks and have lived like royalty in palaces and mansions. (When I said there are many mansions in my Father's house, I did not mean mansions here on Earth for the hierarchy.)

Pope Francis has become a good role model. He lives simply, outside the luxurious papal palace; drives an ordinary car; and has put aside all the papal finery. He dresses simply. He has shown that he is interested in the poor by visiting them and inviting them to eat with him. He has tried to restore my Gospel teachings about poverty. He even took the name Francis, a reference to one of my most outstanding disciples: a truly poor person who served the poor.

Kuan Yin: We have been observing your pope with interest because we have always asked our followers to live simply. The monks and nuns wear rough robes and sandals, which are donated to our community. Each day they carry begging bowls, asking for food from their neighbors in a ritual of mutual love and compassion.

Today Buddhism is often practiced in countries where there is extreme poverty. I do not advocate squalor or extreme deprivation from things needed to live happily. My followers strive to live simply so that they can be free to serve the needs of the impoverished among them.

Jesus: I think that we share similar views on living simply. As the great Hindu Gandhi taught: "The earth has enough resources for our need, but not for our greed." I want my followers to have what they need, but to be focused on the common good of others and dedicated to their needs.

Kuan Yin: To be concerned about the common good requires that there be a oneness among us. And yet all three of us have experienced so many separations and divisions.

Buddha: Divisions among my followers began right after my death. Shocked by my passing, my followers held a council and decided that the monk's form of life was superior to that of the laity. This notion became the crux of serious Buddhist divisions. The older tradition, called Theravada, holds the position that the monks follow a higher state of perfection and that the laity was to support them, to learn from them, and to live a life of devotion rather than strict monasticism. The image of the raft is useful here. The Theravada tradition maintains that only the monks are on the raft, so this group is derisively called the "hinayana," or the small raft. Here, only the select few are called to follow the way of the Buddha. This tradition is popular in Sri Lanka, Myanmar, Thailand, Laos, and Cambodia.

Kuan Yin: The other movement, often called Mahayana (large raft), emphasizes the laity and sees them sharing the raft with the monks. You might say that Mahayana maintains that the monks and laity are "all in the same boat." Here, all are called to live the Buddhist way, not just a select few. They do not seek to flee the world, but to participate in it, and with the help of divine grace, transform it. Mahayana Buddhists view Buddha as a celestial being who came to the Earth as a savior. This movement gained momentum around the same time that you lived, Jesus. It allows Buddhism to be more dynamic and to evolve.

It is the Mahayana Buddhists that are open to the ordination of nuns. The Theravada Buddhists don't approve of women's ordination. This tradition is found in Nepal, Tibet, China, Japan, Korea, Mongolia, Vietnam, and in the West.[18] There are many other forms of Buddhism, including Vajrayana (Tibetan), Pure Land, and Nichiren.

Jesus: Christianity, which is the name that was eventually given to my movement, has also had many divisions and splits that continue even today. We have also had our problems with the division of monks/clerics and laity. Early on, many extremely devout followers fled the cities. They became known as the fathers and mothers of the desert and established religious communities. Over the years, some of these groups evolved into religious orders. Often, a notion developed that the religious led the life of perfection, while the laity led worldly lives, practicing simple devotions. Until recently, it was commonly thought that those who wanted to live a Christian life seriously or serve in ministry would have to leave the world and become a priest or religious brother or sister.

That attitude set up a hierarchical model of church. Even though I taught that the first should be last and the servant of them all, my followers have persistently set up a triangle of authority and holiness with the pope on the top, then bishops, priests, nuns, and finally the laity. The "Church" became synonymous with those in authority in Rome.

Buddha: I can see so many similarities here as we have struggled with models of participation and hierarchy.

Jesus: Fortunately, a great council was held in Rome in the 1960s where all in my church, and indeed all in the world, were declared to be "the people of God." The Catholic Church, which had described itself for so long as "a church of unequals," was now proclaimed to be "a church of equals."

Pope Francis personifies this teaching. On the evening when he came out on the balcony to be proclaimed pope, the first thing he did was to bow and ask the people to bless him and pray for him. Later, he washed the feet of young prisoners, including a Muslim woman.

Kuan Yin: Jesus, those divisions must sadden you. Division can cause feelings of superiority and resentment. Such feelings conflict with our teaching

18. Berry, *Buddhism*, 64–65.

about the importance of love and kindness. What other divisions do you have besides the separation of the clergy and laity?

Jesus: Well, sad to say, divisions have been a perennial problem among my followers. Just a few decades after my death, struggles arose between Jewish-Christians and non-Jewish Christians. My apostle Paul spread my teachings to the non-Jews (Gentiles) and did not want them to be bound by Jewish laws such as circumcision or dietary laws. There was a serious dispute over this among the leaders in Jerusalem, but Paul seems to have prevailed.

In the early centuries, there were disputes over whether to accept the Jewish Scriptures and, especially, over my humanity and divinity. Some held that I was human but not divine, while others taught that I was divine but not truly human. Some saw a contradiction between the oneness and un-changeableness of God and the notion of God becoming human.

Buddha: My followers have also debated whether or not I am human or divine. My Theravada disciples believe that I am a man, an extraordinary man. My Mahayana followers believe that I am divine.

Jesus: So-called Gnostics were also a serious cause of divisions among Christians. Gnostics typically saw the material world as evil and, therefore, could not accept God becoming flesh. Some viewed me as a kind of phantom, or someone who only appeared to be human. Many of these Gnostic communities produced their own gospels. We will discuss these later when we talk about the Christian Scriptures.

Early in the fourth century, after centuries of persecution, Christianity was declared acceptable in the Roman Empire and eventually became its official religion. In 325 CE the Roman Emperor Constantine became impatient with all the doctrinal wrangling within Christianity, a religion he hoped would bring unity and not more division to his empire. He called a council of bishops to meet in the summer palace in Turkey and told them to settle their disputes about Jesus's divinity. Arius, who denied Jesus's divinity, was condemned. The bishops voted almost unanimously that I was consubstantial with the Father and therefore was divine.

The divisions continued, and in 451 CE another council was called to pronounce on my humanity. In Chalcedon it was declared that I was both human and divine—one person with two natures. These definitions have prevailed over the centuries, but they have often been challenged and interpreted in different ways.

Buddha: Consubstantial with the Father? One person and two natures? Lord Jesus, I am afraid this is all Greek to me.

Jesus: Consubstantial? Well, it is difficult to understand, but basically it means to be inseparable from God.

We endured even more tragic divisions in Christianity. The next came in 1054 between Eastern and Western Christianity. The East was a different culture of Christianity and did not want to be dominated by the Roman pope. Both had different approaches to liturgy, theology, and leadership. They went their separate ways and remain so today. That was painful for me to watch.

Even more difficult was the earth-shaking split during the so-called Protestant Reformation. This was a radical division because it was not only about leadership but also about doctrine. The papacy, episcopacy, priesthood, and other doctrines were challenged. The entire sacramental system was shaken. Scriptures, rituals, and laws were in controversy. Protestantism itself became divided into the Lutherans, Presbyterians, Anglicans, Methodists, Baptists, and many other church communities. Catholicism eventually solidified its positions, and then savage religious wars ensued across Europe. The loss of life was difficult for me to observe. All this division was certainly not what I had intended as I set out to reform my religion, Judaism. I had prayed that my people would be one. I taught a message of love and peace.

Buddha: All this violence and destruction in the name of religion is so difficult for all three of us to bear! Buddhists have even had divisions over our sacred text. It might amaze you to hear that Buddhists don't have an official bible the way you Christians do. There are literally hundreds of thousands of Buddhist texts, some originating from me or from my leading disciples, many of whom had learned my teaching by heart.

The Theravada Buddhists have the Pali Canon, which dates back to my time. The Chinese and the Tibetans have their own canon of teachings. Each country where my teachings spread provided their own adaptations and interpretations.[19]

The Mahayana tradition also has its own collection of texts, or sutras. They are believed to be from me directly or from other Buddhas. In that tradition, each person has his or her Buddhahood, which can be a valid source of my teachings. There are also some treasured collections, such as The Golden Light Sutra and the Lotus Sutra.

19. Smith, *The Religions of Man*, 135.

Kuan Yin: I have been told that your Scriptures are unique in that they contain both Jewish and Christian Scriptures. Is that true?

Jesus: Yes, Kuan Yin, that is a fact. The Christian Bible contains both the Hebrew Scriptures and the Christian Scriptures. The two traditions are viewed as being the inspired Word of God and in continuity with each other. My teachings are contained in what is called the New Testament. This collection is composed of four Gospels, some letters written by my early disciples, some early literary pieces about the history of the fledgling church, and prophecy.

The four Gospels appear to be attempts to tell my life story, but in fact are literary creations by later writers based on memories of what I said and did. The first was written about thirty years after my death and is called the Gospel of Mark. The Gospels of Matthew and Luke were written about two decades later. The authors used Mark and a collection of my sayings as their source. The other books of the New Testament are early letters, some of which were written by my apostle Paul, who preached my teachings to some early churches; the Acts of the Apostles, a creative history of the early church; and an apocalyptic piece.

Some of the Gnostic communities wrote their own gospels also, and even though they contain valuable teachings of mine, they were rejected by the mainline communities.

Buddha: There seems to be an ambiguity in our teaching about the relationship of humans to the world. I know that many of your monks and nuns have left the world and worldly matters in order to concentrate on prayer and sacrifice. The same has been true with many of my monks who have gone off into the forests and lived as a community to meditate and seek enlightenment. What are your teachings on this?

Jesus: For me, the Greek word *kosmos*, or cosmos, has several meanings. In one sense, "the world" means the sinful element of the world, which includes greed, selfishness, and the abuse of human appetites such as eating, drinking, and sex. I asked my disciples to leave that sinful side of the world and be people of virtue and love. Another meaning of cosmos refers to the world as God's creation, a world that is considered to be good. I honor all the heavens, Earth, and all God's creatures and people as coming from the hand of the creator. My central teaching on the kingdom of God recognized that the divine loving and saving presence is within all things and all people.

I asked my disciples to reject the sinful side of the world and to live simply in God's kingdom, or presence, detached from everything sinful. When I am quoted as asking my followers to hate their parents, I am asking them to set aside immature dependence, childishness, naiveté, and insecurity. Even though I left home for my mission, my mother, Mary, was always part of my community. She was there when I died and was present at Pentecost, the birth of my church. My brother James actually became the head of the community in Jerusalem.

Buddha: I think we agree on this, Jesus. Even though I originally left my wife, child, and family, they eventually joined me as disciples. Although I spent much time in meditation, I also traveled, taught, and served others. As I have said, we don't want to cling to anyone or anything, but we need to be one with everything and everyone in deep love and compassion.

Jesus: Yes, Lord Buddha, I agree. I want my disciples to be strong, independent, mature, wise, and secure so that they can carry out my mission of teaching and serving others with courage and determination. Even the monks and nuns should not be extreme in their fasting and prayer. Just as you have taught the "middle way," I teach that "virtue stands in the middle."

Religious men and women should be role models of healthy, active Gospel living. I never wanted them to reject their loved ones, but to relate to them in a mature and loving manner. I call my followers to be in the world, active in bringing my message to God's creation, but at the same time, "not of the world," separating themselves from the sin and godlessness of the world.

Buddha: For both of us, religious life has changed, and modern disciples are fully active in the world and in causes of justice and advocacy.

Jesus: I would like to discuss the modern notion of caring for the world. My Jewish tradition speaks about humans having dominion over creation. Often my followers have been led to believe that they were masters over nature and could therefore use it and abuse it for their own use and profit. *Dominion* for me means that humans have been called to stand in God's place to honor, care for, and sustain everything in creation. All living things have come from the hand of the creator and are interconnected, each with its own purpose. Nature is a delicate web linked together by the laws of nature. That web should not be shredded in the name of profit and gain.

Kuan Yin: Our approach is differently nuanced. Buddha did not teach about God or divine creation. But he did teach the interconnection of all things and the importance of right causes to produce right effects. The interconnection of everything is symbolized in the Mahayana texts by a beautiful, many-jeweled net in the heavens. As the heavenly light shines on this jeweled net, the facets of the jewels reflect the many elements of the universe. At the same time, each jewel reflects the entire universe.

Jesus: That is inspiring, Kuan Yin! I am glad that my followers are beginning to deeply understand Gospel values so that they can better sustain the Earth and its resources. My Jewish tradition believes that "the earth is the Lord's" (Ps 24:1) and that "the spirit of the Lord has filled the world" (Wis 1:7). We are called to be co-creators who partner with Abba, the loving and saving God. We are called to serve the poor, who are usually the ones most devastated by extreme weather, scarcity of resources, and the fouling of the air, land, and water.

As the population of the world continues to grow, there will be a shortage of resources. As people continue to disturb the delicate balance of nature and even the weather itself, my followers have to take a lead in sustaining the Earth. I am concerned about the very integrity of nature as well as the future of human existence.

Kuan Yin: We share this concern. Buddha taught that we must live in harmony with all things and recognize our connection with all. The enlightened person recognizes that we all share in the same causes and effects and must be loving and compassionate beings within this network. The mindful disciple is one who understands, responds to, and honors the interconnection of all things. Meditation and the resulting enlightenment reveal toxic thoughts, apathy, and carelessness, which move the disciple to do no harm.

Jesus: Buddha, earlier you said that the long and elaborate rituals of Hinduism were not attractive to you. Do your followers have any rituals?

Buddha: Rituals vary from group to group. Some value the use of bells to encourage mindfulness. Others hang prayer flags to offer homage, letting these flags blow in the wind. Others perform chants and dances to honor me and my teachings. In some areas the monks go to the village with their begging bowls to ask for food. Here they symbolize their humility and give the people opportunity for gaining good karma.

Do your followers perform honored rituals, Jesus?

Jesus: Just as with your followers, Christian rituals differ. My Protestant followers have two rituals that they call sacraments. One is baptism, an initiation rite. The other is Communion, a symbolic meal. Some celebrate Communion every Sunday, while others participate only periodically.

My Catholic followers have seven of these sacraments. Baptism, Confirmation, and Communion are the initiation rites. Communion, also referred to as Eucharist, is central and is solemnly and frequently celebrated, with great reverence toward my presence in the bread and wine. The other sacraments are matrimony; reconciliation, for the forgiveness of sin; ordination, for the priesthood; and the sacrament of the sick, which is for healing as well as preparation for death.

I have heard that prayer is important for your followers.

Buddha: Well, since I did not speak of God, I never advocated praising God or seeking favors. But prayerful meditation is central to my tradition and follows these stages: thought, happiness, serenity, and purity of awareness.

Kuan Yin: Our followers reflect on the causes of their suffering and attempt to root out these causes so that they can be loving, compassionate, and peaceful. During the day, we encourage our followers to be always mindful, to be focused on the present, to be attentive to their connection to everything, and to carefully monitor their actions so that they live good lives.

Jesus, I would like to hear your views on prayer.

Jesus: Prayer has great meaning and value in my tradition. Of course, God is central, and prayer is a means of praising God, being thankful for divine blessings, and asking for what we need. In my own life, I prayed the Jewish psalms and other prayers, even as I suffered the excruciating pain of crucifixion. Often I rose before the sun and went into a deserted place to pray for guidance and protection.

I teach my followers to pray always—being attentive to the presence of the divine within themselves and others, as well as within the world. I guess you would call that mindfulness!

There are progressive stages of prayer. The first is meditation, which has always been an important practice among my followers. This involves reflection on the Gospel and on how my teachings are to be applied. The next stage is contemplation, which involves going to the center of the true self and being open to the experience of the divine presence within. The final stage is union with God, a mystical intimacy with the divine, an experience of God within and being within God.

Well, Lord Buddha and Kuan Yin, it has been an honor to talk with you both. I am more aware now how earnestly we both seek similar goals and struggle with common issues. I have been inspired by your insights and know that more dialogue will offer greater possibilities for justice and peace.

Buddha and Kuan Yin: Namaste, the divine in us honors the divine in you, Lord Jesus.

SUGGESTED READINGS ON BUDDHISM

Dalai Lama. *Ethics for the New Millennium.* New York: Riverhead Books, 1999.
Ghosananda, Maha. *Step by Step; Meditations on Wisdom and Compassion.* Berkeley, CA: Parallax, 1991.
Nhat Hanh, Thich. *The Heart of the Buddha's Teaching.* New York: Broadway Books, 1999.

Chapter 5

Jainism

◆ Jesus with his Mother Mary and Mahavira

"Whoever comes to me and does not hate father and mother, wife and children, brothers and sisters, yes, and even life itself, cannot be my disciple."

—LUKE 14:26

"(For he thinks) I have to provide for a mother, for a father, for a sister, for a wife, for sons, for daughters, for a daughter-in-law, for my friends, for near and remote relations, for my acquaintances, for different kinds of property, profit, meals, and clothes. Longing for these objects, people are careless, suffer day and night, work in the right and the wrong time, desire wealth and treasures, commit injuries and violent acts, direct the mind, again and again, upon these injurious doings.

—AKARANGA SUTRA[1]

Jesus: Namaste, Mahavira. I am so honored to meet you and to find out about your ancient religion. I have brought along my mother, Mary, because she expressed interest in meeting you.

1. Akaranga Sutra, Book 1: Lecture 2, Lesson 1

Mahavira: Namaste, Jesus and Mary. We have a number of Christians here in India, and I have always been fascinated with their beliefs and practices. It is pleasant sitting with both of you next to this lovely river.

Jesus: We know that your religion dates back far before Christianity. Tell us how your movement got started.

Mahavira: Our beginnings are quite unique. I was born in India around the same time as the Buddha, in the sixth century BCE. Though I am one of the main figures in Jainism, I am not considered to be the actual founder. The ancient traditions in India see truth as eternal, so each teacher revives what already exists.

We see the universe as an eternal process with cycles lasting endless years. Each cycle has its own spiritual leader. I am the twenty-fourth spiritual leader of the current cycle. They call us "fordmakers" because we help people ford across the difficult waters from rebirth to salvation. The Buddhist scriptures call me Great Hero (Mahavira) because I started a community of ascetics and taught them detachment and the way to *moksha* (liberation from the life cycle).

Mary: Our Jewish religion also has a similar series of religious leaders. We call them "prophets," and each plays a teaching role for a specific period. They too speak the eternal truth in the name of God. Our prophets begin with Abraham, who received the original call to bring together the "chosen people." Many of our prophets are male, such as Isaac, Jacob, Moses (our greatest prophet), Aaron, Joshua, Elijah, Elisha, Jeremiah, Isaiah, and Ezekiel. We also have outstanding women prophets: Sarah, Miriam, Deborah, and Hannah. All of them spoke for God and guided their people.

Christians recognize that my son Jesus is the final and greatest of the prophets. They honor him as the Son of God, the Messiah.

Jesus: In the Gospels I am often called a "prophet." I recall that when I raised the widow's son from the dead and gave him back to his grieving mother, the people around us seemed to be filled with awe. They cried out, "A great prophet has risen among us!" And "God has looked favorably on his people!" (Luke 7:16).

I remember one time when I had read from the book of the prophet Isaiah in our local synagogue in Nazareth and announced that these prophecies were being fulfilled in me. The locals got so mad they wanted to kill me!

Tell us more about your background, Mahavira.

Mahavira: In some ways my story is similar to Buddha's story. I was born into the noble class and left home as a young man to pursue asceticism. Unlike Buddha's parents, mine greatly admired ascetics and fully supported my leaving home, as well as my search for enlightenment. Like Buddha, I soon became enlightened, gathered disciples, and began my mission.

At first my community consisted of eleven disciples, many of whom were Hindu Brahmins. Soon a community of both monks and nuns were established and led lives of celibacy, detachment from material things, and severe asceticism. I also established a group of lay people, who devoutly followed my teachings and provided the monks and nuns with food, water, and the daily necessities. This service enabled the monks and nuns to pursue the spiritual life full time.

Jesus: It is interesting that you had monks and nuns in your community right away. It took some time before those roles developed in my movement. I gathered a number of women disciples in my lifetime and outstanding women leaders after my death—women such as Priscilla, who with her husband, Aquila, was a leader in Rome and worked with the apostle Paul in Corinth.

It was not until the third century that men and women went into the desert to live a rigorous Gospel life. By the fourth century, Pachomius began to organize these men and women into communities and build monasteries. It was the great Benedict who in the sixth century established religious life and wrote his famous Rule for living it. Today there are dozens of religious orders both for men and women, though these orders are in decline.

Mary: I was just reflecting on the similarities and differences of your story and that of my son. We certainly weren't members of the nobility. We were poor peasant farmers, eking out a living on leased land with farming and trades. My son was a carpenter and builder.

By the time Jesus decided to leave home at age thirty, my husband Joseph had died. The other children in the family were now grown and able to do the work when Jesus felt called to go off on his own. Much as we would miss him, we knew we had to let Jesus go. But when we observed what he was doing—criticizing the Jewish leaders, breaking laws by healing on the Sabbath, and challenging the official teaching authority with his own message—we feared for his life.

We thought he must be crazy to put himself in such danger. We knew that troublemakers usually ended up stoned to death or crucified. We decided to tell him so. But Jesus distanced himself from us and said that if we wanted to be his family, we would have to do the will of God (Mark 3:20–35).

Mahavira: Allow me to tell you about our scriptures.

After my death, my disciples gathered together the Jain teaching into two texts: the Bhagavati Sutra and the Angas. In the Bhagavati Sutra and Angas there are tens of thousands of questions that I have answered. The topics include asceticism, reincarnation, cosmology, as well as the lives of our great spiritual leaders. Even questions on mathematics, agriculture, and politics are addressed.

The central focus of these texts is the essence of life, the nature of bondage, and the way to liberation. Jainism, like all religions, is concerned with the meaning of life and the art of right living. We discuss the causes of misery and pain. We discuss the way to happiness. And we reflect on the nature of soul (*atma*) and the supreme soul (*paramatma*) to which we are all connected.

Mary: We approach scriptural texts quite differently. Our texts are not concerned with science, mathematics, or philosophy. Our Hebrew Scriptures are, in the main, highlighting the sacred covenant between God and his people, as well as God's laws with regard to living a loving and just life. For us, bondage comes from sin, which also causes pain and suffering.

Our New Testament focuses on the life, death, and Resurrection of my son Jesus. It professes his teachings about the Kingdom of God and the loving, saving, and creating presence of God. We believe, based on my son's own word, that he is the Way to salvation, the Truth of God's revelation, and the Life Source of God's grace that sustains us here and hereafter.

Christians were, for hundreds of years, outside the state system as outcasts. Then, in the fifth century, we became part of the state system. Later, we began to dominate the State. In modern times, Christians seem to separate the secular and the sacred more than you do. We have learned that the Church has its own realms of truth, and we consult our hierarchy, theologians, and our people for religious truth. For secular truth, we look to science and the secular disciplines.

Mahavira: We seem to look at reality differently. Jains see the universe and all of its constituents as uncreated and everlasting. Each has its own intrinsic nature: the nature of fire is to burn, and the nature of the soul is to seek self-realization and spiritual elevation. But both realities are eternal.

Jesus: We identify a real difference here. For us, material reality is created and transient. Only the spiritual, that is, spirits and souls, can live on. But spirits have a beginning, although they can live on for all eternity. Only God has no beginning and no end. That which we call "grace," the life of God that is shared with humans, is considered to be uncreated.

Mahavira: In my sacred texts I teach that knowledge and action have equal importance. To have one without the other is like a bird trying to fly with one wing. In addition, one must have faith so that one can be liberated from endless soul migrations. My disciples must exercise their "soul power," whereby they can be detached and in contact with the truth of reality.[2]

Mary: My son also teaches that knowing must be linked to action. He also said that words are not enough: "Not everyone who says to Me, 'Lord, Lord,' will enter the kingdom of heaven, but only the one who does the will of my Father in heaven" (Matt 7:21).

Our tradition teaches that we have been created to know, to love, and to serve God. Our Scriptures condemn those who "profess to know God, but they deny him by their actions" (Titus 1:16).

For you, what kinds of actions are considered to be important for liberation?

Mahavira: Well, first of all, we advocate that people act out of virtues, rather than out of obedience to rules. Some religions get caught up in following many artificial rules and then pronounce condemnation and even execution on those who break the rules. I have heard stories that Christians were condemned for singing in church. I know that the religious leaders of your day wanted to execute Jesus for healing on the Sabbath. All such practices are unacceptable to us!

Our key virtues are forgiveness, humility, truthfulness, straightforwardness, purity, self-restraint, penance, renunciation, non-possessiveness, and—for the monks and nuns—celibacy.

Mary: We Christians would most certainly endorse those virtues. My son taught his followers to be as meek and as humble as he was, to forgive all (even enemies), to be detached, and to be truthful. He did not require celibacy of his disciples, though that was later required for priests in the Western churches. It is not required of the clergy in the Eastern or Protestant

---

2. See Jain, "A Study of the Bhagavati Sutra," http://www.herenow4u.net/index. php?id=67398.

churches, and, strangely, not required of priests who convert from Protestantism to Roman Catholicism. Many think that this requirement of celibacy for Roman Catholic priests is one reason that there is now a serious lack of priests today.

Mahavira, please tell us something about the history of your religion. How did it take hold in India? Didn't it have to compete with other religions?

Mahavira: We had humble beginnings. But, in the fourth century BCE, we found a friend in Chandragupta, the grandfather of Ashoka, the great emperor of India who did so much to spread Buddhism. Chandragupta actually converted to Jainism. This gave us royal patronage in India. Later, unfortunately, the political situation in India became unstable. We had to move south, and we split into two communities.

Jesus: We know what you mean by humble beginnings. Christianity spread through the Middle East, but largely among the poor. Many were martyred by the Romans, and we were not accepted for several hundred years. In the fourth century, the Roman emperor was converted to Christianity, and Christians were accepted. Not too many years later, Christianity became the official religion of the Roman Empire! Contrary to my teaching and example, the persecuted began to become the persecutors of the so-called pagans.

As the Roman Empire collapsed, we found ourselves in conflict with the purported barbarian tribes that invaded the empire. Only when these tribes were converted to Christianity over the centuries did the church stabilize. Meanwhile, we too had many divisions over doctrine. What was the basis of your divisions?

Mahavira: We divided over the authenticity of certain scriptural texts and over how to properly practice asceticism. My original disciples were very strict about detachment and held that almost everything, including clothes, were obstacles to achieving liberation. The monks actually refused to wear clothes and called themselves the Digambara or "sky-clad" monks. You can imagine what consternation that caused! They decided that this practice could not be extended to the nuns for obvious reasons. The other disciples were the Shvetambara. They wore simple white clothing and were more moderate in their detachments.

Mary: I remember a story about one of our great saints, Mother Teresa of Calcutta, and your monks. She was very open to other religions and at times worshiped with some of the local communities. One morning she decided to worship with your monks and came early to say her own prayers. When the monks came in clad only "in the sky," Mother Teresa was quite surprised and had to practice "modesty of the eyes" throughout the ceremony.

Mahavira: That must have been quite embarrassing for her!

The rest of our history had its ups and downs, just as did your religion. We were severely challenged in the seventh century CE when the Hindu kings decided to strengthen Hinduism and its many devotions. In the century following, we had to contend with the Muslims who began to dominate India. During the medieval period, India was invaded by Tamerlane, the Turko-Mongol ruler, and many of our wonderful Jain temples were destroyed.

Things were stable for us from 1400 to 1700, and then we had to contend with the British, who had little appreciation for our traditions. Around 1900, many Jains left India to settle abroad. Today there are about six million Jains worldwide. In India, about 0.4 percent of the population are Jains. There are large groups in England (thirty thousand) and in the United States (one-hundred thousand). There is a small but growing number of Jains in Canada.

Mary: I would like to hear more about your scriptures and how your followers were divided over them. Our Scriptures have also been divisive. Our Bible includes both the Hebrew Scriptures and the New Testament. While Christians accept the Scriptures of the Jews, the Jews do not accept ours. The Protestants and Catholics differ somewhat on which books are to be included in the Bible, and there are both Protestant and Catholic translations. Christians are also divided over the literal and the literary interpretations of the texts.

Mahavira: The Shvetambara Jains have their own canon. These scriptures contain doctrinal statements about the nature of reality, my biography, monastic rules, discussions on karma, mythology, stories that relate positions on piety and morals, accounts of those who ended rebirth and achieved liberation, pieces of my preaching, obligatory rituals, and many other topics.[3]

The Digambara Jains reject the Shvetambara canon and have scriptures of their own. The oldest Digambara text is the *Scripture in Six Parts*, which is based on the oral teaching of a mid-second century monk. The written manuscripts as well as the *Treatise on the Passions*, although revered, were locked away for centuries. In the early twentieth century, they were copied into modern script and eventually published. These writings are technical

---

3. Dobrin, *Religious Ethics: A Sourcebook*, 74ff.

accounts of the nature of the soul and its connection to karma. Although they only date back to the beginning of the Common Era, to Digambara Jains they represent their proud past and provide a connection with the scholars who founded their tradition.

The Kalpasutra also has value in that it contains early texts associated with the life of Mahavira as well as early monastic rules and history. It is recited by monks and read to the laity at some celebrations and feasts. The Digambaras have grouped their texts into four categories. These contain exposition of universal history, cosmology, proper behavior for monks and lay people, and metaphysics.[4]

Jesus: I understand that Jains and Christians differ considerably about God. We believe in One God: a Trinity of Father, Son, and Holy Spirit. Some have said that Jains are in fact atheists. Is that correct?

Mahavira: We Jains are quick to point out that we are not atheists. We do not deny the realm of the spiritual or the divine. On the other hand, Jains do not believe in God as a Supreme Being or Creator of the universe. This is largely because in the Jain tradition the universe has existed eternally in constant and endless process, so there is no need for a creator God or a God who intervenes in human affairs. For Jains, the divine has to do with the "self." Jainism focuses on the liberation of the self from karma (rebirth), thus achieving *paramatma*, the "supreme self." For the Jains, this liberated self, or the soul, in its pure state is the divine principle, and, in fact, is sometimes referred to as God. This divine essence is within all beings, so worship should be directed toward that principle as well as toward the fordmakers who show the way to this liberated state. As one Jain scholar puts it, "We worship this Supreme Essence—the ideal of all life and thought."[5]

Mary: Thanks for clearing up the false notion that Jains are atheists. Though you differ considerably from Christians in your beliefs on God, I see some similarities. Though we make a strong distinction between the human and the divine, we do acknowledge the presence of the divine within human beings.

I know that the Indian religions speak a great deal about karma. I have heard that Jains have a unique approach to karma. Could you explain your approach?

4. Dundas, *The Jains*, 80.
5. Nahar and Ghosh, *An Encyclopaedia of Jainism*, 264.

Mahavira: Jains do indeed have a different approach to the notion of karma from Hindus and Buddhists. For them, karma has a certain moral value and is linked to their actions, as well as to their rebirths. Karma for the Jains is a kind of matter or "sticky substance," which holds the soul in bondage. It is like dirt on the soul and has to be washed away so that the soul is purified and brought to "pure consciousness."

For Jains, all living beings (*jivas*) have the same nature or life force, which includes unlimited knowledge, perception, bliss, and energy. To reach that divine inner self, each individual must be free of karma, which is tied up with desires and passion. Positive karma releases the binding quality and allows for higher ascent in rebirths. Negative karma fouls all the karma, makes the soul heavy, and produces lower rebirths.[6] Ultimately, the goal in Jain purification is to release the individual from all karma and achieve a state of omniscience and bliss.[7]

Thus the monk or nun, the ideal practitioner, must curb frivolous actions of mind, body, and speech; live celibate lives free from desires and passions; strive to be completely nonviolent; and avoid egotism. He or she must be respectful and at the service of others. Passions and desires that prevent individuals from reaching the divine self within are to be avoided. The entire Jain ascetical program, whether it involves a monk, nun, or layperson, has as its goal to free oneself of the burden of karma.[8] From this perspective, no help or grace is needed from a "God." Each human person is "the maker of his own destiny."[9]

The soul takes to renunciation and exercises self-control as a result of which the influx of karma is terminated. After this, the soul takes to austere practices and annihilates karma and becomes perfect and accomplished.

Mary: These notions on karma are quite foreign to Christians. We measure the goodness of persons by how loving they are toward God, self, and others. We speak of "grace," which is the divine life; we assess one's state of soul by closeness to God, through closeness and imitation of Jesus Christ.

At times, Christians have used a merit system, whereby one's place in the afterlife could be measured by the amount of merits one could achieve through good actions or even "indulgences." This was in fact a kind of self-salvation and a departure from the truth that salvation is a free gift from God that cannot be earned.

6. Kelkar and Gangavane, *Feminism in Search of an Identity*, 150.

7. Chapple, *Jainism and Ecology*, 123.

8. Dundas, *The Jains*, 163.

9. Nahar and Ghosh, *An Encyclopaedia of Jainism*, 295.

Jesus: That's true. Christians believe in individual souls, not multiple re-births. The life of the individual begins and can live for all eternity, but remains the same spirit.

Mahavira: Belief in rebirth is common in the religions of India. This is related to the notion of karma and the belief that there is a "wheel of becoming," and that one's karma affects one's wheel and its cycle of deaths and rebirths. There are many interpretations of the process of rebirth in Jainism, but one common view is that "a calm death, free from rancor, frustration or pain, with mind fixed on religious principles at the end of life, will ensure a positive rebirth. . . . The length of the rebirth will be already established by life karma bound six months before death."[10] Jains often see smooth transitions from one life to another, and, therefore, bypass much of the speculation that is found in Hinduism and Buddhism.

Like Hindus and Buddhists, Jains believe that humans wander from birth to rebirth, from one lifetime to another, which is linked to their karma (good or bad) until they attain *moksha*, or liberation, from the process. Generally speaking, for Hindus the goal seems to be union with Brahman or God, while for Buddhists the goal is the "blowing out" of the self and entering into the bliss of Nirvana. Karma for Buddhists is often more a psychological reality; the self is karmic energy that has to be extinguished (achieving the "no self") before Nirvana can be achieved. For the Jains, the goal is *moksha*, or liberation, from the passions that deform the soul.

We believe that life must be a process of controlling the passions and thus freeing the soul from the seeds of destruction that are within. This liberation is achieved through disciplined asceticism that "cooks" these seeds within us and prevents them from bearing fruit.[11]

Mary: In our Scriptures there are some indications that the Jewish tradition had some version of rebirth or at least "re-appearance." While resting with his disciples at Caesarea Philippi, my son Jesus asked his disciples: "Who do they say that I am?" And they answered him, "John the Baptist; and others, Elijah; and still others, one of the prophets. . ." (Mark 8:27–29). This seems to indicate that our people at least expected their religious leaders to return, if not be reborn.

10. Dundas, *The Jains*, 102–103.
11. Long, *Jainism*, 93ff.

Jesus: One of the early theologians, Origen, seems to have accepted reincarnation, but his teachings were not accepted into the mainstream of our tradition.

Mahavira: At this point, I would like to clarify some false impressions about Jains. Not all Jains are monks and nuns practicing extreme asceticism. Many, especially in the United States, have traditionally been involved in business, finance, and commerce. They have regular national conventions in large hotels, where Jain families gather for sessions on conservation, climate change, fracking, as well as economic and social issues.

Jains live in India—as well as in North America, Western Europe, the Far East, and Australia—and are known for their generosity with time and funds for helping youth get jobs, setting up new industries, and helping to reduce unemployment. They are important contributors to society.

Mary: Many Christian churches are beginning to realize that their tradition, which includes a strong creation theology, needs to be applied to being good stewards of the Earth.

With your permission, Mahavira, I would like us to turn our conversation to the topic of nonviolence. I know that my son made some radical statements opposing the belief of "an eye for an eye and a tooth for a tooth" in his conversation about Judaism. He told his disciples to love their enemies and pray for those who offended them. He told them to "turn the other cheek" when struck. And in the garden on the evening before his execution, he told them to put away their swords and not defend him. During his arrest, scourging, and Crucifixion, he made no effort to resist or strike back.

Mahavira: One of the Jains' major contributions to religious truth is their understanding and commitment to *ahimsa*. *Ahimsa* is usually translated to mean nonviolence or "do no harm." For the Jain ascetic, it goes beyond physical harm to avoidance of intellectual violence through lying or harsh words. For them, *ahimsa* is "the absence of desire to do harm to any living being in thought, word, or deed."[12]

The practice of *ahimsa* for the Jain also ties in with the notion of avoiding passions mentioned earlier. They see the passions as being at the root of violence. They seek to moderate and eventually eliminate the passions and thus prepare for a good rebirth. This does not only mean avoiding harm, it also includes positive actions of giving and serving, all of which represent

12. Ibid., 97.

sacrifice of the self and its desires, as well as possessing a sense of duty toward others.

Unlike Buddhists, who are concerned with the motives of actions, Jains are more concerned with consequences. They closely monitor actions to see that they, in fact, do no harm. That is why most Jains are vegetarians or even vegans, who do not consume any animal products. Jains also try to avoid professions that involve the taking of life (for example, butchers or soldiers). For this reason, many Jains prefer the business professions and attempt to be honest and generous in their dealings with others. I put it this way: "To do harm to others is to do harm to oneself. You are he whom you intend to kill. You are he whom you intend to dominate. We corrupt ourselves as soon as we intend to corrupt others. We kill ourselves as soon as we intend to kill others."[13] In carrying out this ideal, the layman will allow violence for self-defense and the protection of others, but monks and nuns are much more extreme in their practice of doing no harm.

It is interesting to note that Mahatma Gandhi, the most influential proponent of nonviolence, was deeply influenced by his mother, who was a Jain.

Jesus: A number of my followers in modern times have been strong proponents of nonviolence. For instance, Martin Luther King Jr. employed nonviolent strategies in his powerful movement to achieve civil rights for African-Americans in the United States. Daniel Berrigan, S.J., and his brother Philip were well-known war resisters during the Vietnam War era. And Cesar Chavez used the nonviolent approach when he led his migrants to achieve justice for the Latino farm workers in the United States. Dorothy Day, who founded the Catholic Worker Movement in the U. S., took an absolute position against war and strongly resisted World War II at a time when this was not at all popular.

Today, John Dear and many other Christian leaders are strong advocates of nonviolence.

Mahavira: The Jains have an interesting history in regard to *ahimsa*. Early on, Jains identified with the heroic warrior tradition of ancient India, but as spiritual, violent warriors. With courage, determination, and rigorous asceticism, they would struggle against desires and attachment to physical things in order to purify and liberate themselves. The emphasis was on spiritual, not physical power—nonviolence, not violence.[14] For the Jains, this peaceful

---

13. Ibid., 107.
14. Hinnells and King, *Religion and Violence in South Asia,* 43ff.

posture included both physical restraint and careful watchfulness over the passions of anger and hatefulness that lead to violence.

The tradition has strongly resisted the killing of any life, even of the minutest organism. I once pointed out that those involved in immoral killing will be reborn as hell-beings or animals. Compassion for all living beings is our standard bearer. The Jain tradition in its discussion of nonviolence goes beyond strategies of passive nonresistance. The tradition develops a thorough analysis of reality that points to the intrinsic value of each living being, the desire of all living things to avoid suffering and destruction, and advocates a spirituality of care and compassion that is the way to liberation.[15]

Some Jains allow for violence in self-defense and even permit participation of laymen in just wars as long as the warrior resists evil passions of hatred and revenge. There have been examples in history where the Jains resisted Muslim repression in the eighteenth and nineteenth centuries and took up arms to defend themselves from oppressors in the twentieth century.

For the most part, Jains put their vigor and power into the spiritual struggle against human tendencies to evil. For the monks and nuns, this requires a rigorous asceticism of fasting, self-control, and intense religious practices. This is the traditional path to "victory" and heroism for the Jain. Cleansing, purifying, freeing oneself of karma, in some cases even fasting unto death, brings the self into a true and enlightened being. For the layperson, this means heroically practicing restraint in the face of the violence that dominates contemporary life.

Mary: Mahavira, tell us about some Jains of our modern day who are strong peace advocates.

Mahavira: We are proud of the contemporary Jains who have been peace activists. For example, Dr. Satish Kumar (b. 1935) has been outstanding in this area. He is a peace activist as well as environmentalist. As a youth he was a Jain monk, but at eighteen he left the monastery and became a follower of one of Gandhi's disciples, working for Indian Independence and land reform. In 1972 he settled in Britain where he established a secondary school and a college dedicated to a curriculum on ecological and spiritual studies. He has walked an eight-thousand mile pilgrimage for peace in Pakistan, India, the Soviet Union, and the United States, protesting nuclear weapons, and a two-thousand mile pilgrimage in Britain to celebrate the beauty of nature and encourage the environmental movement. Dr. Kumar

15. Ibid., 44.

edits *Resurgence* magazine and has written and edited a number of books on peace, ecology, and spirituality.

Bawa Jain (b. 1955) is another notable Jain in the peace movement. He has been the Secretary-General of the Millennium World Peace Summit of Religious and Spiritual Leaders that opened at the United Nations in 2000. Dr. Bawa Jain has been a visionary in the interfaith movement and travels the world giving lectures on peace and interfaith dialogue. He is also the founder of The World Movement for Nonviolence, where he conceived of the Gandhi-King Award, presented to those that foster the practices and principles of nonviolence in daily life. He also helped create the nonviolent youth programs that are operating in fifteen countries and 115 cities in the United States.

Mary: Mahavira, I would like to know how your people deal with women's issues. Such matters have been a challenge for Christians. My son was very open to choosing both women and men as disciples, which was quite unprecedented for Jewish leaders. Early on, the communities that developed were led by some extraordinary women. Once our movement was absorbed into the Roman Empire, the imperial patriarchy began to influence the church. At the same time, many women were appointed to official ministries up until the Middle Ages. After that, an all male clericalism was devised, and women lost their access to official offices and to any positions of authority.

Today there is a strong women's movement in society as well as in all the churches. Catholicism in particular is challenged to implement its theoretical position on the equality of women. For example, Sr. Joan Chittister has been a powerful advocate for the feminine perspective throughout the world. She has written: "It is precisely women's experience of God that this world lacks. A world that does not nurture its weakest, does not know God the birthing mother. A world that does not preserve the planet, does not know God the creator. A world that does not honor the spirit of compassion, does not know God the spirit. God the lawgiver, God the judge, God the omnipotent being have consumed Western spirituality and, in the end, shriveled its heart."[16]

Mahavira: The Jain religion never excluded women from the religious community, which always consisted of monks, nuns, laymen, and laywomen. At the same time, the Jain tradition has carried much negative baggage from its Indian tradition: beliefs that women are weak, deceptive, and unclean. Jain monks have viewed women as a dangerous threat to their vow of celibacy

16. Chittister, *Heart of Flesh*, 112 ff.

and taught that their enticements should be avoided. It has often been assumed that a woman was reborn into such an inferior state because of some sin in a former life. On the whole, the Jain tradition has been written and interpreted by men.

The status of women was a major factor in the split between the Shvetambaras and Digambaras around 79 CE. The debates began before the beginning of the Common Era. The Digambaras took the position that it was not acceptable for women, even nuns, to go naked because they would be raped.[17] It was the Digambara position that detachment from all things, including clothes, was necessary for liberation. Since women could not go naked, they were excluded from liberation. Thus, it was concluded that women had to be reborn as men before they could reach perfection.

In addition, women were thought to have so much bad karma that it was impossible to wash off their karma and reach purification.[18] Women were also believed to be destroyers of forms of life through menstruation and within the hidden orifices of their bodies. All this rendered women impure, weak, incapable of *ahimsa*, and too anxious to properly meditate.

In contrast, the Shvetambaras took the position that detachment is an inner quality and can be achieved by a woman who wears clothes. They point out that a man could set aside clothes, even food, and yet still be attached. The road to emancipation is both an inner and outer way, and therefore the Shvetambaras are not so literal in their interpretation of ascetic detachment. The main path is inner detachment, along with right faith, knowledge, and conduct, and they see no reason why a woman can't follow this path.

Each group has a different version of what they believe is my attitude toward women. The Digambaras maintain that I was a celibate, perfect ascetic who never allowed myself to be subject to the temptations of women. The Shvetambaras, on the other hand, believe that I was married and had a daughter and granddaughter. I was thus a householder and model for the laity before I renounced the world and became an ascetic.

Both sects revere some of the mothers of the *Jinas* (great teachers and perfected beings) and perform devotional rituals and recite mantras toward female deities. Families of both sects often worship female deities associated with their castes or villages, both at home altars and at temple.

Both Buddhism and Jainism were ascetic movements of the sixth century BCE, and both were reacting to Hinduism's denial of full participation in the rituals to women. Buddha took some time before he allowed women to be nuns, but Jainism quickly admitted women into the community of

17. Dundas, *The Jains*, 57.

18. Kelkar and Gangavane, *Feminism in Search of an Identity*, 151.

nuns and laywomen. Eventually, in ancient times as well as today, the nuns came to far outnumber the monks. At the same time, it has to be noted that the nun's life is much more circumscribed, and nuns are considered to be subordinate to the monks.

Mary: I know some of the most important issues in Christianity today are the abuse of women and the struggle to gain equality. In all the churches, especially in the developing countries, there are age-old, patriarchal structures that limit women from participation in ministry. In the Catholic churches, so much of the authority rests in the clergy and hierarchy that it is difficult for women to get access to decision-making. Catholic nuns, who have become quite educated and active in social issues, seem to be threatening to some of the hierarchy. Nuns have been investigated by the Vatican, which seems to be quite disturbed about their feminism and commitment to social issues.

Christian communities are dealing with child abuse, sex trafficking of children and young women, rape on campuses, unfair wages for women, domestic violence, and a number of other problems. What are modern Jains doing about women's issues?

Mahavira: Among the Jain nuns today, there is a serious movement to gain an equal religious education and access to the canonical texts. Nuns in some groups complain they are not allowed to preach, or can do so only when a male is not available. Those nuns who are expected to leave India and minister to Jains in other countries insist on an excellent preparation and a relaxation of some of the rules so that they can better adapt to other cultures. Laywomen, who support the ascetics with money and gifts, are encouraged to be steadfast in their commitment to Jain values and worship and to pass the tradition on to their children. Both women and men are encouraged to organize camps and conferences that will strengthen the Jain religion.

Though Jainism on an institutional level is male-centric, the nuns far outnumber the monks and are greatly admired for their fervor and faith. As one nun puts it, "Jain laywomen exhibit the same conviction in their faith and the same determination in its translation into acts in their daily lives."[19]

Advocates for Jain women maintain that past references to women's bodies being unfit for *ahimsa* are irrelevant to the spiritual life or the process of liberation. They point out that the Jain scriptures say nothing against the possibility of women reaching enlightenment.

19. Sharma, *Women in Indian Religions*, 72ff.

Our history supports their contention. Both in ancient times and now, many nuns are venerated for their learning and high morals. Moreover, women are often considered to be more inclined toward chastity, more adept at controlling violent emotions, at times more compassionate, and often close to nature.

Of course, our members also struggle with many of the issues of abuse and violence against girls and women. So much of this violates our most sacred traditions of "do no harm."

Mary: Please tell us about some of the outstanding Jain women who are today strong proponents for women's rights.

Mahavira: Today we have many outstanding Jain women leaders like Devaki Jain (b. 1933). She was born in Mysore, India, attended Oxford University, and taught at the Delhi University. Early on, she was involved in feminist issues and published *Indian Women* in 1975. Throughout her life, she has been a strong advocate for women's rights and women's employment locally, nationally and globally. She was chair of the Advisory Committee on Gender for the United Nations Centre in Asia Pacific. Jain also championed women's rights in Africa and worked with the United Nations on the feminization of poverty.

Jesus: Mahavira, for my dear mother and me, this has been a marvelous and truly informative sharing on our religious views. My hope would be that many of the members of both our religions would take part in similar discussions.

SUGGESTED READINGS ON JAINISM

Jaini, Padmanabh. *The Jaina Path of Purification*. New Delhi: Motilal Banarsidass, 1998.
Kuhn, Hermann. *Karma, The Mechanism: Create Your Own Fate*. Wunstorf, Germany: Crosswind, 2001.
Long, Jeffery. *Jainism: An Introduction*. New York: I.B. Tauris, 2009.
Nahar, P.C. and K.C. Ghosh, eds. *An Encyclopaedia of Jainism*. New Delhi: Sri Satguru, 1988.

Chapter 6

Sikhism

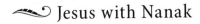 Jesus with Nanak

"One universal Creator God. Truth is the name."

—*SRI GURU GRANTH SAHIB*[1]

"Our Father, who art in heaven, hallowed be thy name."

—MATT 6:9

Jesus: Greetings, Nanak. I know that you founded one of the youngest religions in the world, Sikhism. Could you teach me about your wonderful religion?

Nanak: Very honored to meet you, Jesus. We have had many of your followers come to visit our kitchens to eat, and I have longed to meet you personally.

As you mentioned, our religion, Sikhism (pronounced Seek-ism or Sick-ism), is quite young. It was founded in the fifteenth century, around the time that Christopher Columbus arrived in America. Today there are about twenty-three million Sikhs around the world, many of them living in

1. See the *Sri Guru Granth Sahib*.

Punjab, India. (*Sikh* is the Punjabi word for disciple.) The men are recognizable because they wear elaborate turbans on their heads and have both beards and mustaches. Unfortunately, their turbans cause some people to mistake them for terrorists. Recently, a bigot came into one of our temples in Wisconsin and killed and wounded a number of worshipers there.

Jesus: Tell me something about yourself and how you founded this religion.

Nanak: I was born in 1469 in a little village that is in present-day Pakistan. My family members were Hindus, in an upper caste. I attended a good school, where I studied accounting so that I could work in my father's mercantile business. Besides studying Hinduism, I also learned about Islam.

Like many Hindus, I married young, had two sons, and then took a job as a storekeeper. Store employment put me in touch with both Hindus and Muslims. I learned about their diverse beliefs. I was living a very ordinary life as a family man and merchant.

Jesus: That seems to be the case with so many religious founders. I worked in a small village as a carpenter and farmer. Moses was a shepherd, and Muhammad operated camel caravans. Did something unique happen to you?

Nanak: Indeed! One day when I was about thirty years old, I was bathing in a river, and suddenly I had an extraordinary experience of God's presence and of the awesome power of God's name. I felt a deep and undeniable calling to sing God's praises and spread his word to others.

What was I to do? Was I being beckoned to leave everything and follow this strange calling? I spent much time in prayer. I decided to place my family in the care of my parents and set out on my mission. It was so difficult leaving my dear wife and children. Have you experienced such tensions?

Jesus: Certainly. After my father Joseph died, my mother depended on my income and the work of my brothers and sisters. Like you, I had lived with my family for three decades, and now I felt this strong prompting to call my people to repentance and to tell them that God's reign was in their midst. I had been strongly influenced by a relative called John the Baptist, an ascetic who lived in the desert. Just before he was executed for exposing the hypocrisy of our king, Herod, he baptized me in the Jordan River. That was a deeply moving experience for me, and, after a retreat in the desert, I left my family and started my mission.

Later, I told my followers that they too would have to detach themselves from their families if they wanted to carry on my mission. Perhaps the phrase "hate your families" is too strong because I would certainly want my disciples to love their families.

Nanak: Well, at about the same age as you, I left home with difficulty but with a song in my heart: "Me, a minstrel out of work, and God applies me to his work. Thus spoke the Lord to me: 'Night and day, go and sing my praises.' The Almighty again did summon this minstrel to his exalted court. On me he bestowed the robe of honor of his praise and prayer. . . . Your minstrel spreads your glory by singing your Word."[2]

Jesus: Did you go forth to spread Hinduism?

Nanak: Not really. My revelation has told me that there is but one path to God—and that is neither Hindu nor Muslim. It is simply God's path. None-theless, I have always been open to those two religions. I took Mardana, a Muslim musician friend of mine, along so that we could sing God's praises together and spread the revelation that God gave to me.

Jesus: Did you preach your revelation far and wide, or did you stay in your local area, the way I did?

Nanak: Mardana and I traveled extensively for the next twenty years to the shrines and pilgrimage places dear to Hindus and Muslims. We trekked to India, Gaya, and Varanasi to preach to Hindus; to the holy places of the Jains in India; and to Mecca and the other parts of the Middle East to meet Muslims and Sufis. We called disciples to our Truth.

We never expressed hostility toward other religions; indeed, we dem-onstrated profound respect for the faiths that had shaped us. Nevertheless, we aspired to call them to the truth and simplicity that is the basis of all religions. We had a simple message: we are all called to praise God, live good lives, and serve each other.

Inwardly, I was critical of all the superstitions and idol worship that I encountered. I disagreed with the worshiping of many gods and goddesses as well as the caste system in Hinduism.[3] I was not comfortable with the absence of God and the strict asceticism of Buddhism and Jainism. I liked the strong sense of community, the caring for the sick, and the feeding of the hungry that the Sufis offered, but I was not at ease with their long medita-tions. Islam had become too militant for me. My revelation had taught me

2. Sikh Missionary Society, *Sikh Religion*, 222.

3. Singh Mann, *Sikhism*, 24.

that religion should be a simple way to direct people to God. The rituals should be spare and designed simply for praising God. And the way of life should be one of compassion and service to others.

Jesus: I can relate to what you say, dear friend Nanak. I also felt called to purify and simplify my own Jewish religion. We had become so legalistic that healing a desperate person on Sabbath was considered so sinful that my religious leaders wanted to have me killed for it. Eating rituals and ablutions had become so legalistic and rubrical that the very purpose of the ritual, to praise God, was lost. Yes, our leaders insisted that we believe in one God, but in truth they had other "gods." Money was greedily gathered from taxes collected for money changing, as well as selling sheep and birds for sacrifice. Many also worshiped power, as they lorded it over our people. Hypocrisy was rampant, and, when I called them on it, I ignited a blaze of anger and hate toward myself.

So how long did your mission last? You probably know that mine was short-lived. I was executed after a year or so of preaching and healing.

Nanak: I was blessed with a long life. After twenty years on mission, I was ready to settle down and form a community based on my teachings, which had evolved over time. I bought some land near a beautiful river with a majestic view of the Himalayas in the background. The place was called Kartarpur, which means the town of the Creator.

We were a hardworking, God-praising community, open to all, with no distinction of caste or gender. We valued cleanliness, prayer, hard work, hospitality, and equality. We wanted our lives to be pure and dedicated to the glory of God and the service of others.

Jesus: Your original community sounds much like the early Christian community as it is described in the Acts of the Apostles. It says that they were steadfast in the teaching of the apostles and in the breaking of the bread, shared all things in common, helped the needy, ate together with gladness and simplicity of heart, praising God and being in favor with all the people.

Did you remain the leader of your community until your death, Nanak?

Nanak: Yes, I did. I died at the age of seventy. I had remained close to both my Hindu and Muslim friends, and they came to see me on my deathbed. The Hindus suggested that I be cremated, but the Muslims wanted me to be buried. A cheery visit!

I suggested that the Hindus put fresh flowers on my right side and the Muslims on my left. The group whose flowers stayed fresh after my death could dispose of my body. The next morning, I was found dead and covered with a sheet. When the sheet was removed, the body was gone, and all the flowers were fresh. I had returned to the light from which I had come, and both the Hindus and Muslims together built a monument to my memory.

Were your followers with you when you died, Jesus?

Jesus: Some of them were. You see I was executed by crucifixion. Many of my followers fled, afraid that they too would be killed. But my death was different from yours in that I did not disappear after my death. On the third day, God raised me from the dead, and I was able to appear to my disciples to bring them peace and courage and to commission them to carry on my mission.

Who carried on your mission after your death?

Nanak: Before my death I held a ceremony and appointed my disciple Lehna as my successor. I gave him the name Guru Angad. There would be nine more gurus in succession. Each contributed to the development of this new religion. Some composed verses that celebrated my being a medium for God's revelation. Others sorted out stories about me and continued to organize our scriptures into volumes. Some founded new communities and devised new ways of service such as digging wells for the needy and providing medicine and medical care for the poor. One built the magnificent Golden Temple at Amritsar, which is still a wonderful center for praising God and serving food to all who come, no matter what their religious persuasion.

Jesus: Were these proponents of a new religion well-received? I know that my followers were ostracized by some Jews for accepting me as their Messiah and by some Romans for not worshiping the Roman gods and refusing to recognize the divinity of the emperor. Many of my early apostles and disciples were executed or thrown to wild animals for entertainment in the coliseum.

Nanak: I had always been close to both Hindus and Muslims, so my followers were at first well-accepted.

Eventually, they became a threat to some, especially to the Muslim leaders in India. Some of my supporters were executed, so my Sikhs or disciples began to carry swords to protect themselves. As time went on, we became more militant. Because we were so fit, well-trained, and courageous defending ourselves and the cause of justice, we were often called upon to be part of the military. We engaged in battles with hostile tribes such as the brutal Moguls.

In 1708, the tenth guru, Gobind Singh, was mortally wounded in battle. Before he died, he made a milestone decision about our religion. He would be the last person to be the guru. From now on our book of scriptures, the Guru Granth Sahib, would be honored as our guiding guru. This holy book of stories and songs would be enshrined in every temple and honored as though it were the person who revealed God's message.

The Sikh faith was now complete, just several hundreds of years from my original revelation. We now had our scriptures, leadership, our holy temples with their free kitchens, congregations, martyrs, and the elite Khalsa—trained guards protecting us.

Jesus: Your story brings to mind the complicated evolution of my religion. We began with small communities of Jews in Palestine and the environs. As my movement spread to non-Jews (Gentiles), communities developed throughout Asia Minor and even in Rome. As I mentioned earlier, my followers were often an oppressed minority. By the fourth century, we were so widespread and organized that the Roman Emperor Constantine saw Christians as a possible unifying force in his empire. We eventually became the official religion of the empire.

Our evolution took longer than yours. Becoming integrated into the empire brought with it a strong hierarchical model that was legalistic, militant, and patriarchal. Our elders evolved into bishops, and the bishop of Rome gradually became the pope. A priesthood developed, along with many other ministries. It took until the medieval period before this priesthood took on the meaning of "having special powers," with a required celibacy.

Our book of Scriptures also evolved. It took centuries before our Bible was finalized. Similar to your Guru Granth Sahib, our Bible is now honored as the Word of God, and the Gospels are reverenced as carrying my living presence.

Tell me more about these unusual Sikh scriptures, Nanak, which you now honor as your guru.

Nanak: As you know, Jesus, the word guru comes from *gu*, which means darkness, and *ru*, which means light. In my religion, my scriptures and I are honored as gurus who bring light into darkness.

The Guru Granth Sahib is a large book with 1,430 pages. It is written in various dialects, including Punjabi. In this form it is used in worship. It can be translated and used privately. The book consists of teachings and hymns composed by me and by some later gurus. Some of the hymns are from other religions, because we deeply respect other faiths. The book is treated as a person, with its own room, where it is put to rest at the end of the day.

At times of worship, the book is carefully carried and placed on a raised and decorated platform. A leader sits with the book and leads the singing of selections of holy teachings, prayers, and praises of God. We sing about our search for God: "I am a blind man carrying a burden while the mountainous way is long. I want eyes, which I cannot get. How can I ascend and traverse the journey?"[4] We sing my teachings that religion should be simple and spare, not found in the severe asceticism of a ragged yogi covered in ashes. Nor is religion found in the wearing of jewels, the shaving of heads, the blowing of horns, or elaborate bathings. No! True religion is found in living a pure life in the midst of an impure world and in looking at all people as equals.

We sing in praise of God and about simple faith that is not bound in boatloads of books or elaborate creeds. Salvation lies in deeds not creeds, in serving others in the name of God. Remembering the Divine Name roots out evil and raises us to truth.

My revelation about religion is simple and very practical, Jesus. Salvation is gained by the grace of God and is given to those who keep the name of God on their lips in prayer, lead good lives, make an honest living, and serve others, especially the poor. Salvation is a combination of divine free choice (the grace of God) and our own free "life of activism."[5]

Jesus: Nanak, I find many parallels in your religion to mine. I reminded my Jewish people that God does not want animal sacrifices, but instead wants us to show kindness to people and to stop judging people. This was a radical challenge for some of my leaders who had made a commercial industry out of Temple worship and often stood in judgment of others. I challenged their fancy garments and their luxurious lifestyles enjoyed off the backs of the poor. I confronted their empty legalism and their hypocrisy.

I agree with you that faith should be simple and humble before God. At the same time, I can see the value of creeds as a means of protecting our beliefs and pledging ourselves to them in community. I see nothing wrong with "boatloads of books," as long as books help us deepen our faith and move toward action. My religion has a great tradition of scholarship. Throughout history our theologians have been held in high esteem. Although I regret to say that in the last few decades some of them have been silenced and dealt with rather heavy-handedly.

4. Sikh Missionary Society, *Sikh Religion*, 27.

5. Mittal and Thursby, *Religions of South Asia*, 140.

I wish your people could have had some influence during the Protestant Reformation. You could have helped them see that faith and good deeds go together and that salvation includes the grace of God and the acceptance of that grace by disciples who are open, active, and loving.

Nanak: I can see that we have much in common, Lord Jesus. We also agree with the Hindu and Buddhist traditions that salvation is achieved by destroying the ego and the desires that keep us from being one with God.

Now I would like to share where our religion stands on such beliefs as God, creation, human life, karma, rebirth, death, and the afterlife. We Sikhs have some valuable things to contribute in these areas, and we can learn from each other.

Jesus: I certainly agree that we can learn from each other. The mysteries of God and divine revelation are beyond human comprehension. From the time humans appeared and developed the human capacity to understand and reflect, God has been communicating revelation. Put all our revelations together, and we have but a glimpse of the meaning of Mystery. Of course, my followers honor the uniqueness of my incarnation and revelation. But that is not to exclude the value of God's revelation to you and others.

Nanak, please tell me more about the beliefs of your Sikh people.

Nanak: We are dedicated to the belief in One God, a God who is all-pervasive and personal, one who can be worshiped and loved by all. My revelation taught me that: "There is one God, Eternal Truth is his name, Creator of all things and the all-pervading spirit. Fearless and without hatred, timeless and formless, beyond birth and death, self-enlightened."[6]

Our God cannot be known by the mind, but only by experience. God is "unseen, inscrutable, inaccessible, omnipotent." We have other names for God: *Sat Nam* (true name) and *Sat Guru* (true Guru).

We believe that God dwells within everything and everyone and, yet, is at the same time separate, transcendent, and beyond. God "projected" the divine self on others and draws all back to their Source. The enlightened person is one who is aware of the divine presence in all. I always compare those who don't enjoy such awareness to fish who swim in the water without any consciousness of the water around them.

We believe that God participates in the world, but we do not accept the possibilities of incarnations or avatars, as do Hindus and Christians.

---

6. Cole and Singh Sambhi, *The Sikhs,* 69.

We believe that God is identified with ultimate Truth. The perennial search for truth is, in fact, the search for God. We also believe that it is through the divine will that everything exists, but we still leave room for human freedom. Only God can save, but good actions can render us receptive. As I have said, "Good actions may procure a better frame of mind, but release comes only through His grace."[7]

Jesus: We also believe in the divine presence in the world and in people, but we have unique belief in "Incarnation," that God became human in my person. This belief is central to my Christian tradition. My followers believe that I am the Incarnation, God's Son, and that I, Jesus, am the Christ, the anointed one of God. We also identify God with ultimate Truth. I have identified myself as "the Way, the Truth, and the Life." Those who are in union with me are indeed one with God. As I mentioned before, only God can save, but human freedom and good acts also play roles in this process of salvation.

Nanak: We don't know of incarnation, Jesus, but we do believe in God as the Creator of all. We have no creation stories, but we believe that everything emanated from God in a time of darkness and void millions of years ago. I know that science puts this many billions of years ago, and we are open to science and to the theory of evolution. At the same time, we believe that God sustains all and watches over all, as He casts his glance of grace over all and keeps each constantly in mind.

Jesus: Christians accept the Hebrew creation stories. Some take these stories literally and reject the scientific theories on the development of the universe and the evolution of life. Others see these stories as symbolic myths and view them as compatible with the findings of science. What are your beliefs regarding humans?

Nanak: We see humans as the peak of creation, but left on our own we are separated from God and trapped by our desires for material things. We are like lost and despairing elephants crashing through the forest.

Human ignorance is the main reason for our confusion and despair. Sometimes our family or cultural backgrounds keep us ignorant of our blessedness, teach us to rely on ourselves alone, and deprive us of opportunities for meeting our God.

7. Ibid., 74.

Jesus: We certainly agree on the uniqueness of the human person, but we are cautious that we might see ourselves as "over" creation or simply as "users and abusers" of the Earth and its resources. An air of superiority or dominance produces very destructive results for both the Earth and for many humans who are deprived of good food, air, and water.

Nanak: We should discuss karma because that concept has a strong bearing on how we view human actions. I do not believe that human failures come ultimately from bad karma. Sinfulness, whether it be pride, lust, self-centeredness, attachments, or desires, prevents us from being truly free and blocks us from seeing our dependence on God. It is this blindness to God's presence and grace that is the ultimate cause of our suffering. Only God's grace gives us clear vision, freedom, and the opportunity for union with God.

Jesus: Our tradition teaches that sinfulness is not so much individual actions, but the direction of our lives. Sin is "missing the mark," walking the wrong path. Ultimately, we are either turned toward or away from our God. My teachings reveal the narrow path of justice, compassion, goodness, love, and generosity. I taught that God's grace, the very life of God, can guide and fill the soul. But there must be an openness, as you say, a freedom to embrace God's presence and assistance. There must also be an openness to accept forgiveness when we fail.

Humans are not born "fallen" or "in sin." Children are born innocent, but with the capacity to freely choose sinfulness. I think we both agree that to "be saved" means to be open to divine grace as we travel the perilous road of life.

Nanak: Let's talk about rebirth. I know we have some real differences in this area. As you know, Buddhists and Hindus deal with rebirth. In fact, it seems like the Buddha suggested that through dedicated meditation one could become enlightened and move toward Nirvana. Apparently, he was reacting to the endless cycle of rebirths that some Hindus accept.

My own belief in this area is that one can move through a manifold cycle of lives until one becomes truly human. At that point, there is the opportunity to be liberated from the cycle by surrounding oneself with a holy community and by turning toward God. Only then can one be in union with God.[8]

8. Sikh Missionary Society, *Sikh Religion*, 253.

Jesus: You, no doubt, know that my tradition does not believe in reincarnation or rebirth in that sense. We believe in the individuality of the soul, which has the freedom to move toward or away from God. We view our rite of baptism as a rebirth into a unique relationship with me and my community. Rebirth, for us, does not mean being reborn into another state of existence, but being reborn into a unique relationship with God through me, the Savior. Although this rite moves the soul toward a unique path of salvation, it is not, as some hold, necessary for salvation. For salvation, one needs to live a good life and to be sincerely searching for God.

Nanak: Given these differences, I know we will have diverse beliefs on death and afterlife.

Our ultimate goal as Sikhs is to come to the end of our rebirths and abide in "the Supreme Soul," to become one with the Light. As water can blend with water and light with light, we long to blend with the divine Light. Our scriptures say: "The one who dies in the Word, never dies again and that person's devotion becomes fruitful."[9]

When I died, I wanted to be in the company of God and the saints. I believed that God was both my mother and father, and I yearned to return to my Lord after death. My revelation told me that we all emanate from the divine Light; my prayer was that in death I would become one with the Light.

Jesus: I know that my followers also want to pass from death into the Light. The difference is that they believe that I carry the Light, am indeed the Light, and that through their oneness with me they will be one with God. I told them that I was one with God, and they could be one with us. I promised them that I would give them eternal life.

Nanak: I am sure that your religion has many symbols; all religions do. Let me tell you about some of ours. First of all, male Sikhs carry five symbols, the five "Ks" of our religion. First is the kara, or the steel bracelet, which symbolizes strength, the unity we have with each other, and the wish to be unending with our God. Secondly, there is the kangha, the small comb, a symbol that we are to keep our hair neat and clean but never cut. The third is the kesh, our hair, which is to be left as God intended it and covered with a large turban out of honor to God. (Women are to cover their hair with a scarf). The next item is the kachera, a pair of short trousers that we wear for modesty. Today, these are worn as undergarments. And finally, there is the

9. Ibid., 271.

kirpan, a sword in a sheath—a symbol that we are prepared to defend our faith and those who are oppressed.

Jesus: Interesting symbols, Nanak. Christians also wear symbols. Often they wear a cross in remembrance of my Crucifixion, or medals in commemoration of me or one of the saints. In some areas, women cover their heads in church. Men are usually requested to remove their hats in church. In Roman Catholicism, the pope wears a white cassock and a skullcap (zucchetto). At ceremonies, he and bishops wear tall, peaked miters and carry crosiers (a staff with a cross on it). Both popes and bishops wear special rings signifying their office.

Water is an important symbol for Christians and is poured out at baptisms and at other services. Wine or grape juice along with bread is offered and shared at Eucharistic services. Oil is used for anointing at healing services, confirmations, and ordination as a sign of the coming of the spirit. Incense and bells have often been a part of Christian ritual.

Nanak, tell me your practices of prayer and ritual.

Nanak: Prayer is quite important to Sikhs. Prayer purifies the mind so that it will be open to the Word and experience of God. Prayer is our way of praising God and opening ourselves to the saving graces of God. One of my favorites is: "You are my father. You are my mother. You are my relative. You are my brother and sister. You are my protector everywhere." We pray regularly, both at home and at temple. In our homes we set aside a room where the scriptures are enshrined and the family gathers regularly there for prayer.

Our temples are called *gurdwaras*. These are buildings that house our holy book, the Guru Granth Sahib. It is also where we pray and meet in community for friendship, worship, and education.

When we gather for worship, we greet each other by saying God's name (*Waheguru*), then kneel, touch our heads to the floor as a sign of respect for the scriptures, and sit on the floor—the men on one side, women on the other. Each one brings an offering of flowers, food, or money. The holy book, the centerpiece of our worship, is enshrined on a raised platform, where we place our gifts. On another platform, a group of musicians accompanies us in the singing of the scriptural hymns.

It is all very simple. We have come to praise our God and listen to God's word. The ceremony is led by a *granthi*, who can be male or female. The musicians select and introduce a hymn, and we sing slowly and prayerfully, putting ourselves in touch with our God.

These services are held daily, but the best-attended service is on Saturday. Visitors are always welcome. We serve food from our temple kitchens to all who come. In our Golden Temple at Amritsar, we serve more than forty thousand meals a day free of charge. It is all part of our spirit of hospitality and service. (We offer this same gesture of feeding the hungry at each of our Temples throughout the world.)

Jesus: I like the simplicity of your religion. Such simplicity is what I had in mind for my communities.

However, over the centuries, Christianity has become so complicated with laws, doctrines, and rubrics that often it has lost sight of the heart of the Gospel. Back in the 1960s, St. John XXIII, the pope at that time, called a council to draw us back to the way Christianity was when it was born. I am pleased that Pope Francis wants to simplify the church and call it back to the Gospel ways as a "poor church for the poor." I like your practice of incorporating food kitchens into your places of worship.

Now, dear Nanak, tell me about some of the modern movements in Sikhism.

Nanak: We are starting to get interested in the environmental movement. For instance, one of my followers, Sant Balbir Singh Seechewal, was honored several years ago by *Time* magazine for his heroic efforts to clean up some of the rivers in India.

The Sikh scriptures say: "Creating the world, God has made it a place to practice spirituality."[10] In our religion, our goal is to achieve a state of bliss and be in harmony with all creation. Now, we realize that scriptures were written long ago and cannot be superficially applied to the environmental crises that we face today, yet we have begun to search the scriptures and our spirituality. We yearn to become a part of the movement to sustain the environment.

We believe that all things flow from God and are therefore holy. We believe that God's spirit pervades all creation and that everyone and everything must be held in honor. Humans have a role to play in this world in that we alone are capable of love, compassion, justice, and action.

I have challenged dualism where matter is separated from spirit. All reality is spiritual. Even matter is spiritual.

We have a strict discipline of mind and body, and we are prepared to avoid the excesses that endanger our environment. We are strong and have a firm sense of commitment to the causes in which we believe. We are

10. *Sri Guru Granth Sahib*, 1035.

committed to preserve and sustain our resources by examples of simplicity. You can count on us.

Jesus: As I have said so often in these dialogues, the Earth belongs to the Lord, and my disciples are called to take proper care of it in his name. We too believe that the Creator's spirit is in all things. This is the kingdom of God; the loving, saving presence of God is in all things and must be cherished and honored with love and justice.

What are your views on violence? I know your people have been involved in some violent incidents in recent history.

Nanak: You must be referring to the incidents in the 1980s. A Sikh leader led a militant rebellion against the Indian government and ensconced himself and his followers at our Golden Temple. In 1984 Indira Gandhi, the prime minister of India, sent troops, and thousands were killed on both sides during the government attack on this stronghold. The Temple was destroyed. Mrs. Gandhi visited the site after the battle and promised to rebuild the Temple. Soon after, two of her guards who were Sikhs assassinated her and brought down much reproach on our people. Many of them emigrated.

Today the Sikhs are on much better terms in India. In fact, a Sikh, Dr. Manmohan Singh, was prime minister of India from 2004 through May 26, 2014. He remains a strong advocate for world peace. We have strong principles concerning peace: don't speak ill of anyone; see your enemies as friends; do good deeds for others; consider no one a stranger; make universal sisterhood and brotherhood a goal; and see God in everyone.

Jesus: From what I have heard, Sikhism seems to be quite male-oriented. Are things improving with gender equality?

Nanak: You are right about the inequality. Sikhs have lived in a culture that favors men, and this is reflected in our religion. Tens of thousands of women who visit the Golden Temple plant saplings to urge pilgrims not to abort female fetuses when they appear on sonograms. This has been a serious problem for Sikhs. Our scriptures are both positive and negative toward women. Women are often idealized in scripture as devout women paying homage to a male God. At the same time, we believe that both women and men were created by God.[11] Women are honored for giving birth, but are called to be obedient to their husband's wishes. God is sometimes portrayed as a mother.

11. *Sri Guru Granth Sahib*, 304.

We have not always been faithful to our ideals. At the end of the nineteenth century, Punjab and even the Golden Temple had sunk into the kind of decadence that included pornography, prostitution, and abuse of women.

Gandhi achieved much reform for our women. He advocated for their respect and equality, and honored their courage and strength in resisting British domination. We now oppose female infanticide, child marriage, cremation of widows, the prevention of widows remarrying, dowries, and the requirement of women to veil. Many Sikh women have become heroic activists for women's rights. Yet we still have a long way to go.

Jesus: I can relate to that struggle. Many cultures in North America and Europe have made great advances for women's equality in government, business, the military, education, and the professions. But our churches lag behind.

Church leaders profess gender equality but struggle to implement it in church life. The Catholic and Eastern churches have placed a great amount of authority in the hands of the hierarchy and clergy. At the same time, they oppose the ordination of women, so it is quite difficult to offer women any positions of real authority.

Nanak: Well, Jesus. This has been a wonderful dialogue, and I feel that we have drawn closer and are able to better understand what we have in common as well as where we differ. It has been an honor to dialogue with you.

Jesus: Likewise, dear Nanak. My blessings on you and all your people.

SUGGESTED READINGS ON SIKHISM

Cole, W. Owen and Piara Singh Sambhi. *The Sikhs*. Boston: Routledge, 1978.
Mann, Gurinder Singh. *Sikhism*. Upper River, NJ: Prentice Hall, 2004.
Nesbitt, Eleanor. *Sikhism*. New York: Oxford University Press, 2005.
Sharma, Arvind, ed. *Women in Indian Religions*. New York: Oxford University Press, 2002.

Chapter 7

Taoism

~∽ Jesus with Lao Tzu and Kuan Yin

It achieves its work, but does not take credit

It clothes and feeds myriad things, but does not rule over them.

—LAO TZU[1]

But when you give alms, do not let your left hand know what your right hand is doing, so that your alms may be done in secret; and your Father who sees in secret will reward you.

—MATT 6:3–4

Jesus: Greetings, Lao Tzu and Kuan Yin. It is so pleasant sitting with you both at the foot of this magnificent mountain in China. For so long I have been eager to hear about your ancient Chinese tradition of Taoism.

I guess we should first introduce ourselves. I am Jesus of Nazareth, a Jewish reformer who began a movement that evolved into Christianity after my death. I was born in 4 BCE and was executed by the Roman authorities

1. Legge, *Tao Te Ching*, chap. 34.

thirty years later. I am called the Son of God, and I both taught and embodied the wisdom of a God of mercy and forgiveness.

Kuan Yin: *Ni hao*, Jesus. I am Kuan Yin. We met previously for our discussion with the Buddha. Many in the Taoist tradition revere me as one of the feminine immortals. I am an honored symbol of compassion, especially for those who are suffering.

Lao Tzu: *Ni hao*, Lord Jesus. My name is Lao Tzu. I was born in China, about five hundred years before your birth. Tradition says that I wrote the manifesto that started the religion of Taoism.

Jesus: Please tell me more about yourself, Lao Tzu.

Lao Tzu: Well, I was born into a rather ordinary family. As a young man, I got a job as a state auditor. This work gave me insight into the corruption and violence in my society. Gradually, I became disillusioned with my Chinese culture. Many had refused to live a life of goodness, had lost touch with nature, and were living superficial, or even evil, lives.

As I entered old age, I decided I had had enough. I headed west to Tibet. On my way out of town, I was stopped by a guard who identified me as a wise sage. He requested that I write down my words of wisdom so that they would not be lost.

Before my departure, I collected my thoughts into what is now called the *Tao Te Ching*. Ever since then, that compendium has been the basic text for the Tao religion.

Kuan Yin: Many have encountered Taoism without realizing it. The martial arts practices such as kung fu, the popular exercise t'ai-chi, the Chinese zodiac commonly seen on placemats in Chinese restaurants—for example, the year of the tiger—and the two opposite forces of yin and yang, are all related to Taoism. Taoists worked at alchemy to discover the elixir that would gain immortality. Though they failed, they produced the foundations of chemistry that led to products like gunpowder in China. Even acupuncture, which is still used in healing, can be traced to Taoism.

Lao Tzu: It is my belief that the Tao—which is the basic principle of the universe, the potential of all reality, and the power that develops and changes all things—is a mystery beyond our understanding. Thus I said, "The origin of heaven and earth is beyond the realm of thought. The Tao that can be expressed in words is not the everlasting Tao. . . . The Tao is a mystery. You cannot see its coming or going."[2]

Jesus: Please say more. I am fascinated by this concept.

Lao Tzu: The Tao is a mysterious power that links the entire universe. The true path for humans is to become linked with this power. One of the earliest written expressions of this tradition was the *I Ching* (ca. 300–200 BCE), which describes the flow of the Tao, the indivisible life energy. The power of this energy is described as follows: "The Way gives birth to them, nourishes them, matures them, completes them, rests them, supports them, and protects them. It gives birth to them, but doesn't try to own them; it acts on their behalf but doesn't make them dependent; it matures them but doesn't rule them."[3]

Jesus: You describe the Tao or Way as a power and energy that link our universe and world. In our tradition the closest to that would be "divine grace," the very life of God, which is creative, sustaining, and life-giving. Being life, grace is more personal. Sharing in it is sharing in the very life of God.

I told my followers that I was "the way, and the truth, and the life" (John 14:6). Following me, sharing in my life, death, and Resurrection is the "way" to salvation. In the early days, my movement was called "The Way."

Lao Tzu: I would like to tell about some of the writings in my tradition. The most important is the *Tao Te Ching*, which is a collection of wisdom statements with explanations after each pearl of insight. Its main purpose is to teach how to govern properly and to reflect on the nature of the Tao.

I am emphatic in this document that the Tao is throughout all of reality and that the Tao cannot be defined. "The Tao is like a well: used but never used up. It is like the eternal void: filled with infinite possibilities."[4] At the same time, I am clear that the Tao is beyond all, the source of all, and within all: "It has no equal. It is always present, endlessly in motion. From it, like a mother, everything living has come. I do not know what to call it. So I shall call it Tao. Reluctantly I shall call it the Greatest. Being the Greatest, it goes everywhere. Silently it fills all."[5]

2. Hooper, *Tao Te Ching*, 57.

3. Hendricks, *Te-Tao Ching*, 20.

4. Ibid., 2.

5. Ibid., chap. 25:5ff.

Jesus: I can relate to what you are describing because the God in my tradition is similar—beyond name, description, or human experience. "From ages past no one has heard, no ear has perceived, no eye has seen any God besides you, who works for those who wait for him" (Isa 64:4). And my apostle Paul put it well when he wrote: "What no eye has seen, nor ear heard, nor the human heart conceived, what God has prepared for those who love him" (1 Cor 2:9).

But Christians have some major differences with Taoists in that our God seems to be more personal and has a relational covenant with humans. I know, however, that at times you do describe the Tao as mother, as does Hebrew tradition. For us, God is divine and is to be worshiped and praised.

Uniquely, in my tradition, God has been incarnated in me, Jesus the Christ. I am both human and divine! Uniquely, I embody the divine in a human and personal existence.

Kuan Yin: I would like to point out that the Tao is not only energy, but also a way of life in unity with the Tao. Taoism is the Way of the Tao and that is the way of perfection, the way of becoming one with the Ultimate or the Tao. Lao Tzu taught that the Tao is beyond description and can be found within us. The perfect person is one whose sins are forgiven—one who is One with the Tao.

Jesus: The Christian life is also a way of perfection. I told my followers to "Be perfect, therefore, as your heavenly Father is perfect" (Matt 5:48). My Gospels teach that ". . .the kingdom of God is within you" (Luke 17:21). Seeking forgiveness is also important for me. My initial invitation to potential followers was "Repent, for the kingdom of God has come near" (Matt 4:17).

Uniquely, I taught that my "way" was the way of love, advancing toward union with the God of Love.

Lao Tzu: I am experiencing a strong connection with you, Jesus. I taught that the way should be one of humility, and not of pride or showiness. I wrote, "He who knows the way does not let it show. Neither does he seek to be rewarded by anyone. Those who know the Way find their reward in themselves."

Jesus: I can resonate with that, Lao Tzu. I taught my disciples to "Take my yoke upon you, and learn from me; for I am gentle and humble in heart, and you will find rest for your souls" (Matt 11:29).

I also chastised those who made a show of their generosity. I said, "So whenever you give alms, do not sound a trumpet before you, as the hypocrites do in the synagogues and in the streets, so that they may be praised by others. Truly I tell you, they have received their reward" (Matt 6:2).

Kuan Yin: We are called to be an "unworldly" people. The main reason that Lao Tzu left China was because of the corruption and violence he experienced there. Like so many religious leaders, he withdrew from this world of sinfulness to a more peaceful place within—the Tao. He said, "The Way of heaven is to retire from the world."[6]

Jesus: Many of my followers made the same decision as Lao Tzu. I understand, but I would like to make a distinction. The word "world," or *kosmos* in Greek, the language of the Gospels, has a number of meanings. It can refer to creation, which is from God and therefore good. It can also mean the everyday life of human beings, which calls us to loving care and compassion. Or, it can refer to the world of sin and violence, which we must avoid.

When I told Pilate, the Roman procurator who presided over my execution, that "my kingdom is not of this world," I meant the latter. My followers must separate themselves from materialism and sinfulness and seek my kingdom, where the presence of a loving God reigns supreme.

For us, this God is personal, calling all people to a sacred covenant. For your people, the Tao seems to bring all things into existence and pervades all, but seems to be somewhat remote.

Moreover, for us, the creative dimension of God, the Word, actually "became flesh and lived among us."[7] That is how the Gospel of John describes me.

Lao Tzu: I can't really relate to the Tao as remote, Jesus. Belief in the Tao is central to this religion. Though the Tao is beyond definition, somewhat like God is, I and many others wrote a great deal about it. The Tao is formless, perfect, and eternal. The Tao is the great Mother. . .who gives birth to infinite worlds. The Tao is present with every person and indeed flows through all things. The way to the Tao is to put your own desires and actions aside, empty your mind of your thoughts and being, and become "open as the sky" to the power of the Tao. It calls for a life of simplicity, patience, and compassion.[8]

6. Hooper, *Tao Te Ching*, 45.

7. John 1:14

8. Novak, *The World's Wisdom*, 146ff.

Kuan Yin: The Tao is the basis of all change in the universe and on Earth. The way to flourish is to accept change, to live in accord with the Tao. This calls for personal transformation so that one is in harmony with the very energy that transforms everything in the world.[9]

It is important to note that this is not a process of fate or destiny, but rather "the unfolding of a course of experience that reflects the total collaboration of those participants in the world as they dispose themselves to one another, and who, through their conduct, influence its outcomes."[10] Yet this participation does not demand individual goal-centered actions, as in the West. Rather, participation in the Tao goes along with the natural processes and is concerned for the common good of all. The Way seems to imply that we can't save ourselves or the world, but we can be in harmony with the processes in nature and allow them to save us.

The word *Te* in Lao's teaching—as in *Tao Te Ching*—refers to the power of potency of the Tao. It is this potency that develops and sustains all things. It is the binding force among all things. *Te* is also the capacity that humans have to help sustain and transform both nature and reality. While Tao is the principle of the universe, *Te* is the virtue needed to follow the Tao, to actively live in connection with the Tao. *Te* is also the "way."

Jesus: So we are using similar words to describe our paths. My people debate a great deal about fate and freedom. Some have seen our God as an all-powerful God who controls all things, sending natural disasters and diseases to test people or punish them. They interpret "being subject to God's will" as accepting everything that God sends with resignation and patience. Some even have thought that God required my passion and death as appeasement for original sin and to gain salvation for all.

I would just say that when I said 'Thy will be done'[11] during the agony in the garden, I did not deem it God's will that I suffer and die, but that I keep on with my mission and teaching even though it meant being executed unjustly by those who hated me. I was crucified by Roman decree, not by divine decree. I see, and I want my followers to see, that God only sends love, courage, and endurance to face the natural or human evils that we endure. God only wills goodness, love, and forgiveness for all people.

Kuan Yin: You are giving me much to ponder. Jesus, I have heard that you have a special place in your heart for children. The same is true for Lao Tzu.

---

9. Girardot and others, Daoism and Ecology, 277.

10. Ibid.

11. See Matt 26:39.

He has written that we must seek to achieve the state of a newborn child, who has a clear and pure vision.

Jesus: You are right, Kuan Yin. How I love to have children come to me so that I can hold them on my lap. They are pure and innocent, newly formed from the hand of God. I clearly stated to my disciples that ". . .unless you change and become like children, you will never enter the kingdom of heaven" (Matt 18:3).

Kuan Yin: Another reference to children in Lao's work is one that I love. He teaches the origin of the world as Mother and states that one can come to know the Mother by holding onto the child. And then he says that with this understanding, you will never die. Embracing creation is actually the Way to know creation's Mother and the Way to live forever. I have promised my followers that the Tao will give them eternal life.

To be one with the Tao is to reach eternity, to reach safe haven, and to be whole. Then death no longer has power over you.

Jesus: My tradition teaches that ". . .God so loved the world that he gave his only Son, so that everyone who believes in him may not perish but may have eternal life " (John 3:16). For my followers, I am the personification of God's love, the Son of God, the One who links the human and the divine in my person. To be one with me is to be one with God.

Lao Tzu: I am sure you will agree that meditation is important to get to the heart of things. I teach my followers to close the door, shut out the senses, and center their hearts on the very essence of things. I invite them to enter into ultimate emptiness, stillness, and inner peace.

Jesus: I encouraged my disciples to "pray always" (Luke 18:1). I urged them to realize that they were always in God's presence. Like you, I taught them that ". . .whenever you pray, go into your room and shut the door and pray to your Father who is in secret; and your Father who sees in secret will reward you" (Matt 6:6).

Within themselves, they will discover their true selves, as they have been created in the image and likeness of God.

I encouraged mindfulness not only in the development of the interior life but in seeing daily opportunities to love me in the people encountered each day.

Kuan Yin: Detachment is very important in our tradition. We teach that such things as fame, power, and pride can be our downfall. We encourage our people to live simply, detached from possessions, and "to leave no footprints." Wealth can never bring peace!

Jesus: I too taught the importance of detachment. I urged my disciples to take nothing with them on their mission and to not store up possessions. I said, "...where your treasure is, there your heart will be also" (Matt 6:21). To put it even more strongly: "It is easier for a camel to go through the eye of a needle than for someone who is rich to enter the kingdom of God" (Mark 10:25). I encouraged my followers to store up treasures in heaven.[12] It does not profit anyone to gain the whole world and yet lose one's soul.[13]

Lao Tzu: We Taoists also believe that we should share what we have with the needy. I taught that "true riches come from giving out of one's abundance to those in need."[14] I have also been content with the gifts provided by Mother Tao. I hold that true wisdom is to live for others. Selflessness is the way to fulfillment. I have frequently proclaimed, "The wise do not seek to be first, but to be last."[15]

Jesus: We have much in common here, Lao Tzu. I too urged my disciples to give to the poor. I asked my followers to sell everything and give their money to the poor, so their riches would be in heaven. I also taught them to be selfless: "So the last will be first, and the first will be last" (Matt 20:16). My parable of the Last Judgment demonstrates that those who follow the works of mercy will be welcomed on the final day.

Kuan Yin: It has been inspiring to me to realize that love is central in all religions. It certainly is important for those who follow the Tao. Lao Tzu taught that nothing but good comes to those who love others as they love themselves. He held that the world is actually transformed by those who love all people. He also taught that we should not turn away those whom we consider to be sinful or unworthy.

Jesus: Love is indeed at the very heart of my teaching—love of God, self, and others as the self. I even taught that we must love enemies and those

12. See Matt 6:20.
13. See Matt 16:26.
14. Hooper, *Tao Te Ching*, 97.
15. Ibid., 107.

who revile us. In our Scriptures, we even go so far as to say that you must love in order to know God and that God is actually identified with love: "Whoever does not love does not know God, for God is love" (1 John 4:8). In the beginning, Christians were actually recognized as people who deeply loved one another and shared all they possessed.

Lao Tzu: We might now compare our beliefs on the afterlife. I have taught that to be One with the Tao is to live forever. Even though our body dissolves, the person who is One with the Tao is safe. We do not fear death, nor do we resist death when it comes. Only those who are attached to life fear death.

Jesus: My Resurrection from the dead is the basis for my followers' belief that they too will be given eternal life. I have promised it to them, and that belief is strong enough to help them overcome their fear of death. We believe that resurrection means being embraced by God in a new life and being joined with the communion of saints, including loved ones.

Kuan Yin: I would like to share more with you, Jesus, regarding the development of our movement.

The very early tradition was given great impetus by a legendary Yellow Emperor around 2500 BCE. Under his guidance, the laws of nature were connected with the power of the universe. The people came to believe that a harmony existed within the entire process. A hierarchy was then developed wherein the emperor became the mediator between the spirit and material worlds. The notion of *Tao* (path) emerged, which came to have many meanings, including the path to a proper way of living and also the path to immortality.

As the tradition spread, its writings began to grow. The writings of Chuang Tzu in the fourth century BCE and those of many other sages were added to the canon of Taoist writings.

For many centuries, Taoism existed as more of a philosophy (and still does), which taught individuals the personal development of freedom. Celestial Master Zhang Daoling formed the first Taoist organizations early in the second century during the famous Han dynasty. The original sources for this religion go back thousands of years before that with the worship of deities and ancestors, and with questions about immortality and Chinese folk customs. Many of these traditions seem to have been developed by shamans, who were in touch with the ways of nature and could communicate with the spirit.[16]

Eventually, Daoling became learned in both Taoism and Confucianism. Legends tell of him becoming a magician who could disappear or be in two places at once. There is an account of him meeting Lao Tzu, who by now had been deified; Lao Tzu taught him how to prepare a medicine to make himself immortal. Daoling freed some of his followers of evil spirits, taught them repentance for their wrongdoings, and led them to serve the public with shelters and food kitchens.

Lao Tzu: Eventually, many schools of Taoism and sects were formed. Gradually, these sects merged into two, Zhengyi and Quanzhen.

There is little difference between the two sects, only variations in their norms and regulations. The Zhengyi sect imposes few regulations, while the Quanzhen sect requires more. Quanzhen followers must live in temples too. In the past, these temples were in mountains and forests, but today they are more likely to be found in urban areas. Many followers do not identify themselves as Taoists, but rather see themselves as following a way of life, the way of the Tao.

Jesus: You both are probably familiar with the development of Christianity. It began with my Jewish reform movement and then developed into the Christian religions. It has experienced many more divisions than your religion: East and West, Protestant and Catholic, Orthodox and Uniate, and many Rites and Churches. My prayer that my followers may all be one is so far unrealized.

Maybe we could now discuss your sacred writings.

Lao Tzu: The *I Ching*, or the *Book of Changes*, is the earliest of the Taoist scriptures. This book was written sometime around 300–200 BCE. The text speaks of the ever-changing nature of the world and how to contribute to move things in the right direction. It advises how to adjust to change, take advantage of opportune times, and be adaptable (go with the flow). Here also the process of yin and yang is explained. This book was honored by Confucians and was incorporated into the Confucian scriptures.

Kuan Yin: The *Tao Te Ching* (way-*Tao*; power-*te*; *ching*-classic or the classic way of power) is the masterpiece of Taoism. Many think that Lao Tzu himself authored it. Huston Smith, the renowned scholar of world religions,

16. Palmer, *The Elements of Taoism*, 14–15.

calls this work "a testament to humanity's at-home-ness in the universe. It can be read in half an hour or a life-time, and remains to this day the basic text of Taoist thought."[17]

This book attempts to reflect on the operating principle of the cosmos and teaches how to get in touch with that power. It shows people the way of virtue and gives direction to people's lives. We might say this book is about "let go and let Tao."

As was mentioned earlier, late in life Lao Tzu became disgusted with heads of state imposing their rule on others with absolute laws and requirements. He proposed that leaders, and indeed everyone, put themselves in touch with the mysterious forces of nature and identify with the creative and nurturing powers within the cosmos. He taught "going with the flow" as it were, being adaptive, putting oneself and one's actions in the background, and humbly becoming part of the grand, creative cosmic process. He points out that the Tao cannot be named or described: "The Tao that can be told is not the eternal Tao."[18] The Tao is deep and endless, like a well filled with infinite possibilities.

Lao Tzu: During the centuries after my death, there was a period of immense creativity and vigorous theological debate in Taoism. In the fourth century, a sage named Chuang Tzu wrote down his wise thoughts, which are sometimes irreverent and filled with paradoxes. For instance, he reflects on time: "If there was a beginning, then there was a time before that beginning. And a time before the time which was before the time of that beginning. If there is existence, there must have been non-existence. And if there was a time when nothing existed, then there must have been a time before that— when even nothing did not exist."[19]

Chuang demonstrates the absurdity of those who wear out their intellects on the individuality of things, not recognizing that all things are one. He calls this stupidity "three in the morning." When asked what that means he tells a story about monkeys. The keeper was giving the monkeys three chestnuts in the morning and four at night. They were angry and complained, so the keeper gave the monkeys four chestnuts in the morning and three at night. They were all pleased! Chuang thinks that humans can be as ridiculous as these monkeys.

Chuang Tzu scoffs at how absolute we get about things like standards of beauty and virtue. For him, all things are relative; it is impossible to know

17. Smith, *The World Religions*, 197.
18. Hendricks, *Tao Te Ching*, chap. 1:1.
19. Novak, *The World's Wisdom*, 165.

the standards of beauty, virtue, or anything else for that matter. Chuang Tzu reflects on facing such relativity. The wise sage calls for equilibrium and repose so that the mind becomes like a still body of water that mirrors clearly and accurately. The Tao of the universe can be reflected in the person that is reposed, tranquil and still.

Jesus: You are reminding me of some of our great mystics like Julian of Norwich and Hildegard of Bingen.

Lao Tzu: The *Hua Hu Ching* is another key Taoism resource. It is often attributed to me, but it is a later poet's reflection of my teaching. The author points out that the Tao cannot be fixed in one's mind. He compares this to pinning a butterfly: "The husk is captured but the flying is lost."[20] He says that if one is willing to live by the Tao, one will see it everywhere, even in ordinary things. The author offers direct advice: "If you want to liberate yourself and help save the world, work on your own self-awareness. If you want to awaken all humanity, then awaken all yourself."[21] He calls for self-transformation, finding a good teacher, living a holistic life, and being in harmony with yourself and others. Ching warns about too much austerity and cautions that external dogmas can make one ill.

Jesus: Now I am reminded of the teachings of the Buddha about not clinging and waking up! It is remarkable how much we are discovering in common.

Kuan Yin: By 471 CE the first Taoist canon was compiled and listed more than twelve hundred scrolls. The main themes found in this canon included how to organize a parochial structure; the process of cosmic salvation, which opened salvation to the poor and workers; and the importance of meditation and immortality. In 748 CE another canon was organized with thousands of scrolls. Many more scrolls were added in the following centuries.

Jesus: It is refreshing to hear you speak of "the flow," of ongoing change, and the development of your scriptures. You could teach some of my people about change. So many of them cling to the past and resist change. It is as though their structures and doctrines are frozen in time. Our beliefs and rules are not keeping up with all the major shifts in the world and in society. My people often cling to absolutes, when relativity is basic to all reality. Many of my Catholic leaders consider themselves to be "gradualists,"

20. Ibid., 170ff.
21. Ibid., 75.

meaning that they want centuries to pass before any changes can be made in Catholic teaching or practice. People need change, and so change must occur in religious tradition! And now I am reminded of the Buddha's teaching about impermanency!

Kuan Yin: Taoism does not have a system of elaborate doctrines, but there are other beliefs to complement the Tao. We believe that the Tao produces vital energy, which emanates in the form of Three Purities, or Pure Ones, and many deities and immortals who teach, redeem, and serve as models for humans to achieve Tao. The yin and yang are the two extremes of the dynamic process and, ultimately, can come to balance and harmony.

The three highest deities, the Three Purities, emanate from the Tao and are omnipresent. They are also called the three Celestial Worthies: of Primordial Beginning, of Numinous Treasure, and of the Way and its Virtue. Next in importance is the Jade Emperor, the deity who rules the universe. He is assisted by the four heavenly emperors, who include the Emperor of Longevity of the South Polar Star and Houtu the Earth goddess. The highest goddess is the Queen Mother of the West. There are also Divine Officials—one of heaven who bestows blessings, one of Earth who pardons sins, and one of water who protects against disasters. Popular deities are the god of wealth and the god of war. Certain mountains, rivers, and land areas also have their own deities.[22]

Jesus: Our teaching is somewhat different. We speak of multiple persons in the one God—Father, Son, and Spirit. We note the existence of higher spirits, which we refer to as angels, and we personify the forces of evil as Satan or the Devil. We also canonize certain holy individuals whom we refer to as saints. And, of course, Christians believe that many of the deceased are given eternal life and live in the communion of saints.

Lao Tzu: Most today are familiar with the terms yin/yang as meaning opposite forces. In the Tao tradition, yin and yang are two opposite but complementary forces at work in the universe. The yin is the yielding force—the winter out of which spring comes, the darkness from which light emerges. Yin is the receptive valley into which pours the torrents from the mountains. Yin is the mother aspect of the cosmos. The yang is the active and aggressive principle—the darkness that overshadows the light, the mighty waterfall from above, the father principle. These forces are complementary

---

22. The Taoist Assoc. of China, *Taoism*, 14ff.

and mutually dependent. From their dynamic interplay, new forms emerge: polarity becomes unity and struggle turns into harmony.[23]

Jesus: How exciting it would be to explore these notions as a way to value and welcome change. You are offering me encouragement, Lao Tzu.

Kuan Yin: Lao Tzu listened to the great concert in the universe and wrote: "High and low depend on each other; Sound and silence harmonize with each other; Before and after follow one another."[24] He taught us to be in tune to the process—to be in harmony with the movement inside of all and outside of all.

The early Tao traditions spoke of correspondence among the cosmic energies: the heaven, the Earth, and humans. These energies are identified as the Ultimate Yang (embodied in heaven), the Ultimate Yin (embodied in the Earth), and the Harmonious Neuter (embodied in humans). It is the interaction between the yang and the yin that produces the human. It is clear, then, that if humans are a product of the heavens and Earth, they find their perfection in achieving a balance and harmony with the very sources of their being. Finding balance with the energies of heaven and the Earth thus becomes the "way" to human immortality.

The yin and yang are related to the Five Elements in the natural world: wood, fire, earth, metal, and water. In Chinese cosmology these five elements relate to each other in a yin and yang fashion: earth to wood, water to fire, fire to metal, etc. This magic number of five relates to celestial bodies and is even linked to human internal organs. All of the elements are engaged in the struggle between yin and yang.

Jesus: We struggle so much with this challenge of balance, Kuan Yin. "Being in tune with the process," I think I shall invite you to the next meeting of our church hierarchy in Rome.

Lao Tzu: For Taoism, perfection in nature comes from a balance between yin and yang, the opposites of hot/cold, darkness/light, black/white, and male/female. These opposites struggle with each other, and out of the struggle new things are brought into existence. One opposite gives way to the other. New darkness or new light is born; new winters or new summers are born; new humans, male or female, are born.

23. Fowler, *Chinese Religions*, 5off.
24. Legge, *Te-Tao Ching*, chap. 2:5.

It is the Tao that connects and generates all things and brings balance to the yin and the yang. One scholar puts it this way: "Because of the Tao, all things are linked. Thus we have within ourselves the microcosm of the universe. Thus is the interrelatedness of all living things taken to its ultimate conclusion, that we are all within each other. The fundamental unity of all in and through the Tao is what lies at the center of Taoism."[25]

For followers of Taoism, the Tao is both the reality that energizes the cosmos, as well as the way one must live to be in harmony with this reality.

Jesus: I am wrestling with my own polarity as I experience inspiration and new insight, yet find that some of your explanation appears elaborate and difficult to understand. My tradition believes that all things are interconnected in that everything shares in some form of life. It is life that energizes all things on Earth. Modern science tells us that things are connected by cosmological laws, and that the universe is expanding.

As a rural person, I always felt a deep connection with nature. I used natural symbols of birds, sheep, vines, floods, flowers, and crops in my parables. My notion of the kingdom of God certainly includes all of creation. Many of my followers have been able to perceive the divine within nature. St. Francis of Assisi is an outstanding example of this awareness.

Christian Scriptures speak of opposites: light and darkness, good and evil, blessed and cursed. We believe that God is the source of Oneness and draws all things to the divine. Two Jesuits come to mind. The first was a scientist-visionary, Pierre Teilhard de Chardin, who perceived evolution itself as a movement toward an ultimate convergence. The other, a poet, Gerard Hopkins, wrote about creation gathering to a greatness: "The world is charged with the grandeur of God. It will flame out, like shining from shook foil; It gathers to a greatness, like the ooze of oil crushed. . . ."[26]

Christians observe both a harmony as well as a disharmony in creation. Our Scriptures speak of a beginning and an end, but our scientists question such notions. We also wrestle with the question of 'why bad things happen to good people.' We have not been able to resolve that question.

Kuan Yin: The way of the Tao is a way of life that consists of virtue, "no action," good health, and long life, which includes immortality and life with the ancestors.

Please allow me, Lord Jesus, to speak to the topic of a virtuous life. Taoism insists that humans are not subject to fate, but are in charge of their

25. Palmer, *The Elements of Taoism*, 6–7.
26. Hopkins, "God's Grandeur."

own destiny by living a life of virtue. *Te*, or virtue, is the ideal toward which people should strive; it is the effort one must make to follow the Tao and to let it have power in one's life. *Te* is the conduct of the one who follows Tao. Lao Tzu taught that while curses and blessings come to us, it is we who invite them into our lives. He points out that "the right way leads forward; the wrong way backwards."[27] He directs his followers to avoid the path of evil and forbids them from sinning in secret because "heaven and earth are possessors of crime-recording spirits." He urges them to accumulate virtue and increase merit.

Jesus: Being in charge of one's own destiny, our responsibility for blessings and curses, "crime-recording spirits," the accumulation of merit—these have all been thorny questions for Christians.

We believe that we have been given free will. That is one of the ways that we are made in the image and likeness of God. We can choose good or evil, light or darkness. And yet the power to do good ultimately comes from God's grace.

People can bring good or bad upon themselves, but only good and blessings come from our God. People can choose evil; they can choose to reject God and annihilate their spirits. "Hell" is a choice, rather than a punishment from God.

On the other hand, no one can earn salvation or merit eternal life through his or her good deeds. Christianity has had enormous clashes over this issue. Good deeds or virtuous living as empowered by the grace of God is the way to eternal life.

As for "crime-recording spirits," I did teach that "nothing is hidden that will not be disclosed, nor is anything secret that will not become known and come to light " (Luke 8:17).

Kuan Yin: Lao Tzu recognizes the significance of the yin and yang in virtuous living and morality. He points out: "Mercifulness is recognized by people because they know the opposite, which is meanness. The people only know about good because there is also evil."[28] The virtuous person strives to keep balance in life and thus avoid extremes. One extreme attracts another. One who is not humble attracts disrespect. One who is domineering and repressive attracts defiance and rebellion. Pride comes before the fall. Coldness towards another stimulates anger. Virtue, then, stands in the middle. It is the way of harmony and balance. The virtuous person lets the natural

27. Ibid.
28. Legge, *Te-Tao Ching*, chap. 2:2.

process flow and does not impose his or her will on others. The Taoist ideal is to be humble, tranquil, simple, noncombative, merciful, and frugal. While Tao gives birth, *Te*—or virtue—nurtures life.

Lao Tzu: The notion of "no action" in Taoism is often misunderstood. No action (*wu wei*) does not refer to being passive or inert. No action implies knowing when to refrain from taking action, knowing when to intervene, and when to step back. (Taoism seems to be addressed to the problem solvers of the world.) The Taoist attempts to be in touch with larger forces and allows those forces to prevail. No action is not non-action, but rather *unselfish action*, action that is altruistic. It is no action against the natural flow of things. Lao Tzu put it this way: "I take no action and people are reformed. I enjoy peace and the people become honest. I do nothing and people become rich. I have no desires and the people return to the good and simple life."[29] In part, it seems to be affecting people more by example than by intervening in their lives.

Jesus: How interesting, Lao Tzu. It appears that by not imposing judgment you are offering the freedom to make choices that might require more thought or consideration. My tradition also opposes passivity. Ignatius of Loyola, one of our great teachers, said: "Pray as if everything depends on God, and work as though everything depends on you." The Gospel life is the life of love and service, not withdrawal from the world or a passive submission to the will of God. I told my disciples: "By this everyone will know that you are my disciples, if you have love for one another" (John 13:35). Our Scriptures also exhort: ". . . let us love, not in word or speech, but in truth and action " (1 John 3:18).

Kuan Yin: Please allow me to speak of good health as an important value for those that follow the Tao. We see the body as integral to the spirit. Care for the body in this life is related to life after death. You will notice the Chinese people give priority to good nourishment, regular exercise, attention to health care, and proper rest. Care for the body is necessary for the immortality of the soul. T'ai chi, for example, a meditative exercise that ensures the proper flow of the vital energy force through the body and helps maintain proper balance, is very popular in China, as well as in other countries.

Lao Tzu: Taoists have not been definitive on immortality, but have left it as a mystery. Nevertheless, immortality seems to be an important goal for

29. Ibid.

Taoists, although they interpreted the understanding in various ways. Some have thought that they might escape death altogether by taking some secret elixir, eating special herbs, doing certain exercises, or using a charm. Others were influenced by Buddhism and spoke of karma and rebirth. Some believed that they could peacefully traverse death, while others have held that they would have to face many hells and judgments before they could be forgiven their misdeeds. Here are my words on the matter: "If you hold to the precepts, you will serve as a heavenly official, ascending to immortality. . . ."[30]

Taoists strive to cultivate both body and soul, eliminate selfish ideas, and do good to accumulate merit. Virtue (*Te*) is to be cultivated until the person lives a highly moral life and achieves the purity and goodness that was manifest at birth.

Some traditions speak of two souls: one that lives on with the body and another that is buried. The quest for immortality thus involves meditation; worship at family and public shrines; personal transformation; and also regular, physical exercise.[31]

Jesus: I can see that this conversation has been a vigorous exercise. Since no one has come back to tell us about the afterlife, we need to continue this discussion.

Kuan Yin: Thank you, Jesus. I have a few other distinctions to clarify with you. Taoists have priests who are to be especially dedicated to self-cultivation through discipline and meditation. They are also available to lead prayer rituals on the birthdays of the deities and for festivals.

Priests in the Quanzhen sect have stricter regulations and are required to live in monasteries, remain celibate, and abstain from meat. Priests of the Zhengyi sect can live at home if they wish, can marry, and are allowed to eat meat.

Both sects have an extensive initiation preparation with intense education and elaborate rituals. The initiation ceremony itself is held before the abbot and the eight masters of the monastery. Their ordinary garb consists of dark-blue robes and hats. There are also Taoist nuns who live strict monastic lives and who can lead certain types of ceremonies, such as repentance rituals. They wear orange robes and black hats.

30. Ibid.
31. Ibid.

Lao Tzu: Magnificent Taoist temples are beginning to appear in China, most of which had to be restored after being destroyed by the Communists. As you know, a degree of religious freedom has been restored in China.

Some temples are built on the top of high mountains, such as the Temple of the God of Mount Tai. Others are actually carved into the sides of mountains, like the Nanyan Temple on Mount Wudang or the temple at Mount Kongdong. One of the exotic monasteries is on the top of White Cloud Mountain overlooking a magnificent canyon and winding river below.

Villages and cities celebrate Kuan Yin *jiao* ceremonies regularly. They are preceded by a one-month purification period of fasting, cleansing from sin, and meditation. The priest gathers the people in the local temple and leads them to summon the gods and the ancestors.

Secret ceremonies are held behind locked doors to show intimacy with the gods, and then public rites are held where texts are read, offerings are made for sins, and prayers of forgiveness and healing are invoked. Taoist myths are reenacted, followed by a large banquet to celebrate the blessings of the cosmos.

The Chinese New Year is the most important holiday in the Chinese calendar. It is celebrated during the first month of the lunar calendar. Preparation begins in the homes with cleaning, settling debts, and the preparation of special foods. Incense is burned to pray to the god of wealth, and firecrackers are set off to signal his coming. Festivities continue for two weeks, during which time the gods are given offerings. During this period, the Jade Emperor's birthday is celebrated. He is believed to visit each year to investigate behavior and decide on rewards and punishment. Many offerings of food, candles, and large pieces of paper money are given to him to implore his blessing and protection. More incense and firecrackers are lit to welcome and honor him. The New Year holiday ends with the Lantern Festival, which honors the birthday of the Emperor of the Heavenly Realm. Colorful lanterns are displayed, and prayers are said for blessings and a bright future.

We also celebrate the Feast of the Clear and Bright during the spring, when families renew ties with the dead and strengthen family relationships. A summer feast is the Double Fifth Festival. During the Hungry Ghost Festival, priests symbolically throw open the gates of hell, and ghosts are invited to wander free. They are placated with food, music, and theater and are asked to repent. The Mid-Autumn Festival celebrates the harvest.

After a death, a priest is hired to light the way for the deceased, say prayers, and offer sacrifices to plead for forgiveness for the deceased and to help the person navigate the way through the Land of Darkness.

Jesus: We do not have a similar ceremony in our tradition, except perhaps during the forty days of Lent prior to Easter when we practice fasting, work at conversion of heart and mind and resolve to forgive and change lives for the better.

Lao Tzu: Under Mao Zedong's regime, Taoism was crushed and considered to be a superstition. Its temples were torn down, and its priests and nuns were dismissed. Only since the recent reforms has Taoism begun to rebuild in China. Its followers are again growing in number.

Taoists' main contributions to today's world are in the areas of health. Taoists have always been expert in herbal remedies. Many of their mixtures have become popular among those interested in alternative medicines. Their practice of t'ai-chi has also become popular in many areas of the world, including the United States. It is an excellent exercise, which works on many parts of the body. Its gentle motions are said to work on the central nervous system, to lower blood pressure, to relieve tension, and to stretch the various muscle systems. The movements are designed to balance the body's internal energies, or chi.

Acupuncture is another Taoist contribution to better health. It is an ancient practice that attempts to locate the energy paths in the body and bring them into alignment. When these paths are blocked, physical or mental pain can result. In order to restore balance to the energy centers, needles are inserted at various points (meridians) of the body. Any number of physical or emotional problems can be remedied through the proper use of acupuncture. Today, acupuncture is an accepted practice in modern medicine.

Jesus: Many Christians throughout the world are trying to become more involved in contemporary issues, such as poverty, the plight of refugees, hunger, ecology, peace, and women's rights. Are Taoists also more active today in world issues?

Lao Tzu: The "Three Jewels" of Taoism are compassion, moderation, and humility.[32] This ancient tradition, which was nearly destroyed by Communism, presents an alternative to the modern world with its excesses, anxieties, and tensions. The gentle Taoist call for moderation and balance has much to offer many who suffer the harsh realities of joblessness, homelessness, poverty, violence, and starvation. It is an invitation to be part of, not better than; it is a call to share, not store up.

32. Ibid.

Taoism presents a fresh and dynamic approach to the environmental movement during a time when the Chinese government has done so much to destroy the land, rivers, and quality of air.

Taoism has a perspective that can easily be applied to ecology. According to Taoism, all things in the universe come into being through the transformation of the breath of the Tao. Humans, who are the most spiritual and intelligent of the creatures must be in tune with the Tao and not attempt to shape nature to conform to human desires. They are required to be enlightened about the workings of the Tao and in tune with them. Otherwise, humans distort reality according to their own selfish wishes.

Taoism challenges everything to grow and flourish in its own way. Taoism teaches simplicity, detachment from wealth, and resistance to the insatiable desires that lead to the overexploitation of the Earth and its resources. For the Taoist, true affluence lies in the flourishing of many species, nurtured and cared for; Taoists encourage individuals and governments to cherish and conserve nature.

Kuan Yin: Fu Xiancai is a good example of one who follows the way of the Tao to save the Earth. Fu is a Chinese farmer and civil rights activist. Fu grew up near the Yangtze River. He became politically active in 1994, when his village was threatened by the construction of the Three Gorges Dam. He protested the construction of the dam. In 1997 he was forced to leave his home after it was flooded by water from the reservoir. He campaigned for better compensation for those who had been displaced by the dam. He was warned by local government officials to desist. Following the warning, two separate beating incidents left him with a broken leg and a wound to his head. In 2006 Fu was interviewed about the dam on German television. After further threats, Fu was again assaulted and is now partially paralyzed from his injuries. The German government has protested his treatment and provided for his surgery.

Lao Tzu: Followers of the Tao are usually people of peace. As mentioned earlier, I wrote my first manifesto during a time of corruption and violence in China.[33] My teachings condemned offensive war and the use of arms by the state. I wrote: "Even the best weapon is hateful to living things. So the follower of the Way stays away from it. . . . To enjoy using weapons is to enjoy killing people, and to enjoy killing people is to lose your share in the common good."[34] I urged: "Achieve results but not through violence, for

33. Ibid.
34. Ibid.

it is against the natural way, and damages both others and one's own true self."[35] I taught that all conflict should be met with compassion. The way of the Tao was to follow the way of inner peace, harmoniously in tune with nature, not the way of negative judgments and harmful actions against others. Even though wars prevailed during so many of the dynasties of China, the common folk among the Chinese often followed the way of the Tao and its mission of peacemaking.

Jesus: This is an area of common concern. We seem unable in our world to promote nonviolent response to conflict, to mediate rather than litigate, to take turns talking rather than raising our fists. How have weapons so taken over our lives?

Kuan Yin: Lao Tzu taught that the wise person should not try to rival others by possessing many things. Such rivalry leads to jealousy of the possessions of others and to stealing and harming others. The way of the Tao is to be humble, satisfied with what one has, minimal in one's desires, thoughtful, sincere, and just. Peace ultimately comes from an inner energy within the person who retains the harmony of his inner world, and so remains at peace within himself.

As we have said, the Tao is the source of all things and is within the creative process of life. The Tao is the root of heaven and earth, beyond all yet within all, giving birth to all, containing all, nurturing all. To follow the way of the Tao is to be in harmony with this magnificent process of energy and life. Violence, killing, and war are destructive forces and obviously not compatible with the true way of Tao. *Wu wei*, or "not doing," a central teaching of Taoism, avoids force, manipulation, and indeed any action that interferes with the process of life and creativity.

Jesus: I would like to sit down at the peace table with you and challenge all of the world's leaders to listen, to withhold judgment, to choose life, and nonviolent resolution.

Lao Tzu: Professor Ding Zilin is a role model for Taoist peacemakers in China. A former professor of philosophy at the People's University in Beijing, Ding's seventeen-year-old son, Jiang Jielian, was killed when the People's Liberation Army crushed the Tiananmen Square protests against the oppressive Chinese government in 1989. Her son was shot in the back and was left to bleed to death.

35. Ibid., 30–32.

Following her son's death, Ding became so depressed that she attempted suicide six times. In August 1989 she met another bereaved mother; later, she formed a network of some 150 other families who had lost sons and daughters during the Tiananmen massacre. This group became known as Tiananmen Mothers. She has been collecting the names of those who were killed by the People's Liberation Army in Beijing, and she has been persistent in asking the government to apologize for the deaths.

Ding was forced into early retirement from her university. She and some of her associates have faced imprisonment, house arrest, phone tapping, and constant surveillance.

Despite her multiple arrests and constant surveillance, civil disobedience has been Ding Zilin's persistent choice. She never stops using her voice to speak out in nonviolent ways against the violations of human rights committed by the Chinese government. In 2006, *Time* magazine selected her story, as one of many, to profile in its "60 Years of Asian Heroes" issue.

Jesus: Yes, Lao Tzu, she is a true heroine. She is using nonviolent methods to effect change and to honor her son's memory. We must become more diligent to work together for causes such as this one. Is the fact that she is a woman a detriment to her cause?

Kuan Yin: As with most religions, there are ambiguities toward women in Taoism. In the early sources, the female is honored as the source of life. At the same time, the female is identified with Earth, while the male is linked with heaven, which is higher and identified with the Tao. This identification is made in spite of the fact that Lao Tzu says that heaven and Earth both pass through the doorway of the female. The Tao is spoken of as a mother, and there are many female goddesses in the tradition.[36]

An ancient folk Taoist source calls for equality and maintains that "men and women in harmony reflect the Tao."[37] Traditionally, both women and men are believed to be able to become immortal. The temple at Mount Hua displays an inscription: "All humanity is equal." By way of contrast, author Chuang Tzu, whom we mentioned earlier, wrote: "Men are ranked higher than women, therefore it is noble to be a man."[38]

Today, the number of Taoist women monastics is increasing, and in the large cities they have better access to good education. Taoist nuns in Taiwan and Hong Kong are very supportive of their counterparts in mainland

36. Ibid., 164ff.

37. Metz and Tobin, *The Tao of Women*, 67.

38. Girardot, *Daoism and Ecology*, 36.

China. The modern nuns are not only concerned about personal development but also have achieved leadership in providing service to the larger community.

Many Chinese women who follow the way of the Tao shy away from "feminism" because they view it as a social movement rather than a movement focusing on personal transformation. It is their position that if women place themselves in harmony with the ultimate energy that the Tao represents, they will find their proper role in the world. For them, this is the way of nature and will ultimately prevail.

Remember, we mentioned that yin and yang are the two opposite energies in Taoist thought. The yin, the feminine, is receptive and yields. The other, the yang, the masculine, is active and hard. To keep all things in balance, the two must interact properly and in harmony. Therefore, the energies of both women and men must complement each other and cooperate in accord with each other.

Jesus: I am learning so much from this concept and realizing how my Christian churches need to acknowledge this complementarity to generate more positive energy. Our women do most of the day-to-day labor but they do not get recognition for leadership and charisms that are called for by this generation.

Lao Tzu: Zhang Jie is a good example of a contemporary follower of Taoism who promotes women's rights in China. She does this through her writing of novels and short stories. Zhang is one of China's first writers to produce feminist fiction.

In her writing, Zhang reflects on the radical changes brought about by modernization in China, especially how life has changed for women in her country. Zhang's 1981 novel, *The Ark*, describes the difficult struggle for survival of three professional women who have been cut off from their husbands. It was considered China's first feminist novel. Zhang claims that a modern woman in China has to have money and time to be productive.

Jesus: This has indeed been a wonderful dialogue, Kuan Yin and Lao Tzu. It is clear that both of our ancient religions have touched countless people's lives. My prayer is "that they may all be one" (John 17:21). I know that you both are also advocates of Oneness with the energy and power that permeate and sustain the universe.

SUGGESTED READINGS FOR TAOISM

Fowler, Jeaneane and Merv. *Chinese Religions*. Portland: Sussex Academic Press, 2008.

Girardot, N.J. and others, eds. *Daoism and Ecology*. Cambridge, MA: Harvard University Press, 2001.

Hendricks, Robert G. *Te-Tao Ching*. New York: Ballantine, 1989.

Kirkland, Russell. *Taoism*. New York: Routledge, 2004.

Palmer, Martin. *The Elements of Taoism*. New York: Barnes and Noble, 1991.

Metz, Pamela K. and Jacqueline L. Tobin. *The Tao of Women*. Atlanta: Humanics Trade, 1995.

Chapter 8

Confucianism

～ Jesus with Confucius and Madame Ban Zhao

Tzu-kung asked: "Is there a single word which can be a guide to conduct throughout one's life?" The Master said: "It is perhaps the word *shu* (reciprocity). That which you do not desire, do not do to others."

—ANALECTS 15.24

Do to others as you would have them do to you.

—LUKE 6:31

Confucius: Welcome, Lord Jesus and Madame Ban Zhao, to this beautiful spot on the banks of the Yangtze River. Of course, I know of you, Jesus, from many of my followers who crossed paths with your disciples in China. As you probably know, my movement started about five hundred years before Christianity and has been foundational in the Far Eastern countries.

Ban Zhao: Good morning. I am Ban Zhao, a devoted follower of Confucius. I was born just fifteen years after your death, Jesus. By 45 CE I was a prominent Confucian during the Han dynasty in China. I served as the court historian for Emperor Han Hedi and was an advisor to Empress Deng.

Confucius said very little in his writings about women, so I decided to fill in that gap by writing *Lessons for Women,* an instructional manual on proper feminine behavior. It has been a very popular resource for women throughout the Orient.

Jesus: As you know, I was a Jewish reformer, but ultimately my movement separated from Judaism and became a religion on its own, called Christianity. My religion is more than two thousand years old and has become the largest religion in the world. I am eager to hear more about your backgrounds as well as your teachings.

Confucius: I was born in 551 BCE in Lu, a small feudal state in China. I am a contemporary of the Buddha. My parents seemed to have been, at one time, members of the aristocracy, but at the time of my birth they were poor commoners. My father died when I was only three years old, so I was raised by my mother and a number of teachers.

My home life gave me a love of learning, especially of past teachings. Early on I worked at several jobs: minor local government posts, stable manager, and bookkeeper at a granary. At age nineteen, I married. My wife and I had a son.

Always dedicated to study, I mastered the Six Arts: ritual (proper behavior and manners), music, archery, charioteering, calligraphy, and arithmetic. I also became accomplished in the classics, poetry, and art.

By the time I was thirty, I opened my own school, the first of its kind, where all were invited to learn. My philosophy of education was that it should be open to everyone, not just the rich, and that it should be focused on character building rather than on the mere transmission of knowledge. The aim was to show people how to transform themselves so that they were prepared to serve others as refined people. My goal was to form learning communities composed of people who could help reshape their social and political worlds.

I did not try to start a religion. Rather than be concerned about an afterlife, I concentrated on this life, this human life. My aim was " to sacralize the human community" by forming learning groups that would be guided by the "mandate of Heaven" and that would be determined to change their world.[1] My tradition is a combination of ethics, cosmic outlook, and historical perspective. I provide a way of life, a way of being a good person. My teachings are really not so much religious as they are spiritual. Some say that

---

1. Sharma, *Our Religions,* 51.

my teachings are actually deeper than religion. Often, East Asians belong to different religions, but they all share a Confucian mindset.[2]

Ban Zhao: I can vouch for that. At many times in Chinese history, when there was religious division, our people would turn to Confucianism for unity. That was certainly the case during my time with the Han dynasty. In modern times, Mao Zedong, who tried to eliminate all religion, including Confucianism in Communist China, asked his people to follow the Confucian principle of "self-cultivation" (albeit in the Communist way) in order to strengthen their characters.[3]

Confucius: Your point demonstrates my position that to spread a doctrine one must get to the political leaders.

Early on I became convinced that if my educational message was to be heard, I would have to influence my own leaders. I was able to secure a position as magistrate and then Minister of Justice in Lu. I began to have some influence with the king. Unfortunately, my success became my downfall. Those surrounding the king grew to resent my influence, and I chose to leave office under the pressure.

I returned to teaching. For thirteen years I gathered students to teach them my principles. I especially sought out leaders in the court whom I could influence. However, my message of discipline, study, self-transformation, and loving service did not go well with the nobility, who were focused on gathering wealth and satisfying all their desires.

Eventually, I decided to return home to continue teaching, writing, and gathering classical texts. I passed on at age seventy-three, leaving behind a legacy of many refined and learned students who were concerned about making a difference in their world. I had no idea that I would be recognized as one of the great teachers of all time. Nor did I know that my teaching would shape the Asian culture for the next 2,500 years.

Jesus: I honor good educators. During my time, Hillel and Shammai were outstanding Jewish teachers. As for me, I was more of a preacher and healer. I had very little schooling. I could not afford to attend the fine scribal schools in Jerusalem. I could read the Hebrew Scripture, but could not write. Yet, many look at me as one of history's most influential teachers. Eventually, many other great Christian educators appeared in my movement—giants

2. Ibid., 149.
3. Chai, *Confucianism*, 71.

like Augustine, Thomas Aquinas, Bonaventure, Karl Rahner, and Edward Schillebeeckx.

Who were some of the great teachers who spread your message?

Confucius: Well, one of the most significant was Mencius (372–289 BCE). He had a very upbeat view of human nature and taught my followers how to live virtuous lives. My teachings had convinced Mencius that "the way of heaven" was the ultimate source of goodness and the standard for human behavior.

Another famous teacher, Xunzi (c. 310–220 BCE) took the opposite position of Mencius and held that human nature was inherently evil. He taught that human nature could be improved by teaching morals and rules, but he maintained that hierarchical structures, imposed laws of order, and control were necessary to help people to live good lives.

Jesus: We've had the same debates about whether human nature is good or bad. One of our greatest teachers, Augustine (354–430 CE), taught that humans had fallen natures as a result of the "original sin" of the first human, Adam. He led the way to condemn a teacher by the name of Pelagius, who had a much more positive view of nature. Augustine maintained that because of our fallen nature, we can only be saved by divine grace. Had Pelagius won the debate, people today would have a much more positive view of humans, as well as sexuality.

One of Augustine's followers, Martin Luther, an initiator of the Protestant Reformation, shared Augustine's negative view of nature and referred to humans as "masses of damnation." This was a far cry from my view that humans are beloved children of God. Luther taught that the only way people can be saved is through faith.

Luther and other Protestant deniers of human dignity, such as John Calvin and Zwingli, moved the Catholic Church to a more positive view of human nature, seeing it as "wounded," but not "fallen."

As for being legalistic and controlling, Catholicism has, throughout most of its history, seemed to agree with Xunzi that hierarchical structures, imposed laws, and firm doctrine are needed to keep the people in line. My hope is that the new pope, Francis, will focus more on Gospel values and stress compassion and mercy rather than judgment and punishment toward "the people of God." A certain amount of laws and rules might be necessary, but as Fr. Bernard Haring, one of my great moral teachers, reminded the church, my supreme law is the law of love.

Confucius: I would like to tell you about some of our Confucian texts. The first group of Confucian writings is called the Five Classics. These are records of ancient societies and touch on every aspect of culture, ranging from politics to religion. The first book listed is *The Book of Changes*, a handbook for understanding the nature of the world, largely from metaphysical and moral points of view. This was one of my favorite collections.

The second book is *The Book of Poetry*, a collection of poems written over a period of five hundred years before I was born. Of the three thousand poems in the collection, I collected about three hundred of these that were my favorites; others were added later. I was eager to teach poetry because, as I have written, "It inspires thought, increases one's scope, shows one how to express feelings. . . ."[4]

The next book is *The Book of History*, which is significant to my movement, because I personally arranged the texts and wrote the prefaces. The contents range over three dynasties (c. 2070–857 BCE). The text is a treasure of history, philosophy, and politics. It contains dialogues between kings and their ministers, advice for kings, announcements from kings to the people, and many other interesting pieces.

The fourth book is *The Book of Rites*, which is an anthology of rituals for all kinds of events, banquets, and weddings. It explains how to gesture and use proper etiquette and manners—all that should be part of the cultured person's education.

Finally, there is *The Spring and Autumn Annals*, which records the important events that happened in my State of Lu from 722–481 BCE. In these texts, I present harsh criticism on the violence and corruption during this period. This material offers a thorough overview of my thoughts on good government and the value of peace and unity.

Other books in the Confucian literature, such as *The Great Learning* and *The Doctrine of the Mean*, were written by my disciples.

One of the most popular pieces of Confucian writing is the *Analects*. This was not written by me personally; it was collected by later disciples. It contains conversations that capture the essence of my thought. Here I speak of my love of learning and action, the deep value I place on family, as well as the tremendous joy that I experienced from friends who visit from afar. As I have said many times, "Being filial and fraternal—is this not the root of humanness?" I firmly believe that being clever and pretentious are not ways to become humane. Loyalty, trustworthiness, and openness are of much more value. Good rulers are portrayed as those who are trustworthy and love their people.

4. *Analects*, 17.9.

My teachings offer a vast code (*li*) for living a good life. At the center is a philosophy of education that includes every person from cradle to grave. Other key teachings deal with self-cultivation, using personal goodness to serve society, and following "the choice of heaven," that is, aligning oneself with the positive force in the universe.

A good education is one of my core values. And such education should be for all and continue throughout life. I maintain that everyone, without distinction, should have the opportunity for a good education. I grew up poor, yet had the opportunity for an excellent education. I have always been an advocate for everyone to have the same choices that I had for learning.

It has also always been my conviction that learning should be lifelong. To stop learning at the end of schooling is to become quickly out of touch. New events happen, and new learning continues to develop. I have a saying on the progress of my learning: "At fifteen my heart was set on learning; at thirty I had become established; at forty, I was no longer perplexed; at fifty I knew what is ordained by heaven; at sixty I obeyed; at seventy, I could follow my heart's desires without transgressing the line."[5]

Ban Zhao: Confucius was dedicated to helping people cultivate themselves. He wanted to help people develop themselves to be virtuous (*jen*), respectful of superiors, and dutiful to obligations. The virtuous person places his or her interests after those of others, is sincere and honest in speech and actions, and honest about knowledge. He said, "To say you know when you do know, and to say that you do not know when you do not know—this is wisdom."[6] Confucius taught that a person had to develop courage to both know what is right and do what is right. He taught *shu*, which is translated as sympathy and compassion. It is summed up in a statement similar to the Golden Rule: "not doing to others what one does not want done to oneself."[7] Being a good human being without any hope of praise or reward, even eternal, was the goal for Confucius. It entailed knowing all the rituals and manners of society. It called for avoiding rudeness, pride, deceit, and greed. It was his conviction that the capacity for all this was within every person and had only to be drawn out and practiced.[8]

Jesus: I so agree with your Golden Rule and with all of your teachings about the virtuous person. I suppose where we disagree is how this can be carried

5. Ruggiero, *Confucianism*, 66.

6. *Analects*, 2.27.

7. Ibid., 4.15.

8. Rainey, *Confucius and Confucianism*, 35.

out. I believe that this can only be done with the help of God, while you seem to hold that people can become virtuous on their own.

Confucius: I think my most significant contribution is helping Chinese family life. My teachings have influenced billions of families over thousands of years.

It is my conviction that virtue is first learned in the family and is developed by serving the family. The family is the center of life; therefore, filial piety is of the essence of wholesome family life. Each member in the family must respect and love the other, and the family should be extended to the ancestors.

Each member in the family has to play his or her role with respect and dutiful service. The good person helps shape the family; the good family shapes the good community, and then on to the nation and the world. Bringing peace and harmony to the world is the ultimate goal of the good person.

Ban Zhao: Confucius often uses the term "the way of heaven." That seems to be as close as he gets to speaking about God. The way of heaven carries a number of meanings for Confucius. It can mean that which generates moral power and virtues in human beings. It can refer to the power that takes away the fear to act. The way of heaven might be a call to mission or the powers to carry it out. Some call it a Supreme Being, others the Final Judge, but all life and death was to be governed by this Heaven. Its ultimacy is described in this ancient Confucian teaching: "Those who are obedient to Heaven are preserved; those who are against Heaven are annihilated."[9]

Jesus: I have been much more personal in my teaching about God. In my Jewish tradition, we use images such as father and mother. In my teaching, I usually used the image of father, but in my Gospels, my saving role is likened to a mother hen gathering her chicks.

The notion closest to your "way of heaven" in my tradition would be "the kingdom of God" or the "kingdom of heaven." I use these images numerous times in the Gospels. The kingdom is often described as "the loving, saving presence of God." I teach that it is "within all" and at the same time "beyond all." My fundamental teaching was: "Repent, for the kingdom of heaven has come near" (Matt 3:2).

9. *Mengzi*, 4A:7.

Ban Zhao: The term "the way of heaven" was often politicized in China. At times, the emperors used it as a basis for their rule. During my time in the Han dynasty, the teachings of our master, Confucius, were adopted as State doctrine. Unfortunately, his teaching became distorted, and his wonderful ethics were imposed on the Chinese people in order to control them and to keep public order.

Confucianism gradually became more a political doctrine. State examinations on Confucian classics were required for civil servants. Education for these exams was only accessible to those who had the time and the money. Confucianism became elitist. In many ways, this narrow view of Confucianism helped insulate the Chinese culture, closing them off from the advances being made in the West.

Jesus: It is always dangerous to mix religion with politics. When Christianity became accepted in the Roman Empire, and later its official religion, the teachings became a doctrine that was often enforced on people. Through the years, as Christendom was established, church structures and laws became a means of control. Jews were oppressed and the so-called pagans discovered in the New World were often enslaved and persecuted. 'Convert or be killed' was often the mandate. Inquisitions were initiated. People were threatened with excommunication or even execution if they were unorthodox in their beliefs.

Christian beliefs used for social and political control are still prevalent in modern times. The Bible has been used to legalize slavery, impose segregation laws, and justify the oppression of gays. In the United States, conservative Christians have attempted to make their doctrines, beliefs, and even prejudices the law of the land. Even today, theologians and others are silenced or excommunicated for holding views thought to be unorthodox or for not obeying church rules.

Confucius: It is certainly tragic when our teachings about higher spiritual powers or about living a virtuous life are co-opted by those who want to exercise political, social, or even religious power over others. Both our teachings are about power for service of others, not for power over others.

Another important phase of Confucian development began around the year 1000 CE and lasted into modern times, the Neo-Confucian period. This approach was more philosophical, devising theories on the origins of the universe and human nature. Here the notion of *chi*, the material force in the world, was developed. Then, in the 1800s, Confucianism was used to formulate political reforms that could withstand the onslaught of colonialism.

In 1911 a revolution overthrew the Manchu emperor, ending centuries of imperial rule. During this time of upheaval, it was debated as to whether Confucianism could help overcome the chaos or should be abandoned as a remnant of an elitist system, which resisted change and modernization. In the 1920s the National People's Party was formed. The party wanted to blend Confucian and Western values. During this same period, Chinese Communist revolutionaries set out to impose Marxist-Leninist principles on China.

Eventually, Mao Zedong took over the government of China and cast out Confucianism as belonging to China's archaic past. After Mao's death, a new era began in China. Many in the Communist government see Confucianism as being beneficial. It was thought useful to revive family values, which were suppressed during Mao's regime, and helpful to move the citizenry toward service. For some, this meant service of the nation; for others, it meant service of the people. Where the key Confucian objectives—such as the strengthening of human virtue and the honoring of human rights—fit into a future picture of today's China remains to be seen.

Ban Zhao: Today there is a "New Confucianism," which attempts to adapt the tradition to contemporary times. The economic success in the East Asian countries where Confucianism flourishes has given the tradition new credibility.[10] These countries are trying to build strong families, good educational systems, and develop citizens who are well-cultivated.

Jesus: In many ways, a "New Christianity" is being developed. The churches are attempting to modernize and serve the needs of the contemporary world. Many churches have accepted democratic forms of governing as well as the findings of modern science on evolution, climate change, and health care. Many are open to the teaching of other churches and religions and are willing to participate in ecumenism and interfaith dialogue.

At the same time, there are churches that do not accept these positions and have "circled the wagons." They hold on to world-denying positions on politics and science. They are closed to the truth or saving power of other churches and religions and are not interested in dialogue with them.

Confucius: People often ask us how Confucianism can still be relevant to the modern world. I think that there are two areas in which Confucianism can make valuable contributions, especially in modern China as well as among Chinese who are living in other lands: family and education. Chinese

10. Rainey, 205.

Communism, especially during the reign of Mao, did much to disturb and even destroy the traditional Chinese family system.

Today the Chinese are making great efforts to restore traditional family values, realizing that family, rather than the state, is foundational for many modern Chinese. The former "one child" policy of the government, as well as the need for both parents to work, has been challenging for many extended Chinese families, where three or even four generations live together. Many are looking to traditional Confucian family values to deal with these challenges.

Ban Zhao: Confucianism continues to play a major role in the development of a strong sense of family in East Asia. The Chinese treasure their children. Children receive special care from both parents and grandparents. In the schools, personal attention is given to children in the classroom and on the playground. After school, the grandparents stand by, ready to sweep them up and take them home.

Confucius: The Chinese people struggle with many of these same issues and many have come to realize that Communism has not been very enlightened in dealing with them. Still, it is difficult for Communist leaders to admit that they have been in error. I suspect the same is true for Christian leaders.

Education seems to be essential to developing good family values. The Chinese have perennially valued education, but today the challenges in this area are unique. The rapid industrial and economic development in China calls for a strong educational system that will train an enormous population in the languages, business skills, creativity, and critical thinking needed for such growth. My teaching on the priority for good education has once again become useful.

Ban Zhao: Confucianism has helped shape the cultures of China, Japan, Taiwan, Korea, and others, all of which today are industrialized and mechanized and have the same environmental problems as many other countries. Confucian scholars are beginning to discover that there are many resources in the tradition that can be linked to ecology. The tradition has a dynamic view of a world that evolves and develops and that has amazing resilience and powers of adaptation. Confucians know that the universal process is eternal and can be repaired if humans so choose to act.

The Confucian tradition carries the notion of *chi*—a dynamic, material force within all things that can be nurtured by virtuous human action. It has deep respect for the eternal continuity of life, both past and present, a process of which humans are a part. Confucius' vision was one where all things are interconnected, linked together in an eternal circular motion that is fundamental to all reality.

Confucius: Throughout my life I taught respect for life, especially human life, family life, and life in community. Today all such life is threatened by the current environmental crisis. I have always valued compassion for the suffering, a value that is relevant to the pain that is being imposed on both nature and humans as a result of the degradation of the Earth. I taught the value of study, learning, education, and the cultivation of self for useful action. These values are needed as we face the environmental crisis. And finally, I taught that we must follow the Way of Heaven, the way of the mysterious power and law within all of nature. We must be in touch with this power if we want to understand and prevent the devastation of our world.

Today the Chinese people are deeply concerned about how the pollution in the cities and in the water is affecting their health and their children's health. People in the cities have to wear masks to filter out pollutants, and many Chinese are struggling with lung problems.

The Chinese people are beginning to protest, and at last the government is beginning to respond. Recently, the government adopted a policy to severely limit air pollution, especially in industry.

Ban Zhao: We are very proud of our environmentalists and the progress they are making with our government, which has been slow to respond to this crisis. I am particularly in admiration of Confucian Liao Xiaoyi (b. 1954), a very active environmentalist in China.

She made film documentaries on China's ecological plight that appeared on China Central Television. She also founded the nongovernmental organization Global Village of Beijing. Liao promotes "a life of harmony" through reduced consumption and decreased use of harmful environmental practices in daily lives. She served as an environmental adviser to the Beijing Organizing Committee for the 2008 Olympic Games.

Confucius: I developed my teaching during a time of violence and war, hoping to help restore harmony and peace. I called my people to self-transformation through education and good living to yield an inner peace that starts with the individual, then influences families, and finally the larger community.

In modern times, my teaching has been useful in helping countries recover from stressful circumstances. For instance, after World War II, Asian nations such as Japan, South Korea, Taiwan, and Hong Kong were trying to recover from the horrors of war. To adapt to peacetime and still preserve their cultures, which were becoming Westernized, they often turned to Confucianism. My ancient teaching helped to restabilize their families, develop proper education, preserve respect for the wisdom of their elders, and focus on the common good.[11] They believed that a stable peace could be reestablished through restoring the five relationships of Confucius: husband and wife, father and child, older and younger siblings, ruler and subject, older friend and younger friend.[12]

In today's Communist China, about half of the population still live in villages, largely cut off from the economic boom.[13] Confucian family values and teachings about respect for leaders and government as well as harmony are appealing to many Communist leaders, especially after all the destruction of Chinese culture under Mao Zedong.

Jesus: You might say that I am a pacifist. Note that the word comes from "pacific," which means peaceful and has nothing to do with being passive. For hundreds of years after my death, my followers would not participate in the Roman military or wars. But once they were incorporated into the Roman Empire, they became more militant. Using the "just war theory" developed by the Romans and promoted by Augustine, Christians became even more involved in the military. They have remained so ever since and push to the fringes those Christians who are pacifists.

Ban Zhao: Confucius always rejected the violent ways of despots and held that with good leaders people could eliminate war altogether. He taught: "If truly good people were put in charge of governing for a hundred years, they would be able to overcome violence and dispense with killing altogether."[14] Later disciples, several centuries after the time of Confucius, took strong stands against leaders waging offensive wars and stressed how unproductive and destructive wars actually were, wasting many lives and resources.[15]

Confucius: I want to tell you about a great, contemporary Confucian who was awarded the Nobel Peace Prize in 2010. His name is Liu Xiaobo. Liu has courageously called for political reform in China and the end of Communist one-party rule. He was involved in the infamous uprising at Tiananmen Square in 1989, calling for dialogue and compromise. Tragically, he was not

11. Tucker and Berthrong, *Confucianism and Ecology*, 183.

12. Dallmayr, *Peace Talks—Who Will Listen?*, 161.

13. See http://www.nytimes.com/2013/06/16.

14. *Analects*, 13.11.

15. Dallmayr, *Peace Talks*, 161.

successful, and many students were massacred by the government. He was, however, able to lead negotiations between an army commander and student leaders, so that several thousand students could withdraw peacefully from the square.

In 2008 Liu was arrested. In 2009 he was convicted of subversion of State power and sentenced to eleven years in prison. His Nobel Peace Prize was awarded for his long and nonviolent struggle for fundamental human rights in China.

Ban Zhao: Confucius lived in a male-dominated Chinese society, where education was much more accessible to sons than daughters. Women were subject to their fathers in their youth, their husbands in marriage, and their sons in old age. Though neither Confucius nor neo-Confucianism did much for women's equality, they did set a standard for humanistic respect and equality that can be useful today.

The classical texts are a mix with regard to women. Unlike Buddha, who chose women disciples and taught that women could be enlightened, Confucius does not seem to have women students or disciples. At the same time, he did call for "education without distinction" and indicated that all are called to self-cultivation.[16]

The later traditions tell many stories of well-educated women who became leaders and authors. Yet, they also cast insults to women and tell stories of how they led rulers astray, especially with their female wiles and beauty. During the Han dynasty, women were incorporated in the yin-yang dynamic, identified with yin, which was interpreted as the subordinate or even negative pole, indicating the inferiority of women. In other traditions, the feminine identification with yin indicated their equality and complementarity.[17]

Jesus: It was my conviction that both women and men were the children of God, equal in the eyes of my Father. Jews never spoke of a Fall, where Eve supposedly seduced Adam and brought original sin into the world.

I had no hesitation ignoring the Jewish taboos with regard to women. I freely conversed with women in public, brought healing and forgiveness to them, and even called them to be my closest disciples. I never saw them as unclean, seductive, or weak. As a matter of fact, during my passion and death, my women disciples were more courageous and faithful than the men. None of the women betrayed me, denied knowing me, or deserted me.

---

16. Rainey, *Confucius and Confucianism*, 200.

17. Bell, *Confucian Political Ethics*, 217.

Ban Zhao: I mentioned earlier that I was a significant person in the Han dynasty. Actually, I was a recognized historian.

Because Confucius had written little about women, I chose to express guidelines on how women should conduct themselves. My book was called *Lessons for Women*. Today it might sound rather traditional, but in my day and centuries to follow it set the standards for being a virtuous and noble woman. Many women actually memorized whole sections of my book and kept it by their side.

My goal was to see that women had their proper status in society. I held that, to achieve this, they must be virtuous and have proper speech, appearance, and conduct. Women should not try to stand out above others and should not be sharp in their speech. Neither should they strive to be beautiful or ornamented, nor stand out by being competitive.

My book had seven chapters, and throughout I urged women to be humble, that is, to be in touch with their true feminine selves. I advised women to be devoted to their husbands and to serve their needs. In the yin-yang dynamic, men represent firmness, while women stand for gentleness. I also urged wives to be obedient and in harmony with their in-laws.

I advised young women to control their language and behavior and to guard their virginity. Respect for others and cleanliness is needed for young and older women.

By today's standards my advice may sound rather conservative, but it has certainly helped Oriental cultures build solid family values over the centuries.

Confucius: In my teaching, I emphasize humanistic cultivation and education, which would include both genders. I believe that proper understanding of yin and yang can lead to better cooperation and harmony among the sexes.

Often the birth of a daughter was lamented in Confucian societies, and female infanticide has been practiced throughout Chinese history. This practice still prevails in some Chinese families today. Some parents terminate female fetuses after sonograms. This has resulted in a shortage of females in China. "New Confucianists" advocate the avoidance of these abortions on grounds of human dignity, compassion, harmony, and family values.

The role of widows was dealt with in different ways in the Confucian tradition. Because marriage was the only way for a woman to achieve a social role of her own, widows were often at a disadvantage. In some dynasties, they were not permitted to remarry; in others, they were forced to marry and live as inferiors because they were not virgins. Often, a widow was honored for being chaste and thus loyal to her deceased husband and to his lineage.

Foot binding was almost an obligation for women who wanted to marry well from around 1000 CE until it was banned in 1912; though some women continued to bind their feet until the mid-twentieth century. Foot binding began among medieval court dancers who wanted to have unique ballerina feet. Eventually, the practice spread to the masses, who considered tiny feet to be highly erotic and appealing to men. Little girls at four or five years of age were forced to submit to the painful process of having their four little toes bent backward and their heel bone turned vertical so that the foot was arch-shaped and about three-inches long. This position was tightly bound to inhibit growth. For a young woman, because she had no access to education, this became her sign of civility. Having such feet made her attractive and marriageable. It also rendered her quite immobile, barely able to leave the house. This prepared her for a life of being housebound and submissive to her husband. The thinking was that it also prevented her from being unfaithful. For centuries, women struggled to have the painful process of foot binding stopped. Finally, the practice has met its end. Confucians, who promote the dignity of the human person, rejoice in its demise.

Ban Zhao: Some feminists today think that Confucianism is incompatible with feminism. Others think that such a view is based on a caricature of Confucianism as well as Western notions of feminism. Some advocates for women in China and other parts of Asia believe that traditional concepts, such as Confucianism, can be used to promote virtue-based personhood, filial piety, and complementarity within the yin-yang process to develop a "Confucian feminism."[18]

In the Confucian tradition, women are first and foremost human persons. Gender is always secondary to their human identity. Confucius' main focus was on the self-cultivation of the human person through education and the development of virtue. The cultivation of the person, according to Confucius, is not to be an end in itself, but rather a preparation for service to the family, the community, and the world at large. These principles are certainly useful and can be extracted from the patriarchal structure in which the Sage lived and can be used today to help women take their place in society as equals.

18. Rosenlee, *Confucianism and Women*, 15.

Confucius: My worldview emphasized the interconnectedness of all things—a networking among humans, Earth, and the heavens. Humans were called to cultivate themselves so that they could contribute to the eternal process, or "way" of the universe, the "way of heaven."

Women are often noted for their skills at connecting with others, of drawing people together. Their feminine gifts often seem to be geared toward linking, partnering, and bringing together. Often mothers are the glue that holds families together as well as the energy that sustains people in churches or communities. They are usually more interested in circles (communities) than triangles (hierarchies). This equips women to play their unique role in fostering the cycle of humans, Earth, and Heaven.

Jesus: I have learned so much from our discussion, Ban Zhao and Confucius. You are both teachers for the ages. All three of us teach the eternal wisdom that comes from the "heavens." We all value human dignity, virtuous living, and the treasures of family life. Like all religious leaders, we see all things to be somehow sacred and interconnected.

Hopefully, in the future, we will be able to work together for the good of the Earth, for peace, and for the equality of women.

SUGGESTED READINGS ON CONFUCIANISM

Berthrong, John H. and Evelyn N. *Confucianism: A Short Introduction*. Oxford: Oneworld, 2000.

Li, Chenyang. *The Sage and the Second Sex*. Chicago: Open Court, 2000.

Rainey, Lee Dian. *Confucius and Confucianism: The Essentials*. Oxford: Wiley-Blackwell, 2010.

Tucker, Mary Evelyn and John Berthrong. *Confucianism and Ecology*. Cambridge, MA: Harvard University Press, 1998.

Yao, Xinzhong. *An Introduction to Confucianism*. Cambridge: Cambridge University Press, 2000.

Chapter 9

Indigenous Religions

~~◯ Jesus with Leaders of Indigenous Peoples

"The Earth does not belong to man, man belongs to the Earth. All things are connected like the blood that unites us all. Man did not weave the web of life, he is merely a strand in it. Whatever he does to the web, he does to himself."

—CHIEF SEATTLE

Consider the ravens: they neither sow nor reap, they have neither storehouse nor barn, and yet God feeds them. Of how much more value are you than the birds! And can any of you by worrying add a single hour to your span of life? If then you are not able to do so small a thing as that, why do you worry about the rest?

—LUKE 12:24–26

Jesus: Greetings and welcome! My name is Jesus, and I am the founder of Christianity. I know that the people of your religions have had interactions with my followers, often ones that were brutal and unjust. This saddens me so much!

I invited all of you to this religious powwow so that we could better understand each other's beliefs and practices. You were all outstanding figures in indigenous religions: African, Native American, Aztec, and Inca. I know that there are many other indigenous religions throughout the world, so this is just a beginning of such dialogues, and, hopefully, there will be many more in the future.

I deeply regret that so often Christians have looked upon you as heathens and savages and have not recognized the value and authenticity of your sacred religions.

Please introduce yourselves.

Gadla: My name is Gadla Mphakanyiswa, and I am from the Thembu people, a tribe of the Xhosa clan, who are found mostly in South Africa. I am sure that you know about my famous son, Nelson Mandela, who grew up among my people and is now buried with them. Much of what he learned about equality and collaboration came from his tribal life.

Sacajawea: My name is Sacajawea, and I am a Native American from the Lemhi Shoshoni tribe. I accompanied Lewis and Clark on their expedition West. I was born in 1788. The Shoshoni are indigenous peoples of the Great Basin, who had been in the territory for thousands of years. Our homeland areas include the region now known as Nevada as well as parts of Utah, Idaho, Oregon, California, and Wyoming. Shoshoni people date back to 2000 BCE.

Montezuma: My name is Montezuma, and I was the emperor of the great Aztec Empire, which covered areas now known as Mexico, Honduras, and Nicaragua. There was an Aztec civilization there long before the Spaniards came in the sixteenth century. It was in many ways more advanced than many parts of Europe. When the Spanish came, their leader Cortes captured and killed me. His people proceeded to destroy and pillage our empire and enslave and slaughter my people. Many died from the diseases that the foreigners brought us.

Atahualpa: My name is Atahualpa. I was the emperor of the great Inca Empire in Peru. The Spanish came to us also in the sixteenth century. Their leader Pizarro captured and murdered me. The Spanish then proceeded to enslave and slaughter my people and steal our land and possessions—especially our gold. They spread fatal diseases among us, and they destroyed our empire.

Sacajawea: Before we begin discussing our religions, Jesus, I would like to briefly explain the origin of many of our indigenous people. As I understand it, we humans had our origins in Africa—your continent, Gadla. For millennia, humans then migrated through the Middle East, Europe, and Asia. About thirty thousand years ago, migratory peoples from Asian areas such as Siberia and Mongolia moved across the frozen tundra, which connected with a new continent that had never been inhabited. Migrations spread south through what is now Alaska, Canada, and eventually through the Americas. Tens of millions of differing peoples established themselves in North America, Mexico, Central America, and South America. By the time the Europeans arrived in the Americas, hundreds of tribes of Native Americans had formed in North America. Whole civilizations had been formed in the lower Americas: the Aztecs in Mexico, the Mayans in Central America, the Incas in Peru, as well as many other indigenous peoples across these broad areas.

Tragically, so many of these indigenous societies have been destroyed by European explorers and seekers of wealth and land. Even today they have been subjugated, and attempts have been made to annihilate them.

Jesus: So much destruction and sadness were imposed upon your peoples— done by persons who claimed to be Christians. They often saw you as subhuman, animals that could be slaughtered and pillaged. They described you as pagans and heathens, when in fact, you were all children of God. It distresses me because oppression and killing are against my teachings.

With a heavy heart, I would like to continue with our sharing. Since the first purpose of most religions is to connect people with a higher power, let's start with your beliefs about God.

Gadla: I would be glad to start. First, let me say that Africa is a vast continent with many tribes as well as numerous religions. I can speak for my own people, but I did learn a great deal about the beliefs in other tribes in my dealings with them, too.

In most African religions "everything begins with God."[1] Most believe that God has always been in existence and always will be. A Mbuti hymn from Central Africa says: "In the beginning was God (*Kmvoum*), today is God, tomorrow will be God. Who can make an image of God?"

God has many names in the African religions, each name arising out of experiences of God.[2] In my Thembu tribe, the Supreme Being is called *uThixo* or *uQamata*. Ancestors act as intermediaries with our God and play

---

1. Olupona and. Nyang, *Religious Plurality in Africa*, 71.
2. Hinnells, *A New Handbook of Living Religions*, 566.

a part in the lives of the living. Ancestors are honored in rituals. For us, our dreams play an important role in contacting both God and our ancestors.

The African religions, like many other religions, have a keen sense of "spirit" and usually view God as the Supreme Spirit. In other tribes, such as the Kimbu of Tanzania, God is associated with the sun, which gives life to all things. In the mountainous areas of Kenya (Mt. Kenya) and in Tanzania (Mt. Kilimanjaro), God is symbolized by the mountains. At times, the sky (male) and Earth (female) personify the Supreme Being.

Many attributes are linked with God that would be most familiar with those who belong to major world religions. Often, God in African religions is believed to be all-knowing, all-present, and all-powerful. God is both immanent and transcendent; that is, God is within all and beyond all. God is also one, but with many manifestations. God is called Father, Mother, Grandfather, and Friend. Many African tribes have portrayed God as merciful, kind, loving, and holy.[3]

Jesus: Thank you, Gadla. Sacajawea, could you tell us some beliefs about God among Native American people?

Sacajawea: Well, I have to begin by pointing out that we have hundreds of tribes with diverse beliefs. At the same time, many tribes have similar core beliefs. Central in the religious traditions of Native Americans is the belief in a Spirit that is in all things, often called the Great Spirit.[4]

Most Native Americans believe that there is a Supreme Creator, who is above all the other powers in nature and over other spiritual beings. Among the tribes, there are many and diverse understandings about this Great Spirit. This Creator can be thought of as invisible and ever-present, or remote with little to be said about the Creator's nature. Often the Creator exists in the heavens, which commonly are seen to be held up by a "cosmic pole" or "world tree." In some tribes this Spirit is male, in others female. Various names are used for this deity.

The Algonquins call the Creator the Great Spirit; the Apache, the Life Giver; the Cheyenne and Dakota, the Great Mystery (*Wankan Tanka*); the Hopi, *Taiowa* (Sun God); and the Winnebago, Earthmaker. Some tribes view the Great Spirit as an unnamed and unknown power that creates and allows lesser spirits to guide the world.[5] Often the attitude of the American

3. Mbiti, *Concepts of God in Africa*, 3–42.
4. Deloria, *God is Red*, 151ff.
5. Hirschfelder and Molin, *The Encyclopedia of Native American Religions*, 570.

Indian toward the Eternal and Great Mystery that surrounds all is the "supreme conception" that brings joy and satisfaction to our lives.

This Great Spirit can be experienced in the songs of birds, the scent of flowers, in the mighty waters, or the misty mountaintops, and, of course, in our wonderful people.

Montezuma: For the Aztecs of Mexico, Tezcatlipoca was the most powerful deity—the power within all things, the controller of destiny. This power was closely associated with the royal king. In an early source, an Aztec priest says that it is through the Sacred Spirit that all live, and that the Spirit gives us our daily food, drink, and all that sustains us.

Besides Tezcatlipoca, the all-powerful deity, there were many other gods associated with sustaining the Earth and its peoples. The Aztecs experienced the sacred in all things and developed a pantheon of deities linked to the natural environment: the land and sky, the sun, moon, fire, rain, water, and vegetation.

Jesus: Christians also experience the sacred in all things, but believe in only one God, the Creator of all. Your peoples' belief in God sustaining them reminds me of our prayer, "Give us this day our daily bread."

Atahualpa: The Incas also worshiped many gods from their own traditions, as well as gods whom they brought back from their conquests. Some of these were considered to be secondary causes of creation, especially the sun, water, and the earth. The sun was an extremely important god for the Incas and was viewed as the cause of their many abundant crops.

The Incas considered themselves to be the children of the sun. Mamacocha was the mother goddess of the lakes and water and was worshiped in the fishing areas. She was petitioned for calm seas and plentiful fish. The Incas also had special devotion to Pachamama, the Earth Mother, who gave them abundant crops.[6]

Jesus: I can relate to many of these beliefs. Both Jews and Christians follow the stories in Genesis, where God is revealed as Creator of all. Most see these as religious myths that reveal who the Creator is. But, we rely on science to discover the when and the how of creation.

While we don't see the things in nature as "gods," we do recognize that everything comes from God and that the divine is somehow present in all. Still, we are steadfast in the belief in but one God.

6. Nerburn, *The Wisdom of the Native Americans*, 22–35.

Gadla: In most of the African religions, God stands as the source of life, culture, and religious tradition. God is viewed as the Great Ancestor, the first Founder and Progenitor, the Giver of life, and the Power behind everything that is. God is the first Initiator of a people's way of life—its tradition.

In the African traditions, God is the creator of all. In our creation stories God is always the main actor. In some cases, God can use deputies to shape various parts of creation, as in the Yoruba creation story, where the god Olodumare uses one of his agents to help shape the Earth.

In most of the African traditions there is no clear beginning of creation, nor is there any indication of an end. God creates and sustains; therefore, everything depends on God, who, like a good mother, will not abandon her children. The Mbuti of the Congo believe that if God should die, the world would collapse; but, of course, they know that God will never die.[7]

Sacajawea: For most tribal people of whom I have spoken, there is belief in a process of creation by the Great Spirit, who is the Source of all life. For the Native Americans, all things have a spirit and are, therefore, sacred and interconnected. The Native Americans designated special places as sacred—in the mountains or on the prairies where unique spirits dwelt. Life here on Earth was valued. After death, the Native Americans held that the souls of all things traveled to some kind of a world of the dead.

Our people have many creation stories, and I learned some of them in my travels across the country with Lewis and Clark on their expedition to map what is now the western portion of the United States.

Jesus: The Jews and Christians have two creation stories, both different in their accounts. I presume that the Native Americans have a wide variety of such stories.

Sacajawea: Indeed they do, Jesus. The Navajos describe the creation of the First Man and First Woman in a river, the environment of the Navajos. Often there is a "diving story," where a creature dives below and comes up with land (the Earth).

The Creeks tell a story of a time when all was water. The Above World beings needed land to obtain food, so a council meeting was called. Eagle was appointed chief, and Dove was sent out to find land. Dove failed to locate land, so Crawfish was chosen to dive down deep. On the fourth

---

7. Magesa, *African Religion*, 72–73.

morning, Crawfish came up with some land. It was made into a ball that became the Earth.

The Potawatomis have a story of the Creator flashing his eyes with lightning to produce water and land, and then bellowing thunder to bring forth from the red clay a wonderful bride and groom, kissing in their naked innocence and living in wonder at their new existence.

Other spirits are often believed to perpetuate creation. How this was done varies, depending on the environs of the tribe. These spirits are manifested in everyday life: in the sky, the winds, night and day, the sun, earth, streams, and in hearth fires. The early hunters and gatherers revered the spirits of animals, fruits, and herbs from which they derived shelter, clothing, and food.

I have heard that the Koyukon people of Alaska honored the powerful spirits of the bears, wolverines, and wolves. The later agricultural tribes believed in the spirits associated with crops, as well as the sunshine and water so necessary to nurture these crops. Some Hopis relied on the god Masaw to teach them the correct ways to plant and harvest corn. The Keres people honored the Corn Mother, the goddess of fertility. The Hopi, Pueblo, and Zuni tribes believed in kachina spirits, which were powerful spirits of the dead that come in the form of plants, birds, animals, and other humans.

There are endless stories about these spirits, especially about the so-called culture heroes who assist God in creation. Sometimes they are depicted as a pair of twins, one causing the good events of life and the other bringing about evil or destructive events. Some of these spirits are tricksters who work mischief in creation. They represent the capricious, even dangerous, aspects of the supernatural in the world.

For the Navajo, Coyote is a sometimes obscene jester who plays tricks on humans in the mythical stories. The Apaches tell many stories about Big Owl, and how he helped their ancestors with the daily struggles. There are also guardian spirits, who offer special protection for certain individuals or confer powers of healing, visions, and dreams to shamans. In many tribes, such spirits could be contacted only through special personal gifts or through specific rituals.[8] Often these powers are gained from a specific animal or bird that possessed that spirit.[9]

Jesus: My traditions, both Jewish and Christians, have two quite different accounts of creation. In one, God creates part of the world on a day of the week and then creates humans last in the divine image. God then rests on

8. Deloria, *God is Red*, 170.

9. Jacobs, *Native American Wisdom*, 162.

the seventh day. In the other story, God creates the heavens and the Earth and forms man out of the earth. God then forms a wonderful garden and puts man in charge. Then the Creator makes several attempts to create companions for man (animals and birds). When these fall short, the Lord God puts the man to sleep and forms a woman out of one of his ribs. Now he has a wonderful companion!

Those who take the creation stories too literally often reject the findings of science with regard to the birth of the universe and evolution. Those who take the story where Eve, the first woman, leads Adam, the first man, to eat the forbidden fruit literally have often come to portray women as seducers. Christians, but not Jews, believe in the Fall and an Original Sin that is passed on through humans.

We also have stories about angels, who bring messages from God and protect God's people. Many Christians believe that there are instances where their guardian angels have saved them from harm. They also believe in the communion of saints—people who are with God—and they pray to them. For us, the spirits of the dead are ever-present and active. Catholics canonize outstanding individuals as saints.

Sacajawea, could you explain how your people view nature?

Sacajawea: Because the Native Americans believed that all things come from the hand of the Creator, there was a sacredness about the Earth and its creatures. This reverence for nature is common among the tribes. Lakotas were known to be lovers of nature. Chief Standing Bear of the Lakotas tells how the old people loved to sit or recline on the earth to gain the feeling of being close to their Mother and to be more loosely in touch with its life-giving forces. They often removed their moccasins so that they could feel the earth beneath their feet. They believed that the earth put them in closer touch with the mysteries of life. The soil was soothing, strengthening, and cleansing.

In most Native American traditions, all creation is connected, linked by spiritual, creative power and energy. Humans are thus part of and not greater than. The great Chief Seattle put it this way when asked to sell the land:

> How can you buy or sell the sky, the warmth of the land? The idea of selling nature is strange to us. The rivers are our brothers; they quench our thirst. The rivers carry our canoes and feed our children. The air is precious, to the red man, for all things share the same breath—the beast, the tree, the human, they all share

the same breath. This we know: the earth does not belong to us. We belong to the earth. This we know: all things are connected like the blood that unites one family. Many natives believed that they could talk to tornados and storms and ask for protection from harm. Many talk to animals and nature as they would to a person. We are taught to honor animals in that they provide food and clothing for us. When we kill them, we thank them for giving their lives for us. We are taught to never be cruel to them.[10]

Jesus: Sacajawea, would you explain why totem poles are so important to many of your tribes?

Sacajawea: Many Native American tribes symbolize their reverence for the spirits in animals in their totem poles. These poles represent images of animals and other natural phenomena that are considered to be related to the tribe or clan possessing the totem. The totem spirits are considered to be protectors of these specific people and are often included in their rituals.

Jesus: What role does sacrifice play in your religions?

Montezuma: The Aztecs often see sacrifice as the way creation is brought about. My people believed that the gods sacrificed themselves and were willing to give their own blood and even be dismembered to begin and continue the process of creation. In one creation myth, the god Nanauatzin was even willing to cast himself into the fire to bring about the sunrise.

These beliefs led us to the practice of human sacrifice, which so horrified the Spanish.[11] They did not understand that the Aztec people were imitating the sacrifices of the gods with human sacrifices and in so doing wanted to continue the progress of creation. In addition, blood became the currency in which human beings could trade with gods and so assure the continuance of the Aztec regime.[12] Blood became our way of being united with the gods.

Jesus: It seems to me that your people took their creation myths too literally, and that brought them to the killing of innocent people as sacrifices. My followers have done similar evils. They have actually burned people at the

10. See Chief Seattle, "Speech of 1854," http://www.barefootsworld.
11. Brundage, *The Fifth Sun,* 196.
12. Townsend, *The Aztecs,* 129ff.

stake to show their disdain for "heresy," and they have executed people in horrible ways to "bring about justice." They have gassed and burned people in ovens to "purify" the Nazi nation.

I gave them Eucharist so that they could commune with my risen presence and to symbolize my offering of my life for them in love. But they too took all this too literally and often believed that they were eating my flesh and drinking my blood.

This practice of human sacrifice has a long tradition. In the Hebrew Scriptures, Abraham was asked to sacrifice his son, but then was stopped by God. This story seems to indicate that human sacrifice had been practiced by some Semitic people, but Abraham was shown that it was not the will of God for his chosen people.

The bloody sacrifice of animals was an integral part of Temple rituals, and the blood of hundreds of lambs was sprinkled on the worshipers. "Saved by the blood of Jesus" has been a belief in the Christian tradition, and the word "sacrifice" has been applied to my death on the cross. Though I never supported human sacrifice, I have been described as the "Lamb of God," who was sacrificed on the cross to appease a vengeful God and save humankind. There is such a danger in taking myths too literally. We are called to reverence all life. We worship a loving God, not one who demands human sacrifice.

Gadla: Some of the African creation myths will have a familiar ring to you, Jesus. They often tell of humans being created as one husband and wife. There are even stories of them being created out of earth and shaped like clay by a potter.

In some stories, God creates humans directly, in others, God gets help from the animals. African creation myths often reveal creation as God meant it to be—blessed and harmonious. There are themes that are similar to those in the Judeo-Christian Bible. They tell of a time when heaven and Earth were close together and when humans lived in harmony with God and each other. God provided people with all they needed and intended them to live forever.

Many stories tell how this blessed state was lost. A chasm developed between God and humans as disease, death, and disharmony entered creation. Usually some wrongdoing on the part of humans brought about this breakdown. In some stories, they eat from a forbidden tree. There are accounts of eating a forbidden fruit or a forbidden yam. In some myths, humans were cast out of heaven for their wrongdoing. Other myths tell of God assisting people in surviving the disasters by sending them new knowledge, law, and leaders. In some traditions, humans can overcome their original loss and regain their original immortality through spirituality, marriage, and childbearing.

Often the surrounding nature reveals the existence of the Supreme Being to us, along with the presence of other spiritual beings and powers. These beings serve to link humans with the spiritual world.

The nature spirits are often thought to be in control of the animals, trees, plants, lakes, streams, and rock formations. In the past, this practice was called animism and was considered to be characteristic of so-called primitive religions and, possibly, the basis of early religion. Modern scholars now see the awareness of the presence of spirits as an aspect of many religions, and by no means a primitive element of religion.

The African religions also often believe that all humans were created to learn about and be conveyors of God's truth. This leads many of us to be tolerant of all religions. In this view, God is the source of all Truth and shares divine truth with all humans and all religions. I think we can see this from our dialogue today.

Jesus: Let's talk about our views on afterlife. Christians believe in individual souls. I promised my disciples eternal life if they followed me and my teachings. Eternal life is life with God, beyond time and space, in a state of everlasting joy. Because of my Resurrection, I am called "the firstborn of all creation,"[13] and can promise my followers eternal life.

Sacajawea: In many Native American traditions, death represents a separation of the soul or spirit from the body. The soul or spirit lives on, maintaining its identity. The person is now venerated as an ancestor, who can appear to the family from time to time. After death, our ancestors are supplied with personal possessions, tools, weapons, cooking utensils, and even food, enabling them to continue on in the next life.

The Plains Indians believed that good souls were rewarded with successful hunting, feasting, and dancing—a state that Europeans later characterized as "happy hunting grounds." Some describe the afterlife as the spirit returning to the Great Mystery that breathed life into it. After death, the spirit has the freedom to wander in nature.

The tribal people buried their dead, cremated them, or exposed them to the elements. During a time of intense mourning, tribal members distanced themselves from the dead. Through prayer, songs, and rituals, they assisted the deceased on his or her journey to the land of the dead. There seemed to be little concern about judgment or punishment after death. What was

13. Col 1:15

important was to live a meaningful life and to die with such dignity that the tribe was honored by the person's participation.

Tribes such as the Woodland Indians of Ohio constructed enormous burial mounds, sometimes several stories high. Often, cremations were performed at interior altars, and burials were made at these mounds. These mounds provided places where the dead could be protected and assisted in their journey to another world. Some of these mounds were constructed to be enormous effigies of animals or birds to honor the spiritual forces in nature.

Montezuma: The Aztecs also believed in an afterlife, but the way one died determined one's fate, not the way one lived. Those who died a normal death had to pass through nine levels of the underworld before they reached the realm of the death god. Special consideration was given to those who had unique deaths. Those who died in battle, childbirth, or by way of human sacrifice joined the sun god in the sky. These were honored because of the uniqueness and drama of the deaths.

Atahualpa: The Incas believed in an afterlife and the priests and teachers often taught that there would be rewards or punishments after death for the way they lived their lives.[14] Some believed that the good person would become a star in the heavens, while evil people would suffer eternal punishment in an inferno beneath the earth. Others believed that souls would be born again in other places until, in the end, they would receive the reward or punishment they deserved.

Mummification was widely practiced among the Incas. Mummies, bundled in layers of cotton or even in sheets of gold or silver, are still being discovered and studied. These mummies were often treated as though they were still alive. Their possessions were kept with them. Food and drink were offered to them, and they were at times brought to family or council meetings to be consulted.

Gadla: In most of the African myths, death does not come from God, but from the past sins of humans or from animals or evil spirits. In one myth, similar to the one in Genesis, there is an account of the first people eating forbidden food and bringing death into the world. Death was not intended by the Creator, but came from sickness due to some spiritual cause—or from curses, broken oaths, or taboos. Humans were always at fault when it comes to death!

14. Cobo, *Inca Religion and Customs*, 29ff.

Death is usually followed by a ritual: the body is washed, perhaps anointed, and then buried. It is important that the person be buried in the place where they lived. The land of the ancestors is in their inheritance and is involved with their identity. If the land is taken or destroyed, the spirit has nowhere to go. One can see why being driven from their land was so traumatic for the Africans.

Jesus: Maybe we could now turn to the topic of leadership in our religions. Christianity was originally led by prophets, apostles, missionaries, deacons, and teachers. Those who hosted the Eucharistic meal in their homes usually presided at the table. Both men and women could be ordained to these various ministries. Gradually, the offices of bishop, priest, and pope evolved. These became official positions. By the medieval period, ordination was considered to be the giving of certain powers, such as the powers to forgive sins or to consecrate the host. These powers were reserved for men.

Gadla: The more-settled tribes of Africa usually have some variation of a monarchical structure. The kings of the tribes often saw themselves as directly linked to the ancestors. They maintained that they were descendants of divinities and possessed divine power.

At the same time, these rulers were viewed as servants of the community and were required to consult the community in making decisions. Many tribes have a strong sense of equality and a deep commitment and loyalty to the community.

My son Rolihlahla (Nelson Mandela) learned much about governing from his native people and became our most famous president. He taught equality for all and a sharing of responsibilities. He saw himself as the servant of his nation.

Kings and tribal leaders often presided over the sacrifices and rituals in the African religions. They were regarded as living ancestors and ruled on behalf of the ancestors.

There were other various positions of leadership among the African religions. Commonly, people served as spirit-mediums (sometimes called priests) who were believed to be possessed by nature spirits, ancestors, or hero-divinities (the spirits of outstanding people). These mediums could go into trances and bring messages from the spirit world. Priests performed divinations before ceremonies to determine what God required. They officiated at ceremonies and rituals and maintained shrines.

Rainmakers led the community in prayers for much needed rain in arid areas and, at times, channeled the reasons for the drought from ancestral spirits and made recommendations for solutions to the lack of water.

Healers are also common in the African religions and are often called "medicine men." They are experts in using herbs, roots, and potions for curing diseases. As the West has come to better appreciate the use of herbs in curing, the wisdom of these figures is now admired and appreciated. Harriet Tubman, the great hero of the "underground railroad," whereby countless slaves fled the South to freedom, spent years during the Civil War successfully treating the wounded with herbs and plants.

Sacajawea: Native American religious leadership was often largely provided by medicine men and women or shamans. The term "medicine men" was given to them by missionaries who observed the healing powers of certain individuals. Eventually, it was realized the "medicine" included other supernatural powers to bring back wandering souls, to have visions, and to make contact with the spirit world in ecstatic states. People with these latter powers were often called shamans, a name derived from Siberian spiritualists.

The term shaman was generally applied to those males and females who could go into ecstatic states or trances, make "out of body" journeys, and gain control over spirits. If these spirits are causing illness or misfortune, the shamans can take these spirits into their own bodies and thereby neutralize them. Shamans usually achieved their positions through heredity or through a special calling. A long period of training and asceticism was required before a person could practice this position. A vast knowledge of the curative power of plants and herbs as well as surgical skills were also required.

Montezuma: In the Aztec religion both the royalty and the priests saw themselves as empowered to ensure that the populace had what they needed for their well-being. The king was the son of the gods and was responsible to provide inspired leadership and ongoing conquests in order to gain resources, obtain tributes from the conquered, and provide victims for human sacrifice. The priests designed calendars, plotted astrological movements, and from their personal visions made predictions and issued warnings. Both the royal leaders and the priests presided over temple rituals.

Atahualpa: The Incas designated priests, who were assigned to fast, offer sacrifices, and conduct ceremonies for the great festivals that were often held monthly. The high priests presided at the main Temple of the Sun in Cuzco. The leader of the Inca was considered to be the semi-divine Son of the Sun, as was the main presider in the temple. The Incas and priests were held to be the intermediaries between heaven and Earth.

Many women also ministered in the Inca religion. In the major towns a convent was set up where virgins, usually captured from conquered provinces, lived cloistered lives dedicated to service in the local temple.

Jesus: Rituals seem be integral to all religions. Christians have rituals for various passages such as baptism, marriage, and burial. There is as wide a variety of such rituals among Christians as there are diverse interpretations of them.

Many churches have special ceremonies to celebrate my birth, death, and Resurrection. Some churches have a special time to prepare for Christmas, called Advent. Some also prepare for Easter during a period called Lent.

Gadla: Sacrifice was at the heart of traditional African religious practices. The word "sacrifice" seems to be derived from two Latin words *sacer*, which means sacred, and *facere*, which means to make. Thus the offering of a sacrifice to God, whether it be fruits of the harvest or animals, renders these items sacred. These are given as gifts from God and are now returned in holy sacrifice. Sacrifices were most often made to the Supreme Being to expiate for offenses. These offenses included breaking taboos (having contact with dangerous persons, places, or things), breaking the ordinary laws of life, and anti-social behavior. The sin of any individual involved God, the community, and guardians of the community (ancestors and divinities). Therefore, both individuals and the community had to redress these situations with sacrifices, confessions, and purifications. The offerings were usually connected with the lifestyle of the tribe: herders offered cows, while farmers offered the fruits of the harvest. Formal sacrifices were often made at gravesites and shrines. Offerings of food and drink were made to the ancestors to acknowledge their outstanding knowledge and power. Life passages were extremely important in the African religions, so special prayers and offerings were offered at birth and naming ceremonies, puberty rituals, weddings, and funerals.

Africans are a prayerful people and offer prayers individually or at home, led by the head of the house. Prayers are said to praise God, offer thanksgiving for blessings, or make requests for success, offspring, rain, or recovery of health. Most of these prayers are made to God. The people characterize God as a Father, sometimes as Mother.

Sacajawea: My Shoshoni religion "is based on belief in supernatural power (*boha*) that is acquired primarily through vision quests and dreams. A shaman (*boha gande*) is a person who uses supernatural power to cure others and also leads special group ceremonies, especially at Round Dances. The Eastern Shoshonis also adopted two pan-Indian religions, the Sun Dance, and the Native American Church. The Sun Dance was introduced to the Eastern Shoshonis by a Comanche named Yellow Hand around 1800."[15]

The Creeks celebrated an elaborate Green Corn ceremony that lasted eight days and included a cleansing of the entire village, repairing the ceremonial buildings, and renewing the sacred fire of the village. Long into the night, favorite songs were sung and treasured stories told by the professional storytellers.

Some Native American tribes offer ceremonies before going to war, for safety from approaching storms, before and after hunting, planting, and harvesting. Traditionally, the Mohawks offer sacrifices when crossing dangerous waters. Special ceremonies are held at births, deaths, and marriages. Unique puberty rites are performed for young boys and girls.

Jesus: During my life it was important to me to go to the desert from time to time for prayer and meditation. During my ministry I would rise before my disciples and go off on my own to pray. We also often prayed together while at table. Are there such customs among your people, Sacajawea?

Sacajawea: Yes, there are, Lord Jesus. Often the young are sent on a vision quest in an isolated area, where the individual fasts, prays, and smokes the sacred pipe, with its smoke and accompanying prayers rising to the heavens. Afterward, the individual performs other rituals. During this arduous and lonely quest, the individual hopes to be put in touch with animal spirits, possibly with guardian spirits, who could provide guidance and inspiration.

The vision quest can produce a flash of profound insight. The immensity of space, the sighing of the breeze through the trees, the movement of the winged, or an immense mountain gale that demonstrates the power of nature can all be a teacher as we sit upon a mountain.

Native American rituals are usually led by medicine men or women and consist of dancing, singing, and the reciting of solemn prayers. Drums of all shapes and sizes are beaten, each having its distinctive voice and heartbeat. Elaborate masks and feathers disguise the leaders as animals and birds; they perform symbolic dances and gestures to identify themselves with the spirits of these creatures.

15. See Wisart, *Encyclopedia of The Great Plains*, http://plainshumanities.unl.edu.

The Delawares held a twelve-day ceremony after the fall harvest to celebrate a general thanksgiving and to recognize the mutual exchange of privileges between men and women. Like many tribes, they constructed a *Big House* for such ceremonies, a long building that opened to the east for birth and to the west for death, to symbolize the journey of people from life to death. Faces were carved into its twelve structural posts, symbolizing the levels of the cosmos. The carving on the central post symbolized the Creator who supported all things.

The Sun Dance is still commonly celebrated by Native Americans, especially among the Plains tribes. The ceremony is often held in the summer with elaborate ceremonies and prayers for renewal of the tribe, for successful plans for the future, for fertility of land, and for protection from dangers or diseases. The occasion of this celebration is also an opportunity for clans to reunite, renew old relationships, visit relatives, and catch up on the tribal news.

The use of the sweat lodge is common among Native Americans, especially to prepare for key ceremonies. It is a sacred place to cleanse both the body and the mind. It is usually built as a dome-like structure with a dirt floor and very hot stones in the center. Water is poured over these hot stones to produce intense steam heat. The sweating is thought to be a purification and is used also for curing ailments and preventing sickness. The intimacy of the sweat lodge is also conducive for instruction and storytelling.

Montezuma: As I explained earlier, the Aztecs, and similarly the Incas, believed that human sacrifices were reenactments of the sacrifices of the gods, who shed their blood to bring about creation. The spilling of blood, dismemberment, and consuming the flesh were all required by the gods to continue the process of creation. The victims were often treated as personifications of the gods, and consuming their flesh was viewed as a means of being in communion with the deities.

Gadla: I think we should discuss the environmental crisis that all our people are facing today, and how our religions can use our ancient traditions to improve the situation.

Like so many areas of the world, the continent of Africa is in environmental crisis. Africa's rain forests, which shelter a rich variety of the Earth's plant and animal species, are being rapidly cut down. Most have been destroyed by development, agriculture, and forestry.[16] Slash-and-burn

16. See National Geographic, "Africa: Physical Geography," http://education.nationalgeographic.com.

clearing for agriculture exposes thin soil, which is quickly washed away by heavy rains. Overgrazing and destructive agriculture has turned much of the land into desert. Many of the exotic animals in Africa are moving toward extinction, as casualties of hunting, poaching, ivory gathering, and civil wars. The search for oil, diamonds, and other resources has destroyed much of the natural habitat for these animals.

Sacajawea: The Native American people of the United States stand in dismay to see what foreign invaders have done to our revered land. Parched land, many wild species gone, and polluted waterways and air are their legacy. Vast tracts of land have been displaced by shopping malls and housing developments. The three million Native Americans in the United States often witness the threat of nuclear waste being stored on their lands and see their mountains used for strip mining. As Chief Seattle, a great Chief of the Suquamish put it, "Whatever befalls the earth befalls the sons of earth. . . . All things are connected."

Atahualpa: We have seen that many of the people indigenous to Africa and the Americas, although with different interpretations, believe that creation comes from a Creator God and is therefore sacred. Each facet of creation, whether it be the sun, moon, the waters, animals, or humans, somehow possesses spirit. So often the Earth was seen to be the Mother and given the honor due a deity. Sacred places where the divine was intimately experienced were set aside and cherished.

Many of the indigenous people of the Americas viewed all elements of creation as being linked with the spirit world. Spirits dwelled within all things. Each element of creation has a divinely decreed purpose and is connected with all the other elements. For many, there is a divine energy in all things that sustains an ongoing process of creation. Humans are part of an intricate network and bear responsibility to honor this interconnection of all things.

Jesus: Gadla, I know that for centuries your African people have suffered a great deal at the hands of other conquering nations and that now there is much violence among your own people. How are your people doing in their struggle for peace?

Gadla: Jesus, you are right about our many ordeals. The indigenous people of Africa have, for centuries, suffered conquests by colonial nations, endured the slave trade of twelve million people to other nations, and brutal domination by foreign powers. Only in the twentieth century did the African nations gain independence. Even then, many Africans often fell victim to civil wars, tribal conflicts, and domination by corrupt African leaders. Tribal armies, often recruiting and arming young boys with automatic weapons, ravage villages over land, food, and water rights.

All of this opposes our belief that human life is sacred, and all humans are brothers and sisters to each other, as well as to other living things. Many African myths describe an original blessed state where humans were close to the Earth, a time when there was peace between God and human beings.

Sacajawea: You are all probably familiar with the use of the peace pipe in most of the Native American cultures. The Sioux teach that the pipe was given to them by the White Buffalo Calf woman, a beautiful maiden who appeared to two tribesmen on the road. She gave them the pipe as a sacred gift. She told them that as they smoke the pipe, their voices would rise with the smoke and be sent to the Great Spirit. She taught them that when they smoked this pipe and sent their voices to *Wankan Tanka*, they would pray for and with everything. The pipe would bind all together as relatives.

Maybe we should light the pipe now and pass it around to symbolize that all our religions want world peace.

Jesus: I am sure that all our religions struggle with equality for our women. Throughout history, women have often made gains in this area, but then just as quickly have lost their rights. Christian women seem to be in a perennial struggle to equally participate in the authority and ministry of the churches. The Eastern churches and Roman Catholics have perhaps made the least progress in this area. There is often much positive rhetoric about the dignity and equality of women, but little action is done to back it up.

Catholic leaders maintain that they are acting in my name, but they need to look more closely to how radical and inclusive I was toward women in everyday life and in my ministry.

Gadla: The problem of women's rights is most severe in the African countries. Here women deal with severe poverty, horrible working conditions, and poor health care and education.

In tribal times, women often played key roles in family and community life. There was often no conflict with them being mothers and homemakers and at the same time playing important roles in the tribe. Women could play complementary roles in property matters, in religious leadership, and in the tribal economy.

Colonialism altered the role of African women. The patriarchy of Western nations was enforced on African society. Property rights, economic control, and jobs were largely given to men. Women were to stay home and assume what were now considered to be inferior domestic roles. The tribal structures were seriously disrupted.

Montezuma: As we have seen, in the religions of Mexico and Central and South America, the feminine was often honored for being able to give life. It was common to worship goddesses and to call god both Mother and Father. In the religions of these areas, there were instances where women were guardians of the temple and led ritual dances. Women presided over the domestic rituals, offering sacrifices and incense to the gods. When the Spaniards came, all that ended. Indigenous women were horribly abused physically and sexually. They were forced into slavery and dominated by patriarchal structures that were put in place by their European conquerors.

Sacajawea: Many Native American people honor the feminine in creation and recognize goddesses and women spirits in their religious beliefs. Feminine divine power and energy is experienced in the moon, stars, corn, animals, and in other parts of nature. The Earth is often seen as Mother.

Often the Native Americans honored both male and female spirits. In many tribes, women functioned as medicine women and shamans and were often seen as having more healing powers than men.

In my Shoshoni tribe, men and women were assigned strictly regulated roles. Women were in charge of plant gathering, butchering and preparing bison, household chores, crafting tepees and clothing, and caring for the children. Men were in charge of hunting, warfare, and the political and economic decisions for the tribe.[17]

Socially, women often had their own societies and were quite independent. In fact, some early missionaries complained that Indian women were haughty and independent. Native American women held ownership of their own possessions and had skills that men lacked. In some tribes, if a woman wanted a divorce, she could simply put her mate's things outside the tepee, which was considered to be hers since she made it. There are very few examples of women chiefs, but women did have much informal political power. In the Plateau tribes of the Northwest, women served as warriors, taking care of the wounded but also fighting in combat. In many regions, the women complemented the men.

Jesus: Did the coming of the Europeans affect your wholesome attitudes toward women, Sacajawea?

---

17. See Wisart, *Encyclopedia of The Great Plains*, http://plainshumanities.unl.edu.

Sacajawea: Indeed it did! The Indian cultural ways were suppressed, and the patriarchal ways of the colonists were enforced. Women lost much of the power and independence they had in tribal life. They were taught that they were inferior and that their role was to stay in the background and serve men. Native American men and women lost the complementary roles they held in tribal life. The picture of the Indian woman walking six steps behind her man is of colonial making.

Today, however, many Native American women have access to advanced education, job opportunities, and are once again able to achieve independence. They are working within their communities, along with many men, to restore the treasured old ways of partnership and shared decision-making.

Jesus: I want to thank you all for joining me in this dialogue. It is obvious that we have much in common, share many beliefs, and have a deep regard for one another. At the same time, we have recognized our differences in a respectful and caring way. As "the people of God," we are one. God bless you all!

SUGGESTED READINGS ON INDIGENOUS FAITH TRADITIONS

Bonvillain, Nancy. *Native American Religions*. Munich: Lincom Europa, 2003.

D'Altroy, Terence. *The Incas*. Malden, MA: Blackwell, 2002.

Gill, Sam. *Native American Religions*. Belmont, CA: Wadsworth/Thomson Learning, 2005.

Hirschfelder, Arlene and Paulette Molin. *Encyclopedia of Native American Religions*. New York: Checkmark, 2000.

LaDuke, Winona. *Recovering the Sacred*. Cambridge, MA: South End, 2005.

Laurencich Minelli, Laura and others, eds. *The Inca World*. Norman, OK: University of Oklahoma Press, 1999.

Magesa, Laurenti. *African Religion*. Maryknoll, NY: Orbis, 1997.

———*African Religion in the Dialogue Debate: From Intolerance to Coexistence*. London: Global, 2010.

Mbiti, John S. *African Religions and Philosophy*. Oxford: Heinemann, 1990.

———*Concepts of God in Africa*. New York: Praeger, 1970.

Townsend, Richard F. *The Aztecs*. London: Thames & Hudson, 1993.

Chapter 10

Interfaith Dialogue
~~~⊃ The "What," "Why," and "How"

Pierre Teilhard de Chardin (1881–1955), a renowned scientist and religious visionary, described the movement of evolution as one of divergence and convergence (spreading out and coming together). Humankind moved out of Africa and spread through Europe, the Middle East, and Asia. Later, humans migrated to the Americas. As they moved throughout the world, they developed various religions.

In the so-called Axial Period around 500 BCE, there was a virtual eruption of religions and philosophy: Confucius and Lao Tzu in China; Hinduism, Buddhism, and Jainism in India; Zoroastrianism in Persia; Shinto in Japan; the great prophets of Israel; and the philosophers Socrates, Plato, and Aristotle in Greece. Most of these religions and philosophies eventually extended to other regions. Five hundred years later, Christianity exploded on the scene and proliferated quickly. Seven hundred years later, Islam appeared and spread like a wildfire throughout much of the known world.

Along with this moving out there was division, both within the religions and among the religions themselves. Most religions eventually divided into a number of sects and churches: Vaishnavite and Shaivite Hinduism; Theravada and Mahayana Buddhism; Orthodox, Reform, and Conservative Judaism; and Orthodox, Protestant, and Catholic Christianity.

Conflict among religions has been common. The Israelites fought with the nations surrounding them. In early Christianity, there was conflict between Jews and Christians, as well as Christians and Gentiles. Christians opposed Muslims and Jews in the Crusades; Hindus fought Muslims and Sikhs in India.

In modern times, it has been Muslims vs. Christians in Sudan, Christians vs. Muslims in Bosnia, Hindus vs. Buddhists in Sri Lanka, and Jews vs. Muslims in Israel. Since the 9/11 attack on New York City, the rise of Al Qaeda, ISIS, and the influx of Muslims in Western Europe, there has been much tension between Muslims and some non-Muslims.

None of this speaks well for religions, which preach love, compassion, and peace. Perhaps that is why many faith leaders urgently advocate a coming together of religions to better understand each other and to devise ways that they can work together for peace and justice.

Ewert Cousins (1927–2009), a well-known expert in religions, maintained that we are going through a second Axial Period, which marks a global consciousness on the part of the entire human community. Cousins pointed out that this consciousness is rooted in the Earth, as well as in secular concerns that are political, social, and ecological. He maintained that, during this period, interreligious dialogue is not a luxury, but a necessity; it must be grounded in spiritual energy if the Earth and humanity are to survive. One scholar puts it bluntly: "death or dialogue."[1] Another writes: "The image of the Earth moving peacefully through space can be the symbol of interreligious dialogue and our common spiritual journey as we move into the global consciousness of the twenty-first century."[2]

In modern history, there have been significant signs that such dialogue is beginning to take root. As early as the nineteenth century, Christian missionary groups began to have meetings that considered the legitimacy of other religions. During the two World Wars, people from differing religions fought next to each other and learned of each other's faiths.

The Council for a Parliament of the World's Religions first met in 1893 in Chicago, Illinois, where leaders of the world's religions met to discuss their concerns. Since 1993 the Parliament has met every five years in some major city. The last meeting was in 2009 in Melbourne, Australia, where about five thousand people from eighty nations gathered for dialogue and prayers. Their agenda included extremely relevant issues, including world poverty, global warming, forced migration, and honoring indigenous communities. In 2015 the Parliament of the World's Religions will meet in Salt Lake City, Utah.

In 1948 the World Council of Churches was formed and has since been a force for religious dialogue and unity. Composed of many churches

---

1. Swidler and Cobb, *Death or Dialogue?*, 50.
2. Bryant and Flinn, *Interreligious Dialogue*, 6–7.

and congregations, it has brought about consensus on many doctrinal and theological issues. The WCC has also brought many Christians together to address political and social justice issues.

The Second Vatican Council of the Roman Catholic Church (1962–1965) recognized that truth and salvation exist in all religions and declared that to be saved one must simply live a good life and sincerely search for God.[3] Vatican II strongly advocated dialogue among churches and religions, and soon such exchange became very important among experts as well as among the laity in many churches and religions. Pope Paul VI was a leader in interfaith dialogue. In 1964 he established the Secretariat for Non Christian Religions in Rome to link with other religions. In 1988 it was renamed the Pontifical Council for Interreligious Dialogue (PCID). He also attended an historic meeting with Greek Orthodox Patriarch Athenagoras in 1964 on the Mount of Olives. St. John Paul II, who was pope from 1978–2005, was also a strong advocate for religious unity. Among many interfaith events, he preached in a Lutheran church, walked down the aisle of the Canterbury Cathedral as an equal with the Archbishop of Canterbury, prayed at the Western Wall in Jerusalem, condemned anti-Semitism, and led many interfaith gatherings. Perhaps the most dramatic was his invitation to 120 religious leaders (including an African Voodoo priest) to Assisi in 1986 for joint sharing and prayer. Pope Benedict XVI also made serious efforts to cordially meet with the leaders of other religions. His joint prayer with Muslim leaders in the Blue Mosque in Turkey was most significant.[4] Pope Francis has been a strong and effective advocate for interfaith respect, dialogue, and action.

Other religious leaders have contributed mightily to religious dialogue and unity. Gandhi, a Hindu, was a world figure who respected all religions. He gathered his followers in ashrams and strongly advocated peace between Muslims and Hindus, as well as among all world religions. The Tibetan Buddhist leader, the Dalai Lama (b. 1935), has tirelessly toured the world, meeting religious leaders and advocating peace and religious unity. Jewish leaders such as Rabbi Abraham Heschel (1907–1972), a leading Jewish thinker whose family died at the hands of the Nazis, marched with Martin Luther King Jr. at Selma, Alabama, and engaged in many interfaith dialogues. The present rabbi of the Sinai Temple in Los Angeles, David Wolpe, has led significant, although controversial, dialogues with other religions. The leadership of the World Jewish Congress has also promoted such

---

3. Pope Paul VI, *Lumen Gentium*, http://www.vatican.va/archive/hist_councils/ ii_vatican_council/documents/vat-ii_const_19641121_lumen-gentium_en.html.

4. Bryant and Finn, *Interreligious Dialogue*, 11–16.

dialogues and has met with Pope Benedict XVI. Thich Nhat Hanh (b. 1926) and Ghosananda (1929–2007), Buddhist teachers, have been major figures in interreligious dialogue. Leaders of the Sikhs and Baha'i have also been eager to participate in interreligious dialogue and to work for world peace.

WHAT IS INTERFAITH DIALOGUE?

Before we discuss what interfaith dialogue is, we might consider what it is not. First, such dialogue should not be a debate, where two people are trying to convince the other that each is wrong. We should not come to interfaith dialogue with the notion that our religion is the only correct one.

Secondly, interfaith dialogue should not be a missionary activity where we are trying to convert the others to our religion. This kind of dialogue belongs in mission work, in instructing catechumenates, or in recruiting sessions, where people come to inquire about joining one faith or another.

Nor should this be an activity where differences are ignored or where there is an effort to join all the religions into one big religion. Such an approach ignores the unique and diverse beliefs of each religion. While parallels and similarities will be discovered, religions have always been different and will always remain so.

Authentic interreligious dialogue is a mutual sharing of beliefs, values, and rituals. It is a sincere sharing of religious journeys and searching, where honest and trusting relationships are established. It is a process where mutual respect, understanding, and enrichment are established. It is a time to share one's faith life and one's religious concerns about world issues; it is an opportunity to explore how religions might join together in actions that will make the world better.

Interreligious dialogue recognizes the differences among religions. Different images have been used to accept these differences and yet still be able to relate to and dialogue with those who have other beliefs. Some compare this to climbing a mountain by taking differing paths and not being sure what is at the summit. Others compare this to different individuals pointing their fingers to the same moon or perhaps following different rays to the same light source. We might look at religious dialogue as though we are taking pictures of the sun with others at different times of the day. The sun remains the same, but the cameras are capturing it from different perspectives. Possibly, we might see ourselves joined with others in carrying parts of the same truth, but in different vessels.[5]

---

5. Bryant and Flinn, 11–16.

Interreligious dialogue is stepping out of our comfort zone, our "bubble," and trying to understand what another believes. It is never easy! I remember one humorous story when I took a group of adult students to the local Hindu Temple for a worship service. One woman paused as we went up the steps and said, "I don't think I should be doing this. I was always taught that it was sinful to participate in false religions." I assured her that we were only going into the temple to observe and not necessarily to participate. The woman decided to go in the temple. As the singing and dancing progressed, I could see that the woman was being drawn into the ritual. I saw her accept a tray with candles and begin gesturing before one of the goddesses! Afterwards, she seemed quite pleased with herself and remarked that the whole experience was very moving for her!

Four elements of dialogue

Paul Knitter, an expert in interreligious dialogue, points out that there are four pivotal elements. *First,* there is the willingness to face and experience the differences. If we begin by thinking that all religions are the same, we probably are in for a shock. There is much difference among the notions of God(s) in the Hindu, Shinto, and Jewish religions, for example, and Theravada Buddhism does not mention God at all. And what a contrast between the Hindu and Buddhist beliefs in rebirth, the Christian belief in afterlife, and the common Jewish belief that we live on in memory or achievements.

The *second* element involves trust that our differences can bring us together rather than divide us. We can agree to disagree and be enriched by new perspectives on our own religion by learning about the beliefs of others. We can see that all are searching for "ultimate mystery." That mystery is, in fact, beyond human comprehension and is only partially represented in each religion. We can see ourselves engaged in a common search for truth, but know that we all "see through a glass, darkly" (1 Cor 13:12 KJV).

The *third* element is witnessing. This does not mean that we are trying to convert our dialogue partner, but rather we are trying to honestly share our search, our values, our doubts, and our religious experiences. We may both find that we are truly inspired by the other's testimony, even changed by it. At the same time, it should be clear that no one need reveal anything that feels uncomfortable or too personal. Nor should pressure be put on others to share more than they are willing.

And the *final* element is the resolution to carefully listen, to be open to new insights, and even to be willing to change one's religious perspectives. Often, when we listen to another's view of our own religion, we are able to clear up misunderstandings. On the other hand, we might be brought to notice something in our own tradition that might truly be wrong and be moved to correct it in our own outlook and practice. For instance, Catholics sometimes discover that they can be arrogant and look down on other religions. Dialogue might help such a person make an attitude check.

Four types of dialogue

It has been suggested that there are four types of interreligious dialogue. First, there is *a dialogue of life*, where we share in a trusting and friendly fashion our values, concerns, set backs, and successes in the context of faith. It might be described as "telling our story." Second, we see *a dialogue of action*, where we partner with others in actions to promote peace and justice. Third, we have *a dialogue of theological exchange*, where we share our interpretation and understanding of religious beliefs. And fourth, we offer *a dialogue of religious experience*, where we share religious rituals, prayers, or methods of meditation.[6]

WHY DIALOGUE?

There are a number of reasons for interreligious dialogue and a number of goals that can be achieved by such engagement. Among these goals are:

Self exploration

Interreligious dialogue can benefit us, by helping us explore our own search for beliefs and values. Many college students go on what we might call a "religious leave of absence," in order to assess whether or not they accept the religious tradition that has been given to them by their parents. College is often a time to think through one's beliefs and examine the beliefs of others to see where one stands. Interreligious dialogue provides an occasion for expressing what we believe (or don't believe) and, at the same time, for understanding the beliefs of others. It's an occasion for seeing parallels with other faiths, seeing contradictions, as well as utterly new perspectives, and putting all of this into our own religious perspectives.[7]

6. Fitzgerald and Borelli, *Interfaith Dialogue*, 28.
7. Swidler, Duran, and Firestone, *Trialogue*, 45ff.

An understanding of the faith of others

This type of dialogue is more than just listening to the facts of another religion. It also includes carefully listening to how the other person interprets and relates to his or her religion (or to her opposition to religion). It is an opportunity to listen to another's search for purpose in life and ultimate meaning. We can gain understanding of another's deepest questions, empathy for his doubts (which might be similar to our own), and a deeper respect for the mystery in religion.

Preparing for a global future

We all know that the world is now smaller because of easy travel and communication. Air travel today means that in a matter of hours we can be in an entirely different culture with languages, cultures, and religions that are unfamiliar to us. In our colleges today, we see people from many different cultures and religions coming together to learn. The Internet can instantly put us in touch with diverse people, locally and around the world. Economies and businesses today are global. This reality puts demands on all of us to learn other languages, be comfortable in other cultures, and be familiar with other religions. Dealing with all of this puts pressure on us to become familiar with and respect cultural and religious differences. Thus, we see the need for serious interfaith dialogue in today's world.

Gearing up to make a difference

As we share our ideals and values with others and become more aware of their needs, we can be drawn into action for others. Today we see students going to underdeveloped areas in their own country and abroad to pitch in with a helping hand. Students who share the same faith, as well students who have differing faiths, are teaming up to build houses in Kentucky, build schools in Africa, work in orphanages in India, serve food in Peru, or work in homeless shelters in Nicaragua. Working together, partying together, and praying together, these armies of young people are becoming a force in the world.

HOW TO DIALOGUE

Here we offer a number of suggestions for productive interreligious dialogue. First, let's consider the personal dispositions that are useful in such dialogue. All those involved need to come with attitudes of equality and respect. A "holier than thou" or "my religion is better than yours" attitude militates against good dialogue.

Experts recommend that we come to interreligious dialogue with an attitude of inclusivity, rather than exclusivity. The exclusive Protestant attitude that one must accept Jesus to be saved, or the Catholic view that "outside the church there is no salvation," or that Protestant churches are "defective" are not conducive to productive dialogue.

An acceptance of pluralism is also important in interreligious dialogue, meaning that we accept that there are many authentic religions with their own truth claims and the capacity to lead their constituents to Ultimacy. This final goal might be enlightenment, Nirvana, eternal life, union with God, or liberation: each term has different meanings.[8]

Such dialogue should be approached with humility, honesty, sincerity, openness, and the ability to "beg to disagree." This is a sharing between equals who trust each other and speak to each other as "I to thou" and not "I to it," to use the words of Martin Buber. All participants are willing to be critical of their own tradition and eager to learn about other traditions from those within the tradition.[9]

Most certainly, all participants can remain firm in their own beliefs, but this does not rule out the willingness to listen to and try to understand and experience another religious tradition.[10] At the same time, there can be an openness to change one's mind about other religions' beliefs, possibly to even accept one or the other of these beliefs.

It is useful to begin with personal stories about one's religious upbringing, influences, and experiences. This helps build relationships of trust and respect, a solid foundation upon which to build a productive dialogue. It is also useful to start by visiting churches, temples, and synagogues to experience how the various religions gather and worship. This way we can perhaps "catch" the religion rather than merely hearing ideas.

At the beginning, allow for some tension. Communication experts tell us that there is always a period of "storming" when a group comes together. Patience and perseverance will be needed during this time as well

---

8. See Roozen and Hadsell, *Changing the Way Seminaries Teach.*

9. Mays, *Interfaith Dialogue at the Grass Roots,* 20–4.

10. Fitzgerald and Borelli, *Interfaith Dialogue,* 34.

as throughout. Interreligious dialogue is never easy; it often does not bring about results that can be measured.[11]

Early on, it is important to establish some common ground. This can be done by seeing similarities among religious beliefs. A caution here though, for what might seem to be similar could be quite different. For instance, "rebirth" in the Hindu tradition is quite different from the Christian belief in "being reborn." Seeing Buddha as divine is quite different from seeing Jesus Christ as divine. Nevertheless, by seriously studying different traditions and comparing them, we can find similarities and parallels that are useful to establishing common ground. For instance, it is helpful to know that the births of Buddha, Mahavira, Krishna, and Jesus are described as miraculous births. Discovering the universality of religious myths is useful in understanding the commonality among religions. It is useful to compare the power of the Word to connect with God among Sikhs with the parallel notion among Christians, or to put the Hindu belief in *moksha* (liberation) with Christian interpretations. It is interesting to compare the Hindu notion of Atman with the Christian belief in soul, or the notion of Shinto belief in *kami* with the Native American belief in spirits. (Usually this kind of effort requires the assistance of your teachers.)

We are told that interreligious dialogue involves a crucial "crossing over." It means that we will be moving into another's world of symbol, story, belief, devotion, and living ritual. We will be walking another's path, trying on their moccasins. It might be compared with going to another country, where the culture, language, and lifestyle are different. Often we have "culture shock," and it takes us awhile to ease in and adjust. To be accepted and productive we need to cross over and be open. Otherwise, we remain an outsider, learning little and experiencing less about this country. It takes courage and flexibility to take advantage of this opportunity to expand and to grow. Adapting usually doesn't mean we stay, but we are able to "taste and see" this other land.

When we cross back, we somehow are not the same. We have seen our own land from a distance, heard other perspectives about it, and now see it differently. I remember returning stateside with a group of students I lived with in a barrio in Nicaragua. We stayed with the ordinary folks who lived frugally from day to day. We shared their simple poverty and served their homeless and orphans. We heard other views about our nation: how we disrupted their revolution against a corrupt government; how we have ruined many of their small businesses and crafts with our trade agreements.

---

11. Ibid.

When we returned, we experienced another kind of shock: we had shopped at tiny corner stores and now encountered huge supermarkets overflowing with food. We were stunned by the enormous malls offering every kind of thing to buy. Accustomed to the Nicaraguans being lean and fit, now we noticed numerous obese people everywhere, victims of our fast foods and easy lifestyle.

Crossing over into another religion is similar. We will experience "shock" crossing over into beliefs we have never heard of. And possibly when we cross back, we know that we will never again be the same.

Facing religious differences can challenge our notion of truth. We may think we have truth in a box and that we are absolutely sure of its validity. After dialogue, we know that other religions challenge our absolute truths and, in a sense, make truth relative. Questions arise. Is truth one or many? If truth is one, how can there be so many truths? Are there any absolutes, or is everything relative, so it doesn't matter what you believe? Are the postmodernists correct when they say that all truths are conditioned by culture and language, and are therefore relative?

There are no easy answers to these questions. We only turn to some of our sages. As mentioned in the introduction, Gandhi maintained that truth was indeed absolute, but was at the same time a mystery—a reality that is beyond our comprehension. He spent his entire life searching for Truth. As for religious truth, he believed that one must listen to all religions to catch even a glimpse of the Truth. In the end, he concluded that the Truth was God, beyond our comprehension. He believed that there were many paths to the same Truth. As theologian Monika Hellwig put it: "There are many paths of salvation, many ways of naming and worshiping the same ultimate, transcendent reality, many languages and rituals by which people search for communion with the divine. . . ."[12]

A Digital Approach to Interreligious Dialogue

We urge our readers to make the digital world integral to their interfaith dialogue.

There are many online media presentations, especially on YouTube, that can enhance your learning about other religions and introduce you to many individuals in these religions who are activists in ecology, peace, and women's issues. In addition, there are many interviews of scholars, monks, nuns, and lay people in these religions. We also urge you to dialogue with

12. Swidler and Cobb, *Death or Dialogue?*, 51.

individuals as well as classes at U.S. and international universities through Cisco and Skype.

SUGGESTED READINGS ON INTERFAITH DIALOGUE

Banchoff, Thomas, ed. *Religious Pluralism*. New York: Oxford University Press, 2008.

Bryant, M. Darrol and Frank Flinn, eds. *Interreligious Dialogue*. New York: Paragon, 1989.

Fitzgerald, Michael L. and John Borelli, eds. *Interfaith Dialogue: A Catholic View*. Maryknoll, NY: Orbis, 2006.

Mays, Rebecca K. ed. *Interfaith Dialogue at the Grass Roots*. Philadelphia, PA: Ecumenical, 2008.

Roozen, David A. and Heidi Hadsell, eds. *Changing the Way Seminaries Teach: Pedagogies for Interfaith Dialogue*. Hartford, CT: Hartford Seminary, 2009.

Swidler, Leonard, John B. Cobb Jr., et al., eds. *Death or Dialogue?* London: Trinity, 1990.

———Khalid Duran, and Reuven Firestone. *Trialogue: Jews, Christians, and Muslims in Dialogue*. New London, CT: Twenty-Third, 2007

Epilogue

People who follow a religion generally take one of a variety of positions toward other religions. Some take a stance that their religion is the true one and that the others are false. Others might go to the other extreme and hold that all religions are basically the same and it doesn't really matter which people choose. And we need to also acknowledge the growing numbers who are abandoning religion all together.

Here we take the position that authentic religion is of great value and that each of the religions has its own authenticity and can reveal in part the divine Truth uniquely and differently. Each can fulfill the very purpose of religions: to lead their followers to personal transformation and to union with the divine.

In fact, what our dialogues seem to indicate is that religions cannot be divided into the "true" and the "false," nor are they all the same. Religions have certain areas where they are similar and some areas where they differ considerably. Hopefully, these dialogues have demonstrated that reality.

Let's start with the similarities. As we have seen from these conversations, most religions have seen their beginnings come from a unique revelation or enlightenment to some individual, who generally reveals this revelation to others and then begins to gather disciples. Forming communities to share tradition, lifestyle, and ritual seems to be integral to religion.

Most religions hold to some Ultimate Reality. Religions have called this Reality by a number of names, e.g. God, Yahweh, Allah, the Great Spirit. The divine might be viewed as being singular or multiple, as having different genders, as personal or impersonal. Only early Buddhism and Jainism see no reason to include "God-talk," and yet both maintain that they are not atheistic. Both seem to find a certain ultimacy in Nirvana. Belief in an ultimate Reality often includes viewing this Reality as the source and/or sustaining energy or power within the universe and thus sees all things as being interconnected.

Another universal among religions is the acceptance of some sort of life after death. The afterlife is portrayed in varying fashions from states of rewards and punishments, to the ultimate experience of freedom from desires or suffering. In this area of afterlife, there is notable difference among religions in their posture toward reincarnation. In the case of the Hindu, Buddhist, Jain, and Sikh religions, there is a strong belief in some form of reincarnation, where individuals cycle through other forms of existence before final liberation. In the so-called "religions of the Book," (Jewish, Christian, Islam) on the other hand, there is strong belief in the individual soul, and thus to final afterlife after death.

Religions are also similar in their value of a collection of sacred writings. With the exception of the Quran, which is purported to be direct revelations to Muhammad, these collections are written by or assembled by later disciples. Within most modern religious communities there are different understandings with regard the "truth" aspect of collections. Some take their scriptures literally, while others approach their sacred writings as literature that largely consists of metaphorical writings.

Echoed through religions is admonition for humans to lead a life of detachment from material things, love and compassion, humility, childlikeness, and a commitment to nonviolence. Service to others, unselfishness (no-self), prayer, and sacrifice, individually or within communal ritual, are also characteristic of many religions.

Mahatma Gandhi maintained that all religions testify to the existence of Truth. Indeed, Gandhi came to the conclusion that "God is Truth." When asked what religion he belonged to, he said: "I am a Muslim, a Hindu, a Christian and a Jew." It was his position that all religions reveal some dimension of truth and that we must listen to them all in order to gain just a glimpse of the Truth.

Many of us live in our own religious "bubbles," cut off from the experience and truths of other religions, as well as dialogue with their followers. We rarely share in their faith or rituals. Yet, there is so much to learn from other traditions and the religious experiences of others about the divine, meditation and prayer, faith, and compassionate service toward others. Christians, and indeed those who follow other religions, can hardly imagine the sacred texts from other religions being part of their rituals or reflections!

We have listened to many religions here as Jesus dialogues with their founders and leaders. Hopefully we have gained a better glimpse of the vast scope of divine revelation and have become more aware of how religions today have become more relevant and active in dealing with contemporary issues such as women, ecology, poverty, peace, and social justice.

Could it be that we are entering a new Axial Period? In the first, new religions burst forth. In this new period, religions are awakening to each other's richness and differences, as well as to their interconnection and mission to work for a better world.

Bibliography

Ali, Abdullah Yusuf, translator. *The Qur'an*. New York: Tahrike Tarsile Qur'an, 2007.

Bell, Daniel, A., ed. *Confucian Political Ethics*. Princeton, NJ: Princeton University Press, 2008.

Benstein, Jeremy. *The Way into Judaism and the Environment*. Woodstock, VT: Jewish Lights, 2006.

Berry, Thomas. *Buddhism*. New York: Columbia University Press, 1996.

Bowker, John. *Jesus and the Pharisees*. Cambridge: Cambridge University Press, 1973.

Brundage, Burr C. *The Fifth Sun: Aztec Gods, Aztec World*. Austin, TX: University of Texas Press, 1979.

Bryant, Darrol M. and Frank Flinn, eds. *Interreligious Dialogue*. New York: Paragon, 1989.

Byrom, Thomas. *The Dhammapada*. New York: Random House, 1976.

Chai, Ch'u, and Winberg Chai. *Confucianism*. Woodbury, NY: Barron's Educ. Series, 1973.

Chalmers, Lord, ed. *Buddha's Teachings*. Cambridge, MA: Harvard University Press, 2002.

Chief Seattle. "Speech of 1854." http://www.barefootsworld.net/seattle.html and http://www.halcyon.com/arborhts/chiefsea.html.

Chittister, Joan D. *Heart of Flesh: Feminist Spirituality for Women and Men*. Grand Rapids, MI: Eerdmans, 1998.

Cobo, Bernabe. *Inca Religion and Customs*. Translated and edited by Roland Hamilton. Austin, TX: University of Texas Press, 1979.

Cole, W. Owen, and Piara Singh Sambhi. *The Sikhs*. Boston: Routledge, 1978.

Corrigan, John, et al. *Jews, Christians, Muslims: A Comparative Introduction to Monotheistic Religions*. Upper Saddle River, NJ: Prentice Hall, 1999.

Dallmayr, Fred. *Peace Talks—Who Will Listen?* Notre Dame, IN: University of Notre Dame Press, 2004.

de Lange, Nicholas. *The Penguin Dictionary of Judaism*. New York: Penguin, 2008.

DeLong-Bas, Natana J., et al, eds. *The Oxford Encyclopedia of Islam and Women*. New York: Oxford University Press, 2013.

Deloria, Vine, Jr. *God is Red*. Golden, CO: Fulcrum, 2003.

Dobrin, Arthur B., ed. *Religious Ethics: A Sourcebook*. Mumbai: Hindi Granth Karyalay, 2004.

Doniger, Wendy. *The Hindus: An Alternative History*. New York: Viking/Penguin, 2009.

Dorff, Elliot, and Louis Newman, eds. *Contemporary Jewish Theology.* New York: Oxford University Press, 1999.

Dundas, Paul. *The Jains.* New York: Routledge, 2002.

Encyclopædia Britannica Online, s. v. "al-Qaeda." http://www.britannica.com/EBchecked/topic/734613/al-Qaeda.

Eno, R. *The Analects: An Online Teaching Translation.* Version 2.1, 2012. http://www.indiana.edu/~p374/Analects_of_Confucius_(Eno- 2012).pdf.

Farrer-Halls, Gill. *The Illustrated Encyclopedia of Buddhist Wisdom.* Wheaton, IL: Quest, 2000.

Feldman, Ron. *Fundamentals of Jewish Mysticism and Kabbalah.* Freedom, CA: The Crossing, 1999.

Fitzgerald, Michael L., and John Borelli, eds. *Interfaith Dialogue: A Catholic View.* Maryknoll, NY: Orbis Books, 2006.

Flood, Gavin, ed. *The Blackwell Companion to Hinduism.* Malden, MA: Blackwell, 2003.

Fowler, Jeaneane. *Hinduism: Beliefs and Practices.* Portland: Sussex Academic Press, 1997.

Fowler, Jeaneane, and Merv Fowler. *Chinese Religions.* Portland: Sussex Academic Press, 2008.

Ghose, Tia. "Most Ashkenazi Are Genetically Europeans, Surprising Study Finds." NBC News/Science News. http://www.nbcnews.com/science/science-news/most-ashkenazi-jews-are- genetically-europeans-surprising-study-finds-f8C11358210.

Girardot, N.J., et al., eds. *Daoism and Ecology.* Cambridge, MA: Harvard University Press, 2001.

Griffith, Ralph T.H., translator. *The Ramayan.* Varanasi: Chowkhamba Sanskrit Series Office, 2010.

Harvey, Peter. *An Introduction to Buddhism.* New York: Cambridge University Press, 1990.

Hinnells, John R. *A New Handbook of Living Religions.* Cambridge, MA: Blackwell, 2002.

Hinnells, John R., and Richard King, eds. *Religion and Violence in South Asia.* New York: Routledge, 2007.

Hirschfelder, Arlene, and Paulette Molin, eds. *The Encyclopedia of Native American Religions.* New York: Facts On File, 1992.

Holtz, Barry W. *Back to the Sources: Reading the Classic Jewish Texts.* New York: Summit, 1984.

Hooper, Richard, ed. *Jesus, Buddha, Krishna, Lao Tzu: The Parallel Sayings.* Charlottesville, VA: Sanctuary, 2007.

Hopkins, Gerald. "God's Grandeur." Poetry Foundation. http://www.poetryfoundation.org/poem/173660.

Hussain, Musharraf. *The Five Pillars of Islam: Laying the Foundations of Divine Love and Service to Humanity.* Leicestershire: Kube, 2012.

Jacobs, Alan, ed. *Native American Wisdom.* London: Watkins, 2009.

Jain, Priyadarshana. "A Study of the Bhagavati Sutra." http://www.herenow4u.net/index.php?id=67398.

Johnson, Ian. "China's Great Uprooting: Moving 250 Million Into Cities." nytimes.com. http://www.nytimes.com/2013/06/16/world/asia/chinas-great-uprooting-moving-250-million-into-cities.html?pagewanted=all&_r=0.

Kamali, Mohammad Hashim. *Shari'ah Law: An Introduction.* Oxford: Oneworld, 2008.

Kelkar, Meena, and Deepti Gangavane, eds. *Feminism in Search of an Identity.* Jaipur: Rawat, 2003.

Klostermaier, Klaus K. *A Survey of Hinduism.* Albany: State University of New York Press, 1994.

Lamotte, Etienne, translator. *Samdhinirmocana.* Paris: Adrien Maisoneuve, 1935.

Leaman, Oliver. *An Introduction to Classical Islamic Philosophy.* New York: Cambridge University Press, 2002.

Limaye, V.P., and R.D. Vadekar, eds. *Eighteen Principal Upanishads.* Poona: Vaidika Samshodhana Mandala, 1958.

Long, Jeffery D. *Jainism: An Introduction.* New York: I.B.Tauris, 2009.

Magesa, Laurenti. *African Religion.* Maryknoll, NY: Orbis, 1997.

Mascaro, Juan, translator. *The Bhagavad Gita.* New York: Viking Penguin, 1962.

Mays, Rebecca K., ed. *Interfaith Dialogue at the Grass Roots.* Philadelphia, PA: Ecumenical, 2008.

Mbiti, John. *Concepts of God in Africa.* New York: Praeger, 1970.

Mengzi, 4A:7. Chinese Text Project. http://ctext.org/mengzi.

Merton, Thomas, ed. *Gandhi on Non-Violence.* New York: New Directions, 1965.

Metz, Pamela, and Jacqueline L. Tobin. *The Tao of Women.* Atlanta: Humanics Trade, 1995.

Mittal, Sushil, and Gene Thursby, eds. *Religions of South Asia: An Introduction.* New York: Routledge, 2006.

Muller, Max, translator. *The Upanishads.* New York: Christian Literature, 1897.

Nahar, P.C., and K.C. Ghosh, eds. *An Encyclopaedia of Jainism.* New Delhi: Sri Satguru, 1988.

National Geographic. "Africa: Physical Geography." http://education.nationalgeographic.com/education/encyclopedia/africa-physical- geography/?ar_a=1.

Nerburn, Kent, ed. *The Wisdom of the Native Americans.* Novato, CA: New World Library, 1999.

Neusner, Jacob. *Judaism: The Basics.* New York: Routledge, 2006.

———. *The Way of Torah.* Encino, CA: Dickenson, 1974.

Neville, Peter. *The Holocaust.* Cambridge: Cambridge University Press, 1999.

Noorani, A.G. *Islam and Jihad: Prejudice versus Reality.* New York: Zed, 2003.

Novak, Philip. *The World's Wisdom.* San Francisco: HarperSanFrancisco, 1995.

Olupona, Jacob K., and Sulayman S. Nyang, eds. *Religious Plurality in Africa.* New York: Mouton De Gruyter, 1993.

Palmer, Martin. *The Elements of Taoism.* Rockport, MA: Element, 1991.

Pelikan, Jaroslav, ed. *Hinduism: The Rig Veda.* Translated by Ralph T.H. Griffith. New York: Book of the Month Club, 1992.

PewResearch Religion & Public Life Project. "The Future of the Global Muslim Population," June 7, 2013. http://www.pewforum.org/2011/01/27/the-future-of-the-global-muslim-population and http://www.pewresearch.org/fact-tank/2013/06/07/worlds-muslim-population-more-widespread-than-you-might-think.

PewResearch Religion & Public Life Project. "Global Christianity—A Report on the Size and Distribution of the World's Christian Population," December 19, 2011. http://www.pewforum.org/2011/12/19/global-christianity-movements-and-denominations/.

Pope Paul VI. "Dogmatic Constitution on the Church—Lumen Gentium." Vatican: The Holy See, Rome, 1964. http://www.vatican.va/archive/hist_councils/ii_vatican_council/documents/v at-ii_const_19641121_lumen-gentium_en.html.

Rainey, Lee Dian. *Confucius and Confucianism: The Essentials*. Oxford: Wiley- Blackwell, 2010.

Roozen, David A., and Heidi Hadsell, eds. *Changing the Way Seminaries Teach: Pedagogies for Interfaith Dialogue*. Hartford, CT: Hartford Seminary, 2009.

Rosenlee, Li-Hsiang Lisa. *Confucianism and Women*. Albany, NY: State University of New York Press, 2007.

Ruggiero, Adriane, ed. *Confucianism*. Farmington Hills, MI: Greenhaven Press, 2006.

Saldarini, Anthony. *Pharisees, Scribes and Sadducees in Palestinian Society*. Edinburgh: T.T. Clark, 1989.

Schiffman, Lawrence, and Joel Wolowelsky, eds. *War and Peace in the Jewish Tradition*. New York: Yeshiva University Press, 2007.

Sharma, Arvind. *Our Religions*. New York: HarperCollins, 1993.

———. *Classical Hindu Thought*. New Delhi: Oxford University Press, 2000.

———, ed. *Women in Indian Religions*. New Delhi: Oxford University Press, 2002.

Sikh Missionary Society. *Sikh Religion*. Detroit: Sikh Missionary Center, 1990.

Singh Mann, Gurinder. *Sikhism*. Upper Saddle River, NJ: Prentice Hall, 2004.

Ska, Jean-Louis. *The Exegesis of the Pentateuch*. Tubingen: Mohr Siebeck, 2009.

Smith, Huston. *The Religions of Man*. New York: Harper and Row, 1958.

Sri Guru Granth Sahib. http://www.sikhs.org/english/eg14.htm.

Swidler, Leonard, and John B. Cobb Jr., et al., eds. *Death or Dialogue?* Philadelphia: Trinity, 1990.

———, Khalid Duran, and Reuven Firestone. *Trialogue: Jews, Christians, and Muslims in Dialogue*. New London, CT: Twenty-Third, 2007.

Swinson, P. "Be A Light Unto Yourself." *Mahaparinibbana Sutta*. http://artofdharma.com/be-a-light-unto-yourself.

Thomas, E.J. *Buddhist Scriptures*. http://www.sacred-texts.com/bud/busc/index.htm.

Townsend, Richard. *The Aztecs*. London: Thames and Hudson, 1993.

Tsomo, Karma Lekshe, ed. *Innovative Buddhist Women*. Richmond, Surrey: Curzon, 2000.

Tucker, Mary Evelyn, and John Berthrong, eds. *Confucianism and Ecology*. Cambridge, MA: Harvard University Press, 1998.

Tzu, Lao. *Tao Te Ching*. Translated by J. Legge. http://www.sacred-texts.com/tao/taote.htm.

Tzu, Lao and Robert Henricks. *Te-Tao Ching*. Translated by Robert Henricks. New York: Ballantine, 1989.

Van de Weyer, Robert, ed. *366 Readings from Buddhism*. Delhi: Jaico Publishing, 2003.

Winter, T.J., and John A. Williams. *Understanding Islam and the Muslims: The Muslim Family, Islam, and World Peace*. Louisville, KY: Fons Vitae, 2002.

Wisart, David, ed. *Encyclopedia of The Great Plains*. Lincoln, NE: University of Nebraska–Lincoln, 2011. http://plainshumanities.unl.edu/encyclopedia/doc/egp.na.105.